Visible Mantra

To Naomi
with love
from
Jayarava.

Other books by Jayarava

Pilgrimage Diary
Nāmapada: a guide to names in the Triratna Buddhist Order

Visible Mantra

visualising and writing
Buddhist mantras

Jayarava

Visible Mantra Books
Cambridge
2011

Published by
Visible Mantra Books
25 Newmarket Rd
Cambridge
CB5 8EG
UK

ISBN 978-0-9566929-1-7

For the Triratna Buddhist Order

For the Triratna Buddhist Order

Contents

Acknowledgements 9
Abbreviations 11
Introduction 12
Pronouncing Sanskrit and Pāli 15
Scripts 20
Siddhaṃ: The Perfect Script 24
Punctuation 26
Anusvāra and Visarga 32
Anusvāra 32
Visarga 33
The Arapacana Alphabet 35
Arapacana 36
Meditating on the Arapacana Alphabet 37
Arapacana Alphabet in the Pañcaviṃśatisāhasrikā sūtra 43
Background Reading. 48
What is Mantra? 49
On the Etymology of the Word 'Mantra'. 55
Phonosemantics 60
Dhāraṇī - origins, meaning, and usage. 66
Non-lexical utterances, stobhas, and mantra 69
Mantra, Magic, and Interconnectedness. 71
Words in mantras that end in –e 73
Tadyathā in The Heart Sūtra 76
Buddhas 78
Śākyamuni 79
Vajrasattva 82
Bhaiṣajyaguru - the Medicine Buddha 90
Vairocana 94
Akṣobhya 99
Ratnasambhava 102
Amitābha and Amitāyus 104
Amoghasiddhi 109
Ākāśadhātvīśvarī 111
Locanā 113
Māmakī 115
Pāṇḍaravāsinī 117
Bodhisattvas and other mythic beings 120
A note on the word Bodhisattva 120
Acala Vidyārāja 121
Ākāśagarbha 124
Avalokiteśvara / Guānyīn 127
Caturmahārāja: The Four Great Kings 131
Kṣitigarbha 136
Kurukullā 138
Mahāsthāmaprāpta 140
Maitreya 142
Mañjuśrī / Mañjughoṣa 144
Prajñāpāramitā 148
Samantabhadra 151
Tārā 153
Tārā - White 156
Vajrapāṇi 161
Vajrayoginī Ḍākiṇī 163

Mantras of Historical Figures and Teachers of the Past 166
- Dr. Bhimrao Ramji Ambedkar 167
- Kūkai (空 海) aka Kōbōdaishi (弘法大師) 169
- Milarepa 174
- Padmasambhava 176

Bīja mantras – Seed Syllables 180
- The Seed Syllable *a* 181
- The Seed Syllable āḥ 185
- The Seed Syllable dhīḥ 186
- The Seed Syllable hrīḥ 188
- The Seed Syllable hūṃ 190
- The Seed Syllable ma 193
- The Seed Syllable oṃ 194
- The Seed Syllable tāṃ 196
- The Seed Syllable traṃ/trāḥ 198
- The Seed Syllable vaṃ 199
- Complex Seed-Syllables 200

Mantric Words 203
- Namas 204
- Phaṭ 206
- Svāhā 207

Miscellaneous Mantras 208
- The Alphabet as Mantra 209
- Oṃ āḥ hūṃ 211
- Heart Sutra Mantra 212
- Jaḥ hūṃ vaṃ hoḥ 215
- Karaṇḍamudrā Dhāraṇī 217
- Nīlakaṇṭha Dhāraṇī 220
- The Śānti Mantra 223
- The Śūnyatā Mantra 224
- The Śuddha - Purity Mantra 226

Sūtras 228
- Thus have I heard 229
- Karaṇīya Mettā Sutta 231
- The Last Words of the Buddha 236
- Prajñāpāramitā Ratnaguṇasaṁcayagāthā 237
- The Doors to the Deathless are Open 238

Buddhist Chants & Phrases 240
- Ye dharmā hetuprabhava – Causation 241
- May all beings be happy! 244
- Truths of the Noble Ones 245
- This being, that becomes... 246
- The Three Refuges 248

Glossary 252

Names 256

Bibliography 258

Index 266

The Author 270

Acknowledgements

Many people have earned my thanks in the years this project has been active. I'm grateful to Saṅgharakṣita for spreading the Dharma in the West in a way I could immediately begin to understand, and, perhaps more importantly, to fall in love with. My preceptor Nāgabodhi for his *kalyāṇa-mitratā*, for witnessing my 'Going for Refuge', and for his constant encouragement to keep writing, especially in the face of disappointments and difficulties – of which there have been many.

I'd like to take this opportunity to express my gratitude to all those visitors to the website that made donations, especially the very generous John Scherer. And also to Paul Powell who hosts the website on his server.

Special thanks are due especially to Maitiu O'Ceileachair for stimulating and insightful discussions about mantra and tantra, as well as advice on Chinese, Japanese and Tibetan Buddhism, language, spelling and orthography; and for the many times he has consulted the Chinese and Tibetan versions of the *Tripiṭaka* for me. Special thanks also to Samudraghoṣa for making it possible for Visible Mantra Press to have its own ISBN numbers, and to Emma Chopourian for providing me with desktop publishing softeware. Thanks to Vidyavajra for his friendship and interest over many years, and for his cover art. Śākyakumāra provided some valuable feedback on an early draft that lead to big improvements in the overall design of the book.

Thanks to Dhīvan for his encouragement to both persevere and maintain high standards of research and scholarship. Thanks to the members of the Triratna Buddhist Order I was ordained with in 2005 who collectively asked the questions that made it clear that some kind of reference work was needed – this was first and foremost a book I wanted to read, rather than write! Thanks also to all those other friends whose ears I've bent while I tried to clarify the mysteries of mantra, most of which remain.

Many scholars have informed my thinking about mantra and tantra, and my practice of Buddhism. They are cited in my published and unpublished essays, and/or listed in my bibliography. Without them I'd probably have nothing to say. There are not many Buddhist calligraphers, but I've drawn inspiration from the work of Tashi Mannox and Nathaniel Archer, and enjoyed a friendly correspondence with both of them. I'm grateful to John Stevens for his book *Sacred Calligraphy of the East* from which I initially learned Siddhaṃ calligraphy.

I spell badly in every language I know, so I am very grateful to Tejasvini for proof reading the book, and also for suggesting structural changes. Amanda Katz also proof read parts of the book. Several readers of the Visible Mantra website and blog, some of whom are anonymous or use pseudonyms, have kept an eye on my spelling and written comments on errors they've seen. I'm grateful to all of them, but in particular to Vinodh Rajan who reads all of these scripts, and whose convertor produced the Sinhala script in the book, and to Tống Phước Khải who has been helpful over the years, and who provided the Rañjana script interface I use to create mantras in that script.

Any remaining errors, inaccuracies or infelicities are my responsibility, though there would have been many more without all this help.

Jayarava
Cambridge, UK.
June 2011.

Abbreviations

BHS	Buddhist Hybrid Sanskrit
BHSD	Buddhist Hybrid Sanskrit Dictionary, Edgerton.
DN	Dīgha Nikāya.
G.	Gāndhārī
J.	Japanese
MAT	Mahāvairocana Abhisaṃbodhi Tantra, aka Mahāvairocana Sūtra.
MWD	Monier-Williams Sanskrit English Dictionary.
P.	Pāli
PED	Pali-English Dictionary, Pali Text Society.
PIE	Proto-Indo-European (see glossary)
S.	Sanskrit
STTS	Sarvatathāgata-tattvasaṃgraha
T.	Tibetan
Vin.	Pāli Vinaya. References are to the Pali Text Society Edition.
Vism.	Visuddhimagga.

Introduction

THE CONCEPTION OF THE *VISIBLE MANTRA* PROJECT occurred during my four month ordination retreat in 2005, and the website[1] began to be built almost as soon as I returned to the UK. It grew haphazardly for the next three years, until it dawned on me that there was enough material there for a book.

This is a book *of* mantras more than it is *about* mantras, though the reading section at the end provides some of the fruits of my research. A book like this can be misleading. I may seem to suggest that there is one mantra or one seed-syllable (*bījākṣara*) for each figure but the situation is this: there are hundreds, if not thousands, of figures, each of which may have a dozen different names and dozens of iconographic forms (with each tiny detail symbolising something). There are sometimes dozens of associated mantras and seed syllables for each figure as well. The scale of it is staggering. What we have in this book are some common mantras – mantras that tend to exist outside the context of a particular text or ritual and have come to be generalised. Some of them come from *Mahāyāna sūtras*, some from *tantras*, and the origin of some is obscure. Some of the 'mantras' are not mantras at all, but are used in the way that a mantra is used, for example the chant: *sabbe sattā sukhi hontu*.

I see this book as a companion to Vessantara's books *Meeting the Buddhas* and *Female Deities in Buddhism*, where he gives proper introductions to the Buddhas and Bodhisattvas.[2] My initial aim was to provide a formal representation of mantras visualised in the course of Triratna Buddhist Order *sādhana* practices, as well as providing a resource for people who might want to take up mantra calligraphy, and also for artists painting thangkas. These still form the core of the book, but I've also gone beyond that initial brief by including deities and mantras from both Shingon and Tibetan lineages which will be less familiar to some readers. An important extension has been the linguistic analysis where it is possible, which grew out of my own interest in such matters. The limitations of this approach are considerable and I discuss them to some extent in context and in the reading material.

While mantra calligraphy practice is still popular in Japanese Buddhism, it has not yet taken off in the Western forms of Buddhism where handwriting itself, let alone calligraphy, is a dying art. Here one is more likely to have a mantra screen saver than be interested in mantra calligraphy.

Another early interest was to demonstrate and popularise the Siddhaṃ script used by Shingon Buddhists for writing mantras. It is elegant, and designed for writing Sanskrit – the name Siddhaṃ means 'perfected' suggesting it is the perfect script for writing Sanskrit, the perfect language (*saṃskṛta* means 'polished, perfected'). However it became apparent that most of my colleagues had a strong preference for Tibetan and so I started to learn the Tibetan script. Sadly my Tibetan has never reached a high standard, but with the advent of the Unicode standard for encoding non-Roman scripts the whole thing was simplified – I use fonts for Devanāgarī, Tibetan, Japanese, Chinese and most other languages where they are available. However it must be said that some of the computer encodings are different from printed or handwritten scripts. In Devanāgarīn for instance the fonts do not always support vertical

[1] http://www.visiblemantra.org
[2] Vessantara's work was originally published as a single book *Meeting the Buddhas*, but has since been re-published as three separate books.

stacking of conjunct consonants. I have retained my Siddhaṃ calligraphy because there is no good font for it yet, and for my own enjoyment.

Conventions.

Words from at least six different languages appear in this book. When non-English words occur in my text I will capitalise them using English conventions. There is a tendency to capitalise significant technical terms such as 'enlightenment' or '*nirvāṇa'*. I see this as an affectation.[3] Mantras will be transliterated in all lowercase because Sanskrit does not use capitals, and although there is a trend for using block capitals to transliterate mantras, I find it inelegant and, when the mantra is long, difficult to read.

Following scholarly practice non-English words, except for personal names and Anglicised words, are italicised: so '*maṇḍala*'; but 'mandala'. Publication titles are in italics. I have tried to avoid creating plurals by simply adding a 's' to a Sanskrit word – thereby creating a monster which is neither Sanskrit nor English – and will leave Sanskrit words in the singular e.g. *dhāraṇī* rather than *dhāraṇīs* (the nominative plural of *dhāraṇī* is in fact *dharaṇyaḥ*).

Sanskrit verbal roots are prefixed with √, and any roots which have been conjectured or hypothesised but not found in practice are preceded by * (used for instance when referring to the putative Proto-Indo-European language). When phonemes, sounds as distinct from letters, are discussed they are written between forward slashes: so the letter c in English can represent two phonemes /k/ and /s/ – in cake and ceiling respectively.

When writing mantras in non-Roman scripts I have followed the conventions for that script. Siddhaṃ leaves no spaces between words for instance. Tibetan does not leave spaces for words in mantras, but does use the *tsheg* (also spelt *tsig* etc.), a small dot to indicate syllables, and two syllables without a *tsheg* are read as one, often dropping the final vowel e.g. *padma* (པ་དྨ) becomes *pad ma* (པདམ). That said the *tsheg* is often left out of mantras which introduces some ambiguity. Devanāgarī, by contrast, almost always supplies spaces between words, but due to *sandhi* can combine two words into one long sequence. The ends of lines of poetry are marked by the *daṇḍa* '|' and this is also used irregularly as a universal punctuation mark in manuscripts.

Transliterating Tibetan can be a problem even for experts because pronunciation varies widely across Tibet. As in English, writing and pronunciation often differ, for instance *vajra* is transliterated as *badzra* (with no *tsheg)* and pronounced like *benza.* Tibetans regularly substitute *ba* for *va* when writing Sanskrit, similarly *jra* is transliterated as *dzra*; and *ca* as *tsa.* I have tried to stick to the Wylie scheme when transliterating Tibetan. The main Tibetan script I use is *dbu can,* pronounced 'uchen'. Where there is a significant difference from Sanskrit orthography I will note it. Wylie didn't include the special characters for writing Sanskrit in his transliteration scheme. The *Tibetan and Himlayan Library*[4] extended Wylie scheme avoids diacritics by using capitals: e.g. *dznyAna* for *jñāna.* I use diacritics where there isn't a standard Wylie transliteration when I'm transcribing text, e.g. *dznyāna.*

There are a number of different schemes for transliterating Chinese – I have favoured Pinyin over Wade-Giles because it is becoming the scholarly standard. I follow the widely used Hepburn scheme for transliterating Japanese. A table is provided at the end of the book with the names of the various figures in Tibetan and Japanese. Names are often transliterated rather than translated, i.e. the combination of characters is an attempt to capture the sound, rather than the

---

[3] It seems to me that Buddhists are following a Victorian habit of aping the King James Bible in capitalising words of religious significance. Indic scripts do not capitalise or otherwise mark Buddhist technical terms.

[4] http://www.thlib.org.

meaning of the name. Both Japan and Mainland China use sets of characters that have been simplified by reducing the number of strokes needed to write them. In Japan they are called *Shinjitai* (新字体) and the writing reforms were introduced after the Second World War and have been updated periodically since. In China they are called *Jiantizi* (简体字) and they were introduced in the 1950s. Both sets use traditional variants (e.g. Chinese has simplified 網 "net" with 网, and Japanese has simplified 佛 "Buddha" with 仏) and use simplified elements taken from handwriting and calligraphy (e.g. the character 見 "to see", is written 见 and then is incorporated as an element in many other characters, e.g. 观, 觉 and 规). Sometimes the simplifications correspond in the two systems but often they don't. Most of the simplifications don't appear in canonical texts as they were printed from wood blocks and the characters were written out in full but many of the variants do. Often Buddhist texts contain variant characters that have fallen completely out of use and some that are so rare that they are not supported by any computer encoding. For instance in his Chinese translation of the Large Perfection of Wisdom Sutra Kumārajīva uses a character 咤(*zhà*) which is not found in Unicode, so the CBETA Online Tripiṭaka represents it using two characters like this: [口*宅].

The difference between traditional forms, *shinjitai* and *jiantizi* is greater than the difference between British and American spellings. Some variations are easy to see but others are only obvious once they've been learnt. If you know the traditional form of *ying* 應 it's not obvious that the Japanese *shinjitai* is 応 and probably less obvious that the Chinese *jiantizi* is 应. Out of context there is little way of knowing that 応 and 应 are the same character. [5]

When transliterating mantras into Roman script I will give the syllables as well as the words because this makes it easier to decipher the Indic scripts which are syllabic.

[5] This explanation of Chinese and Japanese orthography is by Maitiu O'Ceileachair.

Pronouncing Sanskrit and Pāli

PRONOUNCING SANSKRIT and other Indic languages such as Pāli accurately can be quite difficult for native English speakers. Some of the Indian sounds such as the various nasal consonants are indistinquishable for most of us, and the retroflex stops are difficult to distinguish from dental stops. Since a wrongly pronounced word usually means something different, it is worth making the effort. Diacritics are important.

A rough guide

About 80% of pronouncing Sanskrit can be covered by a few basic rules

Pronounce all the letters. So Bud-d-ha, c-handa.
C is always soft as in church.
Curl your tongue back when there is a dot under the letter, except for...
ṃ, ḥ and ṛ which you can treat as though English with no dots.
A dash over a letter makes it longer.
If an‘s’ has diacritics - ie ś or ṣ - pronounce it ‘sh’.
Pronounce ṅ, ñ and ṇ as English ‘n’.
Sangha rhymes with sung, not sang. (*the* most common vowel mispronuciation).

Follow this and your mantras won’t sound too awful. If you are a bit more ambitious read on.

Comprehensive Guide

While a good enough approach will suit most people I hope that some will be interested enough to attempt a more accurate pronunciation. What follows provides a guide to all the sounds of Sanskrit (and Pāli which is actually a subset).

Vowels

a as in u in c<u>u</u>t
ā as in f<u>a</u>ther
i as in b<u>i</u>t
ī as in b<u>ee</u>t
u as in p<u>u</u>t or f<u>oo</u>t
ū as in br<u>u</u>te
e as in b<u>ay</u> (e.g. deva). In Pāli before a double consonant as in b<u>e</u>d (e.g. metta)
ai as in s<u>i</u>gh
o as in h<u>o</u>pe
au as in s<u>ou</u>nd
ṛ as in cu<u>r</u>

ṃ nasalise preceding vowel so that *oṃ* as in the French bon (although it is very common to hear it rhyme with bomb, I believe this is technically incorrect).
ḥ softly echoes the preceding vowel
ṝ rarely used in mantra, pronounce as for ṛ but longer.
ḷ and ḹ very rare in mantras. The tongue on the alveolar ridge (see diagram below). Sounds like the Japanese l/r. ḹ is longer.

Consonants

Sanskrit groups consonants by the position in the mouth where they are pronounced. Velar consonants are pronounced at the back of the throat with the tongue against the velum. Palatal consonants with the tongue pressed up against the patal. Retroflex consonants with the tip of the tongue bent back to touch the palate or alveolar ridge.[6] Dental consonants with the tongue on the teeth, and labial made with the lips. Because the Sanskrit alphabet has a few more letters than English, we employ some extra marks (called diacritics) to indicate the other letters when using the Roman alphabet. Most letters are pronounced like English consonants except for the following:

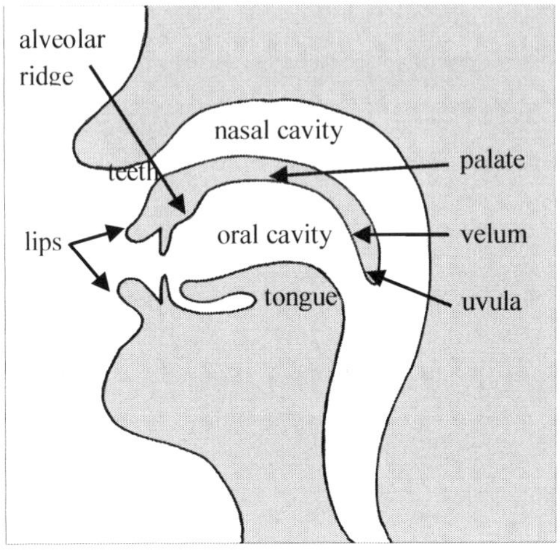

The Vocal Tract

v closer to w
c always soft as in church
ṅ (velar) like sung
ñ (palatal) as in canyon
ṇ (retroflex) like renown

Aspirated consonants
(kh, gh, ch, jh, th, dh, ph, bh)
The h's are pronounced. Especially note: th as in hothouse, not as in theatre, or there; and ph as in tophat, not as in philology.

The **dental consonants**
(t th d dh n)
Pronounced with the tongue on the teeth. In English our tongue is often on the gum behind the teeth, or on the alveolar ridge, making our dental stops sound like something between a true dental and a retroflex.

Retroflex consonants

[6] In Sanskritist circles, retroflex is sometimes called 'cerebral', a translation of the Sanskrit term *mūrdhanya*, 'made in the head'. This is now considered incorrect, if only because Latin *cerebrum* means 'brain'

(ṭ ṭh ḍ ḍh ṇ ṣ)
The tongue is curled back to touch the palate.

Sibilants
(ś ṣ s)
In practice the palatal ś and retroflex ṣ sibilants have not been distinguished since ancient times. Both are pronounced like the English phoneme /sh/. ś as in shame, ṣ similar to dish.

Stress

The ancient Vedic language, like ancient Greek, had pitch accents, that is to say that some syllables were pronounced at a higher pitch than others. These were gradually changed to stress accents not unlike those we use in English, though in English we can move the emphasis around in a sentence to alter the meaning (particularly in ironic statements).

Sanskrit stress accents are determined by heavy and light syllables. A syllable is light unless it has a long vowel (i.e. ā, ī, ū, ṝ, e, ai, o, au)[7] or it has a short vowel followed by a conjunct consonant – for example the 'ṛ' vowel in dṛṣṭi is short, but because it is followed by *ṣṭ* the syllable *dṛ* is heavy.

Stress falls on the last heavy syllable (shown in bold) up to four syllables back from the end. So **dhā**tu, Mahā**yā**na, **Ā**nanda. In a name like Satyānanda is falls on *yā* because of the long ā: Sat**yā**nanda. Similarly Ākāśa**gī**ta. However note: **Ā**ryadhara, but Ārya**ke**tu and Āryaku**mā**ra. Also Ma**hā**sukha (*kha* is an aspirated consonant, not a conjunct, so *su* is light); Saṅgha**ra**kṣita (the ra is heavy because it is followed by a conjunct); and Avaloki**te**śvara (e is a long vowel, and it is followed by a conjunct). Where there is no heavy syllable the stress falls on the penultimate syllable, e.g. Caruna**la**ka, Dṛḍha**ma**ti.

In the *Teach Yourself Sanskrit* (used as an introductory text in Universities around the world) Michael Coulson encourages us to dwell on heavy syllables in an exaggerated manner; and to draw out long vowels but skip lightly and quickly over short ones. Although this results in a somewhat dramatic pronunciation it is a good way to start.

Opinions of scholars on stress in Pāli seem to vary, but the consensus seems to be to follow the stress patterns of Sanskrit.

Notes

To hear the Sanskrit alphabet spoken try the sound files which go with *Samskrta-Subodhini: A Sanskrit Primer*, spoken by the author, Madhav M. Deshpande.[8]

It is worth noting that those traditions which use mantra are inconsistant on the subject of pronunciation. The old traditions and the texts themselves speak of the absolute necessity of correctly pronouncing the syllables for the mantras to have the desired effect. The Chinese are sensitive to this issue and retain the Siddhaṃ characters in the Taisho edition of the Tripiṭaka to ensure that the original pronunciation is not lost in transliterating mantras into Chinese characters.

However in practice those not born to Indic langauges may never really get the hang of the sounds and tend to incorporate 'fudges' into their pronunciation. So the Tibetans apparently

[7] e and o are long vowels, but do not have the macron – ē and ō – because the short ĕ and ŏ were long ago assimilated into the short a, so they don't need to be distinguished.
[8] http://www.umich.edu/~iinet/csas/publications/sanskrit/audio.html

struggle with *svāhā* and pronounce it *soha*; while the Japanese who have quite a restricted palette of sounds pronounce it *sowa*. In fact around India there is variation in pronunciation of Sanskrit, so that a Bengali will pronounce *namaskar* as though it is written 'nomoskar' (ie the vowel becomes rounded towards an /o/ sound). Also Bengali and Tibetan speakers regularly confuse /b/ and /v/ which are also often confused in writing Siddhaṃ and Tibetan.

There is an old story about someone who mistakenly was pronouncing their mantra incorrectly, but was making great progress with it. When a passing lama corrected their diction, the progress ceased! In one version the person runs across the top of the lake to catch up with the lama because he has forgotten how the mantra is supposed to sound. When Donald Lopez quotes this story in *Prisoners of Shangrila* (p.114) he notes that it is a short story by Tolstoy called The Three Hermits. Tolstoy apparently picked this story up from a wandering story teller in 1879, and its origins are obscure. Was the source in Tibetan, or has it been adapted by Tibetan Buddhists to explain changes in pronunciation? The story is reproduced in *The Autobiography of a Yogi* (p.309) by Paramhansa Yogananda, first published 1946. I suspect that this is the immediate source of the story in Buddhist circles.

There are good aesthetic grounds for attempting to pronounce a language as it is supposed to be pronounced - think how we often wince to hear our mother tongue mangled by a non-native speaker, and how we value words well spoken. Imagine that Sanskrit is the language of the Buddha or Bodhisattva whose mantra you are chanting... would it not be a good idea to pronounce their name well?

However it is also true that if you change the sound of a word, substituting a dental for a retroflex consonant, or a long vowel for a short one, you are frequently using a different word which may well exist indepently and have a different meaning. For instance: *dharma* is the teachings, reality, and phenomena; while *dhārma* (long ā) is "justice"; *dāma* (close to how *dharma* is frequently pronounced by English speakers) is "a donor or giver"; and *darma* is "a demolisher" (so don't drop that h!). Our English /d/ sounds a little like the Indian /ḍ/ and this can make a huge difference: *ḍama* for instance means "a despised mixed caste".

Finally I may say that in attempting to pronounce Sanskrit accurately, in paying attention to what our tongue is doing when we speak, and paying attention to the details of Sanskrit generally, we are more likely to fulfil the Buddha's injunction that we are mindful of our speech.

Using Diacritics

Diacritics are those dots, dashes, and squiggly lines above and below letters which one sees when Sanskrit, Pāli, and Japanese are transliterated using Roman characters, i.e. the letters we use to write English. Throughout this book I have opted to include all diacritics for Roman script transliterations of Sanskrit, Pāli, and Japanese. Why? Isn't this just being pedantic? No, it isn't. Diacritics convey important information. It is important for instance to distinguish between 't' and 'ṭ' because they are completely different letters of the alphabet, and are pronounced differently. If you look at the table of Siddhaṃ characters you can see that the two letters have nothing in common when written in Siddhaṃ. In Devanāgarī they are: त and ट

It may be argued that English speakers will inevitably pronounce them the same anyway so why bother? There's a story about a person who goes to a Chinese restaurant and orders a steak. The waiter comes along a few minutes after it's delivered to the table and asks how the steak is. The person says, "it's rubbery". The waiter says: "Rubbery? Oh that's good, I'rr go and terr the chef, he'rr be so preased to hear it". The Chinese can also poke fun at us: for instance the syllable 'ma' can mean mother, numb, horse, or scold, depending on the tones used and it takes time to master tones when one is not a native speaker.

The point here is not to make fun of other people's pronunciation, but that as it makes a difference in English, so why would Sanskrit be different? Precision in pronunciation is desireable because it aids communication, and reduces the chances of being misunderstood. Wrtng Snskrt wtht dcrtcs s bt lk wrtng Nglsh nd mssng t th vwls.[9] It may be possible to correctly reconstruct and understand the original... or it may not.

[9] i.e. writing Sanskrit without diacritics is a bit like writing English without the vowels.

Scripts

IN THIS BOOK SEVERAL SCRIPTS are used for mantras. The main are Siddhaṃ, Tibetan (*dbu-can*), Lantsa (or Ranjana) and Devanāgarī. These four are the most common scripts one is likely to encounter, although other scripts have been, and still are, used. The diagram below shows how some of the more prominent scripts are related. Note that the relationships between the scripts does not imply the same kind of relationship between languages.

Script Family Tree

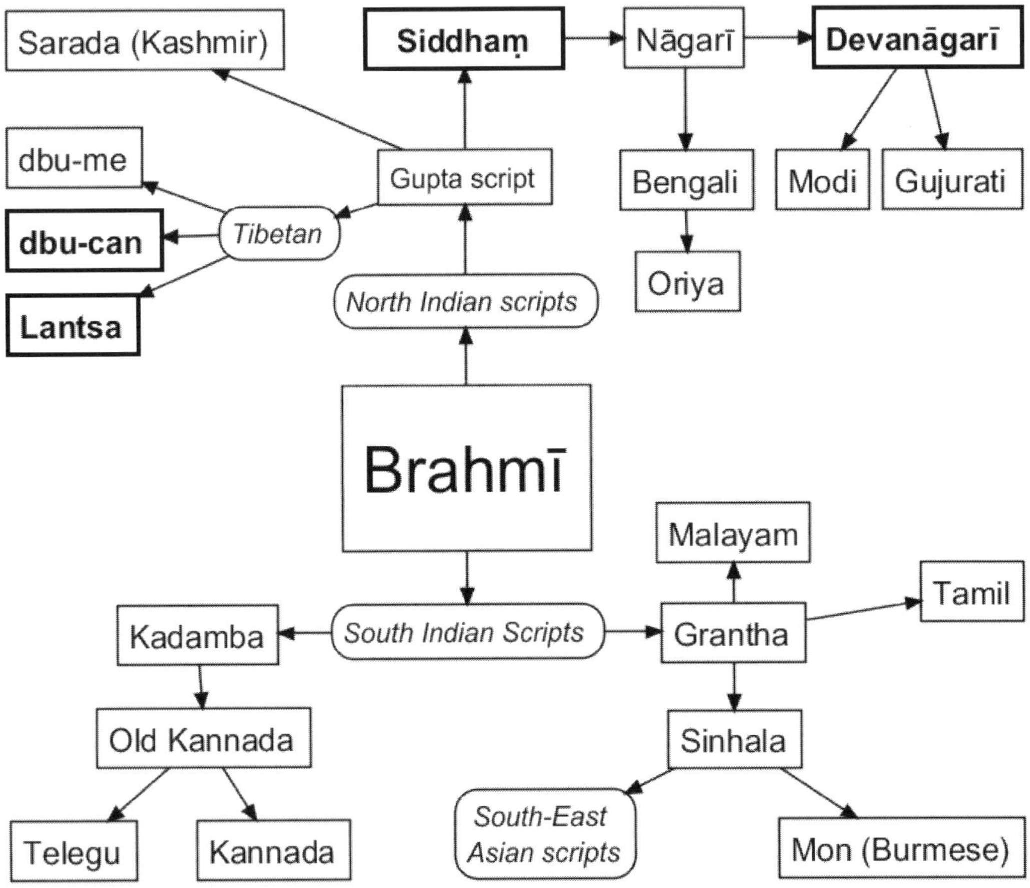

Brahmī

All Indian scripts are derived from the Brāhmī script which came into wide-spread use during the time of King Aśoka. Buddhists initially resisted the use of writing, only resorting to writing down their texts some four or five centuries after writing was introduced to India. However once they started using writing, Buddhists became envangelists for its use and spread the use of writing throughout South, and South East Asia as they spread the Buddhadharma.

This example of Brahmi script below was transcribed from the fragment of pillar 6, an inscription by King Aśoka formerly at Meerut, about 100km north-east of New Delhi. The fragment is dated to mid-3rd century BCE, and now housed in the British Museum. The bottom line is part of a stock phrase which is found in other inscriptions:

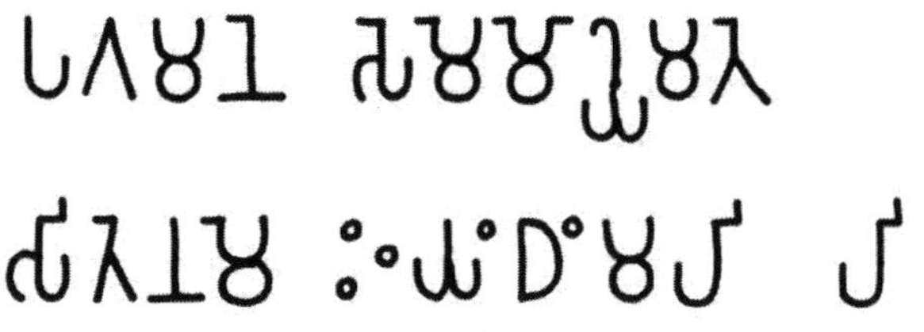

...pagamane sememokhyamate...
...sitename iyaṃdhaṃmali ... li

[saḍuvīsativābhi]sitena me iyaṃ dhaṃmma li[pi] li[khāpita]

"when I had been consecrated twenty-six years I ordered this inscription of the dhamma to be engraved".[10]

Siddhaṃ

After Aśoka's Empire writing continued to develop. During the Gupta Empire (ca. 3rd – 6th century CE) the script used in the Northeast was distinctive enough for historians to name it 'the Gupta script'. Siddhaṃ is a descendent of the Gupta script. It was the form of writing used in the centuries following the collapse of the Gupta Empire, roughly the period from the 6th to 12th century CE. The name Siddhaṃ comes from the practice of teachers writing the word *siddhaṃ* 'perfection' at the top of a writing tablet for students to copy as a prelude to learning the rest of the script. A number of variations on this script are preserved in manuscripts.

A form of Siddhṃ is preserved by the Shingon School of Japan where it is known as Bonji (梵字) '*brāhmī* chracters' or Shittan (悉曇) which transliterates '*siddhaṃ*'. Siddhaṃ is also used in the Taisho edition of the Chinese Tripitaka to record mantras. The image below is from Taisho No. 913 and reads *oṃ a mṛ ta hūṃ pha ṭ* - ie *oṃ amṛta hūṃ phaṭ*. *Amṛta* means 'immortal' or 'undying', and can also refer to a kind of elixir of life. Below the Siddhaṃ is the Chinese transliteration, with information on pronunciation. T. 913 is a *homa pūja* (or fire ritual) manual.

[0935a04]
[5] 
唵 [6]阿[合*牛] 密[7][口*栗](二合) [8]多 [合*牛] [打-丁+市] 吒(半[9]音)

It can be written with a pen or a brush – pen calligraphy is used in this book. In Japanese sources you sometimes see Siddhaṃ spelt Siddhāṃ (with the long ā) but this is incorrect. A more detailed account of Siddhaṃ is included below (p.25).

---

[10] c.f. the 1st pillar in A. L. Basham *The Wonder that was India* p.395. A translation of what is left of pillar 6 is available in *The Edicts of King Asoka: An English Rendering* by Ven. S. Dhammika. http://www.accesstoinsight.org/lib/authors/dhammika/wheel386.html

Tibetan

In Tibet the Gupta script developed into a number of different scripts ,Uchen (*dbu-can*) and Ume *(dbu-med)* are used in this book. There are also Drutsa (*'bru-tsha*) and Chuyik (*'khyug-yig*) and Bamyik (*'bam-yig*). The relationship of the Tibetan scripts to the varieties of spoken Tibetan is complex, much like the relationship of spoken to written English.

Uchen (*dbu-can*)

This script is what most people think of as "Tibetan". It is a formal script that has become the standard for printing. It is quite good for calligraphy though more demanding than Siddhaṃ

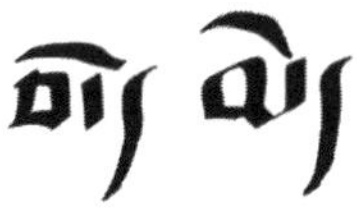

Ume (*dbu-med*)

Ume (literally 'headless') is a cursive script for hand writing, which has general as well as sacred uses.

Lantsa or Rañjana

Although these two scritps are often conflated because they are quite similar, there are subtle distinctions in writing them. They both emerged around the 10th century and derive from the Gupta script. The Tibetan variant is called Lantsa (ལན་ཚ་) which derives from the Nepalese *rañjā*, and it is mainly used for ceremonial purposes, such as writing mantras or special Sanskrit phrases. Rañjana is the Nepalese script. Additionally, Lantsa is written in several different styles. In this book the CBETA Ranjana font is used as representative of these scripts.

Devanāgarī

देवनागरी

Devanāgarī is the chief script in use in North India for writing Sanskrit and Hindi, as well as some other languages, such as Marathi. Some scripts, such as Bengali and Gujurati are very closely related. Devanāgarī first appeared about the eighth century, but did not finally displace Siddaṃ until about the tenth century.

Other Scripts

Amoung the other scripts used for mantras or related writing you will find some Kharoṣṭhī (read right to left), which is important as probably the earliest form of writing in India. The Arapacana alphabet, which became associated with Mañjuśrī Mantra, originated as the alphabet of the Gāndhārī language written in Kharoṣṭhī. In recent years, a number of caches of very old manuscripts written in the Kharoṣṭhī script have been found in the old Gandhāra area in the North-west of Pakistan.

Sinhala was used for recording the Pāli texts and is therefore very important for Buddhism. It is derived from southern variants of Brahmi. Similarly Pāli is recorded in Thailand and Burma in their local scripts, which are both derived from Brahmi.

සිංහල

For a bit of fun I have included some made-up scripts, Klingon and Elvish versions of the Avalokiteśvara mantra for instance.

Links between Aramaic and Kharoṣṭhī, and between Kharoṣṭhī and Brāhmī, and between any of them and the Indus Valley script (if it is a script[11]) are conjectured, but while interesting theories abound, none is proved, and with the paucity of evidence none seems proveable at present.

Further Reading on Scripts

There are several websites which catalogue scripts and give details of how they came into being, and where and how long they were in use.

- Probably the most useful and comprehensive is *Ominglot.*[12]
- The *Ancient Scripts* website compliments Omniglot and has useful info on relationships and timeframes.[13]
- *Indian Scripts in Tibet* is very detailed.[14]

Richard Salomon's review article: *On the origins of the Early Indian Scripts*[15] is full of useful information. It was originally published in the *Journal of the American Oriental Society*, 115.2 (1995), 271-279 .

Judicious use of search engines will turn up more, of course. There are active projects to include many of these scripts in the unicode specification.

---

[11] The experts Michael Witzel and Steve Farmer have recently concluded that while the symbols may be meaningful, they are probably not writing.

[12] http://www.omniglot.com/

[13] http://www.ancientscripts.com/sa_ws.html

[14] http://www.lantsha-vartu.org/index.html

[15] http://indology.info/papers/salomon/

Siddhaṃ: The Perfect Script

Siddhaṃ Sanskrit Alphabet

Siddhaṃ means 'perfected' or 'accomplished' and is believed by some Buddhists to be the perfect script intended for writing the perfect language: Sanskrit.

Ancient Indians did not use writing for spiritual purposes. Scripture was heard at the foot of the master, and committed to memory. Writing was introduced, probably from Persia, by merchants who used it for commerce. King Aśoka (273-36 BCE) chose writing to communicate his message by having it carved on large pillars of stone and rocks. He wrote in a vernacular Prakrit and mainly used the Brahmi script, although Kharoṣṭhī and even Aramaic and Greek scripts were also used. However, around the 1st century BCE, Buddhists began to write down their scriptures and writing became an increasingly important medium for Buddhists after that.

Siddhaṃ is descended from the Brāhmī script, which also gave rise to the Devanāgarī scripts as well as a number of non-Indian scripts such as the various Tibetan scripts, and most of the scripts of Southeast Asia. It was an influence on the development of the Japanese kana script and on the Korean Hangul script.

The story goes that when a student was learning to write during the Gupta era (ca. 3rd - 6th centuries CE), the teacher would write *siddhaṃ* 'perfection' or *siddhamastu* 'may there be perfection' for the student to copy out.[16] Gradually the writing became known as Siddhaṃ, and by the 7th century it was a distinct script. However Siddhaṃ continued to change and develop. As well the form of Siddhaṃ found in stone inscriptions is often slightly different to written Siddhaṃ because of the demands of the medium. The calligraphy in this book is in a form of modern Siddhaṃ that owes a lot to Japanese aesthetics.[17]

The Buddhist scriptures that were taken east by Indian missionaries and Chinese pilgrims were written in a number of languages and scripts. Siddhaṃ is really only remembered because the Japanese monks Kūkai and Saichō studied it in China and transplanted it into Japan in the early 9th century. Kūkai and Saichō founded, respectively, the Shingon and Tendai schools of Buddhism. Shingon is a purely esoteric, or Mantrayāna school, whereas the Tendai school is primarily an exoteric school focused on the *Saddharmapuṇḍarīka Sūtra*, but incorporating esoteric elements. Both still use Siddhaṃ for writing mantras.

[16] This story is repeated in John Steven's book *Sacred Calligraphy of the East* (p.33) where he notes that the form used in Japan – *siddhāṃrastu* – is not "strictly speaking, grammatically correct". In fact it is simply incorrect. The problem is that *siddhāṃ* should have a short *a* i.e. *siddhaṃ*; and there is no word *rastu*. The verb √*as* 'to be' in the third person imperative is *astu* 'may it be. Sandhi dictates that *ṃ* followed by *a* combines into *ma*.

[17] Though fluent in this style of Siddhaṃ I find I cannot read ancient manuscripts for instance.

An important change occurred in China. In India, even though they did begin to write scripture down, it was always as an aid to memory – writing was secondary. The Indians had solved the problem of a large number of dialects and languages by using a lingua franca - Sanskrit, and to a lesser extent Pāli. In China, however, which also boasts a large number of dialects, the problem was solved by a common writing system which could be pronounced according to dialect, but read the same everywhere. By the time the Buddhist scriptures arrived in China, nothing was worth anything unless it was written down. So Siddhaṃ came to be more important in its own right.

Not long after Kūkai's and Saichō's visits to China in the early ninth century, the Tang dynasty collapsed and Buddhism almost died out in China - certainly esoteric Buddhism, in which the Siddhaṃ script was particularly used for writing mantras, did die out in China. However, esoteric Buddhism, along with the study of Siddhaṃ, still survives in Japan. Siddhaṃ also survives in Korea, although books on Siddhaṃ do not record this fact. A photograph turned up recently on Flickr.com[18] which shows a Korean *bīja mantra* which clearly originates from the Siddhaṃ script. I corresponded with the author of the photo and discovered that they are relatively common, but no more information has surfaced since.

Another place where Siddhaṃ survives is in the Taisho version of the Chinese Tripiṭaka. In the days when the canon was compiled it was still considered essential to preserve the correct Sanskrit pronunciation. Rather than transliterating mantras with Chinese characters, as was done with names for instance, the Siddhaṃ was therefore preserved alongside the Chinese translation.

Attitudes to pronunciation have shifted over time, and now both the Tibetans and Japanese (not to mention English speakers!) regularly pronounce mantras with no regard for the Sanskrit. It is sometimes said that the mantras 'still work' but I've never been very sure what that means and prefer to learn to attempt to accurately render the Sanskrit rather than accept the cop-out (c.f. my comments on pronunciation p. 25).

The copying of sutras, mantras and seed syllables, known as *shakyo* is still an important spiritual practice in Shingon Buddhism. Although Siddhaṃ is primarily intended for writing Sanskrit it can be used to write any Indic language - see the Pāli phrase *sabbe sattā sukhi hontu* for instance (p.237).

[18] http://www.flickr.com/photos/parrhesiastes/487612545/

Punctuation

Mantras in Indic scripts were not usually punctuated, even when punctuation began to be used. However ancient inscriptions and texts often have special symbols or signs at the beginning and end. These do not appear to have names in Indic languages, or even specific 'meanings', though in general terms they fit the category of *maṅgala* or auspicious marks along with the *svastika*. In 1904 Georg Bühler observed that it was a Brahmanical maxim that a composition should have a *maṅgala* at the beginning, in the middle and at the end.[19] In Tibetan scripts, including Lantsa, mantras do get some punctuation in addition to *maṅgala* symbols. This section explores the types of symbols and marks we might encounter in written mantras.

The most common beginning marker is known as *yimgo* (i.e. *yig mgo*) in Tibetan, and since I have found no certain name for it in Indic language I will call it by the Tibetan name. The earliest versions of the *yimgo* are a simple spiral curve, though the orientation varies over time. The first non-Indian commentator on this feature was al-Bīrūnī[20] (973-1048) who interpreted the sign as *oṃ*.[21] His observation seems to have been accepted by most observers until the matter was reconsidered by Nalinikanta Bhattasali in 1923. Bhattasali put forward the idea that in fact the *yimgo* represented the word *siddhiḥ*. He had three reasons for this: 1. it is commonly used in old manuscripts; 2. in Gupta inscriptions either the symbol or the word *siddhi* appear at the head, and never both; and 3. in many inscriptions it appears before oṃ and the two are unlikely to appear together.[22]

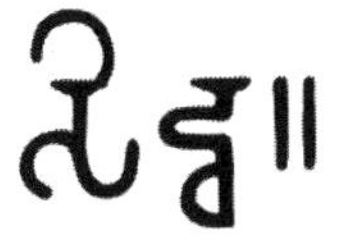

siddha in the Brāhmī script style of the inscriptions at Sanchi.

D.C. Sircar (1965) accepts as certain the identification of the *yimgo* with *siddhiḥ*, or *siddhir astu*.[23] The subject is taken up in 1986 by both Roth and Sanders who present several dozen examples between them which bolster the conclusion that the *yimgo* stands for *siddhiḥ* or *siddhaṃ*. Roth notes that *maṅgala* symbols are rare on Aśoka inscriptions. We know from Cunningham's records of the inscriptions at Sanchi that by the Common Era inscriptions were often accompanied by maṅgala.[24] The word *siddhaṃ* appears at the head of an inscription for the first time between the 1st and 4th centuries in Mathurā. By the early Gupta period (ca. 4th century) *siddhaṃ* is used in the majority of inscriptions. Indeed the fact is what gives the post-Gupta script it's name. Contrary to Bhattasali, Roth finds one example of the occurrence of the symbol along with *siddhi* in a manuscript of the *Pañcakrama*, a tantric text attributed to Nāgārjuna.[25] He interprets it as "explaining" the symbol, but c.f. Bhattasali's conclusion that the sign and *oṃ* are unlikely to occur together. Finding the two together actually weakens the conclusion that the symbol stands for *siddhi*. Roth discusses, but dismisses the idea

[19] Bühler (1904) p.109.
[20] Also spelled Al Beruni, or Al bērūnī.
[21] Bhattasali (1923-4) p.352.
[22] Bhattasali (1923-4) p.352.
[23] *Siddhir astu* 'may there be perfection'. Sircar (1965) p.92-93. The phrase is also used by Hindus as a mantra for Gaṇeṣa. On some websites the words are incorrectly parsed from the Devanāgarī सिद्धिरस्तु as *siddhi rastu*. The *sandhi* rule is that when *–iḥ* is followed by a vowel it becomes *–ir*. So in effect the r here stands for *visarga*.
[24] See e.g. Cunningham (1854), plate XLX, p.449.
[25] Roth (1986) p.240.

that the *yimgo* is a form of the Brāhmī *o akṣara*. By the end of his article Roth is referring to the *siddhaṃ* symbol, though does not establish the identification beyond doubt.

Where Roth draws on a wide variety of Indian manuscripts and inscriptions, Sander looks specifically at manuscripts from Gilgit, Kucha and Khotan. Here she finds that while in Kucha and Khotan the word *siddhaṃ* is used, the Gilgit manuscripts mainly use the *yimgo* symbol. However she also notes that the symbol and the word *siddhaṃ* often occur together. The fact of their occurring together I again take as weakening the argument that the symbol indicates the word.[26] Salomon (1998) writes that it is "probably more accurate" to treat the *yimgo* as *siddhaṃ*. He bases this on the same sources that I have just reviewed, but his treatment is merely a few sentences amidst a very broad exploration of epigraphy – he has no time to dwell on this kind of detail, especially when there is no solid evidence.[27] The selections below convey the variations shown by Roth and Sander. The top line is from Roth's early manuscripts, while the lower examples are from Sander's Gilgit manuscripts.

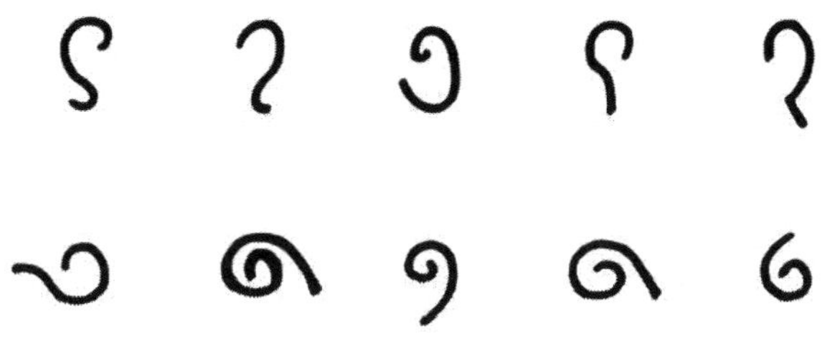

This shape, especially the top line, is also found in another context which appears not to have been considered by epigraphy scholars. Coins from the Indian Kingdom of Kuninda (ca. 2nd century BCE to the 3rd Century CE) often have Buddhist symbols on both sides. The reverse often has *svastika*, tree in railing, and other *maṅgala* symbols. On the obverse often appears a deer with a sign of two cobras between his horns.[28]

Not much appears to be known about this symbol, and it does always appears between the deer horns. However, the similarity is striking. If we identify the two cobras with the *yimgo* symbols then perhaps the *yimgo* is in fact a serpent, a *nāga*, perhaps even related to the legend of Mucalinda the cobra who spread his hood over the meditating Buddha to keep the rain off him.

We find the *yimgo* symbol in Rañjana/Lantsa and Siddhaṃ scripts.

In Tibetan the symbol becomes more elaborate:

[26] See Sander (1986) esp. p.257-8.
[27] Salomon (1998) p.67-68.
[28] Fishman (2006).

The first symbol here is *bdra rnying yig mgo mdun ma* which seems to mean 'old orthography header', so-called since it is used in early texts. Clearly this is more or less identical to the Siddhaṃ script *yimgo*. The second symbol is the *yimgo* accompanied by the *yig mgo sgab ma* 'following *yimgo'*. The third and fourth symbols are the modern version of these symbols.[29] In addition there are some *yimgo* which combine other symbols:

These are first: the *yig mgo phur shad ma* or '*yimgo* decorated with a *shad*' (see below for the *shad*); second: *yig mgo tsheg shad ma*, the old style *yimgo* with both shad and *tsheg*; third and fourth : the *gug rtags gyon* and *gug rtags gyas* or opening and closing brackets.

Furthermore the *yimgo* is combined with other punctuation marks, but I need to introduce these first. Punctuation is rare and usually entirely absent in the earliest Indian inscriptions.[30] As time goes on the *daṇḍa* – a single vertical stroke | – is introduced, but it is still used sporadically and irregularly. It is not until the Gupta period that regular use of punctuation begins to be seen. Eventually two marks were used. In verse the single *daṇḍa* | was used to mark the end of a line or *pada*, and the double *daṇḍa* || was used to mark the end of a stanza or *gāthā*. In prose the *daṇḍa* was, and is, used variably where in English we might use a comma, semicolon, colon, or even a full-stop. The double *daṇḍa* is used at the end of paragraphs, sections, and texts. The Rañjana/Lantsa script has forms of the *daṇḍa* and double *daṇḍa*:

The Siddhaṃ script also has *daṇḍa* and double *daṇḍa* but they seem to be used quite rarely in either mantras or texts. Modern Japanese Siddhaṃ has a modified *daṇḍa* which my Japanese Siddhaṃ manual describes as an incomplete letter *da*.[31] For reference they look like this:[32]

daṇḍa double daṇḍa alternate daṇḍa

In Tibetan the *daṇḍa* is called a *shad* (pronounced *shé*) and performs more or less the same function, though some manuscripts start each line a shad as well as ending it. As with the *yimgo* there are some decorative variants

[29] See West (2005) & (2006a).
[30] Salomon (1998) p.66.
[31] i.e. "*da* 字の省略". Kodama (1991) p.222.
[32] C.f. Stevens (1995), p.41.

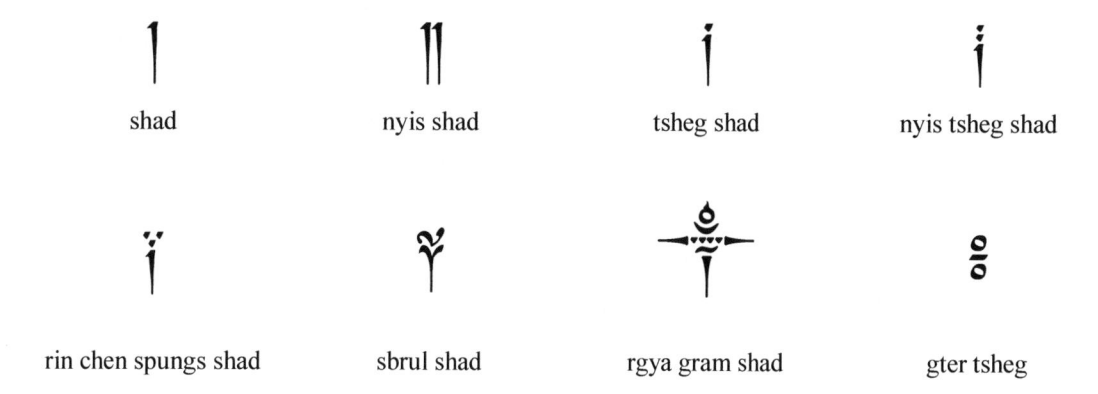

shad | nyis shad | tsheg shad | nyis tsheg shad

rin chen spungs shad | sbrul shad | rgya gram shad | gter tsheg

The *shad* and *nyis* (double) *shad* are the same as the Indic *daṇḍa* and double *daṇḍa*. These are the most common seen forms in mantras. The *tsheg shad* decorates the *shad* with a dot (similar to the syllable marker also called a *tsheg*). The *nyis* (double) *tsheg shad* has two *tshegs*. Along the bottom row we have the *rin chen spungs* (mound of jewels) *shad*; the *sbrul* (snake stroke) *shad*; the highly elaborated *rgya gram* (cross) *shad*; and finally the *gter* (treasure) *tsheg* – a decorative form of the syllable market that is sometimes used in place of a *shad* at the end of mantras. Some of these symbols do have distinct functions in texts, but apart from the *shad*, double *shad* and *gter tsheg* they are seldom seen in mantras.

We often see combinations of *yimgo* and *shad* in Tibetan such as:

These are used at the beginning of pages of manuscripts. In Rañjana or Lantsa mantras we also see the *yimgo* and *daṇḍa* combined at the beginning of mantras:

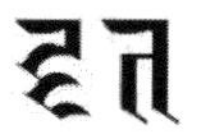

Finally there are a number of auspicious marks used at the end of texts or chapters of texts. These range from a simple circle to a variety of very elaborate signs. Some are just geometric; others are obviously based on the lotus flower, or the *vajra*.

In ancient inscriptions other auspicious marks are used along with mantras. Of these the *svastika* is still in common use in Tibet and East Asia, though the association with Nazi Germany has lead to its suppression in the West. One sees the *svastika* in both clockwise and anticlockwise orientations and also decorated with dots. [33] These four symbols have been included in the Unicode standard for computer encoded Tibetan *dbu can* script.

࿕ ࿖ ࿗ ࿘

The *svastika* is also used in China as a *hànzì* (漢字) or ideograph: 卍 卐. Andrew West relates that the Empress Wu decreed in 693 CE that the symbol should be pronounced like 萬 (wàn). In writing it's generally only used in the form 卍字 (wàn zì) meaning the *svastika* character.[34] Another story one sometimes see about the svastika is that it is a monogram. This story is repeated in Monier-Williams Sanskrit dictionary which may account for how it became popular. A bit of detective work shows that General Sir Alexander Cunningham, later the first director of the Archaeological Survey of India, makes the claim in his book *The Bhilsa Topes*. Cunningham surveyed the great stupa complex at Sanchi in 1851, where he famously found caskets of relics labelled 'Sāriputta' and 'Mahā Mogallāna'.[35] *The Bhilsa Topes* records the features, contents, artwork and inscriptions found in and around these stupas. All of the inscriptions he records are in Brāhmī script. What he says is:

> "The swasti of Sanskrit is the suti of Pali; the mystic cross, or swastika is only a monogrammatic symbol formed by the combination of the two syllables, su + ti = suti."[36]

There are two problems with this.

1. While there is a word *suti* in Pāli it is equivalent to Sanskrit *śruti* 'hearing'. The Pali equivalent of *svasti* is *sotthi*; and *svastika* is either *sotthiya* or *sotthika*. Cunningham is simply mistaken about this.
2. The two letters *su* + *ti* in Brāhmī script are not like the *svastika* at all. This can easily been seen in the accompanying image below, where I have written the words in the Brāhmī script. I've included the Sanskrit and Pali words for comparison. Cunningham's imagination has run away with him.

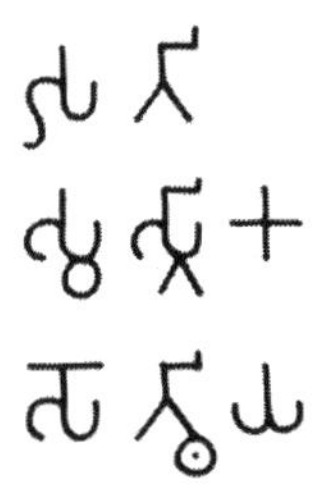

suti

svastika

sottiya

[33] The notion that the Buddhist svastika is a different orientation to the Nazi one is unfortunately incorrect. Indian svastikas go in both directions as seen above.

[34] West (2006b).

[35] This story is well recounted in Allen (2002), see especially p.214f.

[36] Cunningham (1854) p.18, note.

A few other marks are seen in early inscriptions and on coins. These include the three jewels symbol and the tree in railings.

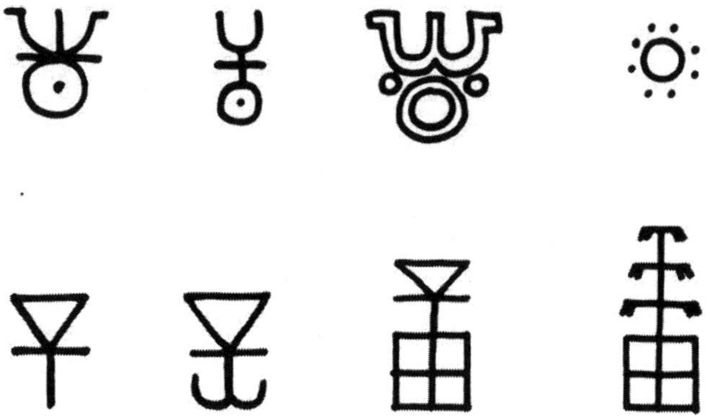

The first three symbols on the top left are referred to as symbolising the Three Jewels. The top right hand symbol is probably solar. Along the bottom are variations on the bodhi tree, particularly surrounded by a railing. The symbol at bottom right is from a Kuninda coin and second from the right is from an inscription at Sanchi. Fishman says the two symbols on the bottom left are usually refered to as ‘the standard’, but the similarity with the Sanchi tree symbol does suggest the tree. Another possibility is that it is the umbrella that is a symbol of royalty.

Anusvāra and Visarga

THESE ARE THE MARKS that one frequently sees attached to syllables which indicated nasalisation and aspiration respectively. In Roman script these are *ṃ* and *ḥ* respectively.

Anusvāra

Anusvāra means 'after-sound'. In Japanese it is *kū-ten* (空点), the 'void point'.[37] When the *anusvāra* is used it means that the vowel of the syllable is nasalised – for instance, the 'a' (ə in the phonetic alphabet) sound in *but*, changes to the 'ang' sound in *bung*, or the first syllable in *onion*. In the Brāhmī script the *anusvāra* was indicated by a dot to the right of the syllable, but this gradually moved to sit above the letter. A dot above the syllable is the way it is used in other Indic scripts including Tibetan. In Roman transliteration anusvāra is written as *ṃ*. So *aṃ* would be written:

Siddhaṃ Devanāgarī Tibetan

The esoteric significance is indicated by the Japanese name: it symbolises *śūnyatā*. Adding *anusvāra* to a syllable indicates that the syllable never quite ends, but fades into a nasal hum, and by analogy the concept conveyed by the syllable merges into emptiness.

One also sees a more elaborate version of the *anusvāra* in which a half-moon shape sits under the dot, e.g.

This is known as *anunāsika* meaning 'from the nose' a more general term for nasal sounds in Sanskrit; or *candra-bindu* literally 'moon & drop'. The symbolism of the candra-bindu was elaborated in Tantric Buddhism. When Devanāgarī is used to write Sanskrit the *candra-bindu* is only used in special circumstances such as nasalised semi-vowels: v, l, y. These are seldom if ever used in practice but can be created by *sandhi*. In Tibetan and Siddhaṃ the *candra-bindu* is routinely used for seed syllables.

lṃ[38] aṃ

The old way of writing *auṃ* with the *candra-bindu* is often retained in Devanāgarī.

[37] The syllable 空 *kū* is also found in Kūkai's name (空海). Adrian Snodgrass (1988) transliterates 点 as *den*, which as far as I can ascertain is incorrect. John Stevens refers to this as *bodai ten* but gives no kanji.

[38] It's not entirely clear how this nasalised vocalic *l* would be pronounced.

ॐ

In Hindi *chandra-bindu* is used unless the syllable has a vowel mark that rises above the line. So with the syllable *ha*:

हँ हाँ हिं हीं हुँ हूँ हृँ हें हैं हों हौं

haṃ hāṃ hiṃ hīṃ huṃ hūṃ hṛṃ heṃ haiṃ hoṃ hauṃ

In transliteration *anusvāra* is written as *ṃ* or *ṁ* following the syllable – either is correct but the underdot tends to be used more often. This reflects contemporary usage since the *ṃ* is often given a distinct /m/ sound with the lips coming together. *Baṃ* technically rhymes with the French *bon*, not with the English *bomb*, let alone English *ham*. However even in India the distincton is often lost.

Sometimes the *anusvāra* is used to replace nasal consonants in words, usually on the grounds that it saves having to write a conjunct and is often much easier and takes up less space. A good example is the word *saṅgha*. It is very common to see this word spelt saṃgha. A nasal in combination with another consonant always takes on the value of the consonant for that series. So for instance *ṃ* before *ka*, *kha*, *ga*, or *gha* is always *ṅ*, and before *ca*, *cha*, *ja*, *jha* is always *ñ*. So although it is not as explicit, the practice doesn't result in ambiguity. A slight problem may occur when the word *saṅgha* spelt *saṃgha* would be incorrectly romanised to samgha, but this is rare.

Visarga

The word *visarga* means 'sending forth' or 'letting go'. The root is √*sṛj* meaning 'to send forth'. The suffix *vi-* probably functioning as an intensive in this case, though it can also mean 'out, away from'.[39] The *visarga* is an unvoiced aspiration – a small puff of air after the syllable. Sometimes following 'a' it is a faint echo of the 'a', and other times it is a barely discernable breath. In practice pronunciation of *visarga* is variable and irregular.

In Indic scripts and Tibetan the visarga is indicated by two dots like a colon to the right of the letter, and by a *ḥ* in Roman script. So *aḥ* is written:

𑖀𑖾	अः	ཨཿ
Siddhaṃ	Devanāgarī	Tibetan

This 'sending forth' is interpreted in esoteric symbolism as 'blowing out' i.e. *nirvāṇa*. In Japanese it is called *nehan-ten* (涅槃点) '*nirvāṇa* points' and as it is unvoiced it represents the 'serene and eternal silence of *nirvāṇa*'. In Shingon mantra theory adding a *visarga* to a *bīja* indicates that the symbol is transposed to the level of *nirvāṇa*.

[39] Adrian Snodgrass (1988, Vol.1, p.54) says it is √*srig* which is an incorrect spelling – his definition is correct however.

Compare the esoteric significance with the ways in which the four variations on the syllable *a* are related to the stages of the path and Buddha's of the *maṇḍala* in the section on the *bīja a* (p.172).

The Arapacana Alphabet

One of the most fascinating aspects of Buddhist mantra is the Arapacana alphabet, its importance is seldom recognised. The ideas which underlie the Arapacana are crucial in later Tantric practice. What follows is amalgamated from several short essays I wrote for my blog. Until very recently the Arapacana was assumed to be a mystical construction. I summarise the research which shows that it was far more mundane, and trace the history of its use over time. I also try to show how it would have been used in practice in the Mahāyāna phase (as opposed to its use in Tantric practices).

The Arapacana Alphabet in Siddhaṃ Script

Arapacana

WHAT IS NOW CALLED the 'Arapacana Alphabet' after the first five letters (*a ra pa ca na*), has also sometimes been called the 'Wisdom Alphabet' because of its association with the Perfection of Wisdom tradition. The earliest references to the Arapacana occur in Gandhāra in the first centuries of the Common Era. Particularly important are a collection of texts found in 1998 near Bajaur in what is now Pakistan.[40] These birch-bark manuscripts from the 1st or 2nd Centuries contain a fragment which has a series of lines with keywords in the order of the Kharoṣṭhī alphabet. Other important sources include bas-relief stone carving depicting scenes from the *Lalitavistara Sūtra*, and engravings on the back of some of the carvings. Richard Salomon (2006) has used the latter to confirm that the order of vowels in Kharoṣṭhī is the same as Aramaic and different from other Indian scripts.

Salomon places the origins of Kharoṣṭhī in about the 4th century BCE, and Brahmi about the 3rd century BCE (Salomon 1995). The model for the Kharoṣṭhī script is thought to be a form of Aramaic writing used by Persians. Several features, including the order of vowels, writing right to left, and the form of some letters, make this seem very likely. In addition, the use of the alphabet as a mnemonic probably demonstrates outside influence, since no other Indian texts use this method, while Manichean and Hebrew texts do. We know that Gandhāra was subject to many invasions through the Khyber Pass, and at the time of the earliest references to the Arapacana Alphabet the rulers were the Kushans. It is notable that also at this time images of the Buddha in human form were first made, using Greco-Roman sculptural models.

The earliest uses of the word *dhāraṇī* probably refer to the mnemonic use of the Kharoṣṭhī alphabet.[41] Each letter of the alphabet reminded the reciter or meditator of a word, which in turn served as the key for a reflection on the Buddhadharma. The most obvious sources of the alphabet for many years were texts written in Sanskrit, but preserving the Gāndhārī alphabetical order for the keywords. Until the discovery of the Bajaur collection, the oldest example of an Indian alphabetical mnemonic was in the *Lalitavistara Sūtra*. The well known Sanskrit version uses the Sanskrit alphabet, but a lesser known Chinese translation which may be older[42], retains the Gāndhārī order. The key source is the *Pañcaviṃśatisāhasrikā Prajñāpāramita Sutra*, The Perfection of Wisdom in 25,000 lines, which Conze translates in his book *The Large Sutra on Perfect Wisdom*. The meanings for the first syllables is:

> *a* is an opening because of the primal quality of not arising of all mental phenomena.
> *ra* is an opening because of absence of impurity of all mental phenomena.
> *pa* is an opening because it points to the highest truth about all mental phenomena.
> *ca* is an opening because of the non-perception of the causes of falling of any mental phenomena.
> *na* is an opening because of the absence of names of any mental phenomena.[43]

Across the various texts there is variation in the make-up of the alphabet, the order, and the number of letters. Most, but not all, of these can be explained by the process of transplanting the Gāndhārī into a Sanskrit milieu, followed by a loss of knowledge of the original language and/or script. Others may be scribal errors. A complete explanation is still needed. The complete Arapacana Alphabet in the *Pañcaviṃśatisāhasrikā* is:

---

[40] See Strauch (2007-8).
[41] Nattier (2003) p.291-292, n.549. In Tibetan the word *dhāraṇī* is translated as *gzungs* meaning 'retention'.
[42] See Brough (1977).
[43] My translation.

a ra pa ca na la da ba ḍa ṣa va ta ya ṣṭa ka sa ma ga stha ja śva dha śa kha kṣa sta jña rta ha bha cha sma hva tsa bha ṭha ṇa pha ska ysa śca ṭa ḍha.

The first sentence from the *Pañcaviṃśatisāhasrikā* verses – *akāro mukhaṃ sarvadharmāṇāṃ ādyanutpannavāt* – went on to become a mantra in its own right. In torma offering ceremonies for instance we find the mantra: *oṃ akāro mukhaḥ sarvadharmāṇāṃ ādyanutpannatvāt.*[44]

Meditating on the Arapacana Alphabet

The Arapacana Alphabet is the foundation of a Buddhist meditation practice on the nature of experience. It is expounded in a number of sūtras but the *locus classicus* is the *Pañcaviṃśatisāhasrikā Prajñāpāramitā Sūtra* (PPS) – translated into English by Edward Conze.[45] The Arapacana Alphabet occurs in a chapter of the PPS which begins by spelling out the thirty-seven *bodhipakṣyā dharmā* (wings to awakening) in a slightly expanded form. The two lists often appear together though it is not clear what the relationship is. The text introduces the Alphabet:

> "And again, Subhūti, the *dhāraṇī*-doors are the great vehicle of the Bodhisattva, the great being. Which are they? The sameness of all letters and syllables, the sameness of all spoken words, the syllable-doors, the syllables-entrances. What then are the syllable-doors, the syllable-entrances?"[46]

The letters of the Arapacana Alphabet appear next in the text (they are listed at p. 42f. for reference). Having listed the letters the text says:

> "Hence there are no higher practices of the undying. For what reason? Because there is not in any name that by which he should have intercourse, or speak about, announce, write, or see. Subhuti, 'just as space' that is called. All experiences are discovered to be like that. Subhuti: this is the method of *dhāraṇī*, the method of instruction in sounds and syllables. Subhuti, any awkening-being great-being who knows this method of instruction in sounds and syllables is not anywhere beaten down by any sounds. All should meditate on this essence, and speak [when] skilful in the knowledge of sounds."[47]

---

[44] See e.g. Beyer (1973), p.146.

[45] We should also note that though the main part of the text is from the PPS Conze has often used alternative passages from related sutras to fill in unreadable passages in what he refers to as "often unbelievably careless and corrupt late Nepalese manuscripts". In the case of the passages that concern us here he Conze has used a parallel chapter from a Gilgit manuscript of the Sanskrit *Aṣṭādaśasahāsrikā Prajñāpāramitā Sūtra* (the 18000 line version) with reference to Chinese and Tibetan versions of the PPS to reconstruct the original. (Conze 1975b. p.160 n.6).

[46] c.f. Conze (1975b) p.160 [PPS I 9,15,]. My translation.

[47] c.f. Conze (1975b) p.162 [PPS I 9,15,]. My translation. Conze is more free with his rendering: "No letters or syllables are in conventional use except the foregoing. And why? For no word that is not composed of them is used when anything is conventionally expressed, talked about pointed out, written about, made manifest or recited. Simply like space would one pursue all dharmas. This, Subhuti, is called the entrance into the door of the dhāraṇīs, the entrance into the exposition of the letters A, etc. Any Bodhisattva who cognizes this skill in letters A, etc. will not be tied down by any sounds, he will accomplish everything through the sameness of all dharmas, and he will acquire the skill in the cognition of sounds."

In other words all of these reflections are aimed at realising the same thing about experience: it is *śūnya* or empty. Compare another brief extract from the text:

> More over Kauśika: *samādhi* is empty of *samādhi*. The *dhāraṇī*-gates are empty of *dhāraṇī*-gates, the bodhisattva is empty of bodhisattva – thus the emptiness of *samādhi*, *dhāraṇī* and bodhisattva are not two, not divided.[48]

Twenty advantages will come to the Bodhisattva who masters this teaching, including: being mindful, clever, intelligent, steadfast, not being assailed by doubts etc. This teaching is called, like the other teachings in the sutra, a great vehicle (i.e. Mahāyāna) of the Bodhisattva. Sameness (*samatā*) in this context is a synonym for *śūnyatā* or emptiness, i.e. all things are the same because they are empty of any essential nature. The sutra, then, seems to be saying that the way to realise the sameness of all sounds is to contemplate the sounds of the letters as being linked to aspects of the Dharma.

Curiously, the rest of the commentary on the practice is at the end of the *sūtra*. This may be because the two bits were composed at separate times, or that they were split up for some reason, possibly inept editing, or to obscure the practice from the uninitiated. We don't know. But we have to jump ahead several hundred pages in the text where we find, immediately after a list of the 32 major and 80 minor marks of the Buddha:

> Further more, Subhūti, the bodhi-being, great-being, on the path of the perfection of wisdom admonishes and teaches those beings thus: you family-sons should have the skill of accumulating the letters. You should be expert in one letter, in two letters... up to expertise in 42 letters. Through one letter, two letters... up to 42 letters may you obtain the the state of having moved away from everything (*sarvavyayopagatān*).[49] Make the 42 letters included in the single letter, and the one amongst the 42.[50]

This is what tells us that the Arapacana Alphabet is a meditation practice, and gives us an idea of how one might have meditated on the letters. It's not always clear from the text what is intended, but with a background in Buddhist ideas and practices it is possible to make some sense of it. One uses the alphabet as a mnemonic to remember the list of keywords. The keywords tell you what you are reflecting on, but they are all some aspect of the *śūnya* nature of experience. Having memorised the list, and learned the meditation in linear fashion, the practice culminates in reflecting on the sameness of each of the reflections. Everything is pointing towards *śūnyatā*, and by reflecting that all of the keywords mean the same thing in this sense, one gets a glimpse of the way things are. In this way the practitioner, the Bodhisattva, masters the practice.

---

[48] PSP 2-3:7. My translation (following Conze).

[49] PSP_6-8:67-8. My thanks to Dhīvan Thomas Jones and Elisa Freschi for helping me to understand the Sanskrit here. Conze (1967) defines *sarvavyayopagatān* 'may you come to the state which is free from all passing away'.

[50] The text does say 42 syllables here (*dvācatvāriṃśad akṣarāṇi*), even though 43 syllables are given in the earlier section. Is this an artefact of using different versions of the text at different places? Conze (1975b) translates "Furthermore, Subhuti, the Bodhisattva, great being, who courses in perfect wisdom, admonishes the Bodhisattvas as follow: 'Sons of good family, may you become skilled in the consummation of the letters! May you become skilled in one letter, in two letters, etc. to: in forty-two letters! May you through these forty-two letters come to a state which has moved away from everything. May you meditate on the 42 letters as contained in one letter, and may you meditate on one single letter as contained in 42 letters!" (p.587)

> Just as the Tathāgata, skilled in dharmas, skilled in letters, demonstrates Dharma; and demonstrates with letters a Dharma which is without them. And yet that Dharma is not quite free from the mode(?) of letters.[51]

This is to say that we use the concepts represented by the letters to get to the gnosis which is beyond concepts. The experience of Awakening is beyond words. However the experience of having had that experience is communicable, as are the various methods for having that experience one's self.

Comments

The PPS appears to me to consider this meditation as one of many which one can employ to experience Awakening. It is found appended to discussions of the thirty-seven (or more) *bodhipakṣyā dharmā* and the list of major and minor marks (related to the *buddhanusmṛti*, a meditation practice involving recollection of the Buddha). However two things make me think it might not have originated in this text. Firstly the meditation instructions which are tacked onto the beginning of section VIII.5.3 do not seem to be in an appropriate place since the Alphabet itself occurs in section I.9 (they are separated by more than 400 pages in Conze's translation for instance). The previous section, VIII.5.2, is a repeat of the expanded *bodhipakṣyā dharmā* list, and although the instructions would have made some sense at the end of that section, we find them at the beginning of another section, where they do not fit the context. After the paragraph from VIII.5.3 quoted above the text goes off in an entirely different direction and does not mention the letters of the alphabet again. However, we need to take into account that the published editions are based on a redaction of the PPS which has been rearranged to fit the categories of the *Abhisamayālaṅkārakārikā*[52] and this may have broken up the bits we are interested in order to make the text fit. However if this process did break up our practice, then it suggests that the redactor was unaware of the significance of the passages, that is they were unaware of the meditation practice.

Secondly, as already mentioned, although the PPS is written in Sanskrit, the alphabet is that of the Gāndhārī Prakrit. Conze makes the point that in the various surviving manuscripts and translations (spanning 200 CE – 900 CE) there are shifts in the associations (i.e. the keywords) with the letters. However, the letters themselves remain stable, apart from some minor variations easily explained by absorption of Gāndhārī into a Sanskrit milieu. Other texts which have an Arapacana alphabet also associate the letters of the alphabet with different keywords.

The Gāndhārī alphabet was retained in many of the Sanskrit texts, though clearly at some point before the composition of the PPS the knowledge that the alphabet was the Gāndhārī alphabet was lost by Buddhists, along with the significance on this fact. One version of the *Lalitavistara* and the *Mahāvairocana Abhisaṃbodhi Tantra* (MAT) both use a Sanskrit alphabet, although MAT retains the pattern of only using the 'a' vowel which is a feature of Gāndhārī associated with the Kharoṣṭhī script. The people of Gandhāra used Gāndhārī written in Kharoṣṭhī script for Buddhist texts in the first few centuries common era. A number of caches of these texts have been found and some have been published by Salomon and others.

The Arapacana Alphabet developed along several lines, most of which were dead ends. For instance there is aa Arapacana Alphabet in the *Gaṇḍavyūha Sūtra* but the keywords have

---

[51] (PPS VIII 5.3; c.f. Conze (1975b) p.587.

[52] Dutt (1934) p. 5

become (phonetically) disconnected from the letters of the alphabet. The line develops positively in the *Mahāvairocana Abhisaṃbodhi Tantra* (MAT) an early esoteric scripture (mid 7th century CE). In the PPS the letters are abstract symbols of abstract and abstruse concepts. In the MAT there is another level of abstraction. As well as a meditation similar to the PPS, the MAT instructs the meditator to imagine placing the letters on the body while visualising oneself as a Buddha – the object being to literally transform yourself. The letters on the their own have become transformative in MAT. The practices associated with the letters in the MAT are mainly associated with the master conducting the *abhiṣeka* as he prepares to give the initiation. A full discussion of the way the Arapacana Alphabet is used in the MAT is beyond the scope of this book. However, we can say that the loss of the knowledge that this was simply the Gāndhārī alphabet most likely contributed, along with the adoption of ideas from Brahminical linguistic philosophy (both *Mīmāṃsā* and Grammarian), to treating the alphabet as having an intrinsic significance. Hence Dr Conze could refer to it as a "mystical alphabet", because it continued to be used in meditation practices as a mnemonic, but its mundane origins were already obscure.

A Practical Approach to Arapacana Meditation

In Nov 2007 I led an evening on the Arapacana Alphabet at the Cambridge Buddhist Centre which involved a led meditation and a talk which looked at the recent research on Arapacana, especially the work of Dr Richard Salomon. In order to lead the meditation I took the text of the verses associated with the Arapacana in the *Large Perfection of Wisdom Sutra* (*Pañcaviṃśatisāhasrikā Prajñāpāramitā Sūtra*), and attempted to put them into an idiom which conveyed what I perceived to be the intention of the verses, in a way that would be familiar to an Triratna audience.

For the purposes of this exercise I decided to use "experience" as a translation of "*dharma*" – that is, *dharma* in its aspect as phenomena or element, and in particular mental phenomena or element. I also made the caveat that in a meditation one often makes categorical statements which are not meant to literally describe Reality, but simply to be the subject of reflection. Finally I had to admit that this is simply my reading of a text, and that as far as I know there is no living tradition of meditating in this way.

We began with some *samatha* meditation focussing on the body and breath. Then having calmed down and become concentrated to some extent we reflected on each of the letters (or more accurately syllables) in turn, although only the first five: *a ra pa ca na*. As you may know each letter is the initial letter of a word in Sanskrit, which fits into a sentence that provides a reflection on the nature of experience. My method will become more clear as we look at the examples.

The letter A (the short vowel sound in the English word cut), according to the text, is a door to the insight that all dharmas are unproduced from the very beginning (*ādya-anutpannatvād*). I take this to mean that even though we undeniable have experiences, no 'thing' - no ontologically solid and lasting entity - arises as a result. So rather than thinking, for instance, there is "the in-breath" and "the out-breath", we can reflect that there is no 'thing' called breath, there is just the experience, the physical sensation of breathing. Instead of thinking in terms of "this feeling is in my body", try to think in terms of "there is a physical feeling". Using verbs rather than nouns helps this I think. Focus on the experience, that is the flow of sensations and perhaps mental activity, rather than extrapolating from the experience to something solid.

RA is a door to the insight that all dharmas are without dirt (*rajas*). In this stage of the meditation we reflect that although we have experiences which are either pleasant or unpleasant or neutral, the feeling tone is not intrinsic to the experience. Something done once might be pleasant, but done a dozen times may be unpleasant; one day it might thrill us, the next it might bore us. Experience is just experience, and therefore it is "pure". We tend to be attracted to pleasant, and repulsed by the unpleasant. We want to hold onto what attracts us, and to push away what is unpleasant. It is these attempts at holding and pushing away which cause us to suffer, not the bare experience of pleasant or unpleasant. Ultimately experience is just experience.

PA is a door to the insight that all dharmas have been expounded in the ultimate sense (*paramārtha*). This aspect took me a little time to understand. What I think it means is that when you reach out to determine what underlies experience, or what lies behind it, you can only have another experience. So for instance although I feel embodied I might want to confirm that I have a body. I might reach out my hand and touch myself - this is simply a touch sensation; or I might look down at my body, and this is simply a sight sensation. It's as if we look behind the mirror to see if we can find the object in the mirror, only to find another mirror. This is the true nature of things, the ultimate (*paramārtha*) explanation - we are immersed in experience, and there is nothing beyond this.

CA is a door to the insight that the decrease (*cyavana*) or rebirth of any dharma cannot be apprehended, because all dharmas do not decrease, nor are they reborn. Because we now know that no 'thing' arises, then we should see that the corollary is that no 'thing' ever ceases. The best we can say is there is experience. Once we start trying to talk about this experience, or that experience; my experience or your experience we are already dividing things up (*vijñāna*) and attributing thingness to them. If there is just experience, then what is it that arises, what that dies?

NA is a door to the insight that the Names [i.e. *nāma*] of all dharmas have vanished; the essential nature behind names cannot be gained or lost. Since all we can be aware of is a ceaseless flow of experience, changing from moment to moment, a name cannot apply to anything since there is no 'thing' for it to apply to. By the time we have though of a name, the experience has passed and been replaced by another. The very act of conceiving a name is simply a mental experience.

There are of course another thirty-nine letters[53] in the Arapacana alphabet and each was associated with an aspect of experience and meditated on in turn. At the end however the text makes it clear that one is to contemplate how each letter is merely a facet of a larger truth, that each letter is in the long run identical in meaning to all the others. All experiences are impersonal and impermanent. And they are all we have.

One thing I did not mention in my talk was the way in which this meditation practice developed after the *Large Perfection of Wisdom Sutra*. In the *Mahāvairocana Abhisaṃbodhi Tantra* the meditation begins in the same way (although substituting the Sanskrit consonants for the Gāndhārī ones), but then one imaginatively places the letters around the body while visualising oneself as the Buddha. The *Sarvatathāgata-tattvasaṃgraha Tantra* pares the whole thing down to just meditating on the letter a. It is this latter meditation which became important in Shingon, and other Vajrayāna lineages - the whole shebang boiled down to contemplating that no things arise.

---

[53] Various versions of the alphabet differ. There are 44 in the Large Perfection of Wisdom Sutra, although the same text when discussing the meditation practice talks about the 42 letters! Other texts have 43 letters. The variation is likely to be related to difficulties representing the sounds of Gāndhārī from a Sanskrit perspective.

A recording of my talk[54] and the led meditation[55] are available on the Cambridge Buddhist Centre website.

[54] http://cambridgebuddhistcentre.com/resources/files/20071101_Jayarava_Wisdom_Alphabet_talk.mp3
[55] http://cambridgebuddhistcentre.com/resources/files/20071101_Jayarava_Wisdom_Alphabet_meditation.mp3

Arapacana Alphabet in the Pañcaviṃśatisāhasrikā sūtra

This is my translation of the Sanskrit edition of PPS produced by Takayasu (1986-2009). I have also consulted the Sanskrit edition by Dutt (1934); the Chinese translations by Kumārajīva (T.223) and Xuánzàng (T.220)[56] as found in CBETA online version of the Taisho Ed. of the Chinese Tripiṭaka[57]; and Edward Conze's English translation (1975b), particularly his notes on translation and ms. variants. Conze cites Mokshala [sic] which I take to be a reference to T.221, the translation of the PPS by Mokṣa (or Mokṣala); and Yüan-tsang [sic; i.e. Xuánzàng] which I take to be a reference to T.220. Maitiu O'Ceileachair also provided extensive notes on the Chinese and Tibetan translations many of which I have included verbatim.[58] I have also used Brough's (1977) discussion of the Arapacana in 普曜經 (*Pŭ yào jīng = The Lalitavistara Sūtra*; T. 186), translated by Dharmarakṣa in 308 CE, to shed light on Chinese translations. Brough himself also refers to Kumārajīva's translation of the *Mahāprajñāpāramitopadeśa* (T. 1509[59]) a commentary on the PPS attributed to Nāgārjuna[60] which appears not to coincide with T.223 in every detail; and Xuánzàng's various translations of the large Perfection of Wisdom text contained within T.220.[61] Salomon (1990) is invaluable for understanding the alphabet in any script or language. The Sanskrit editions, and presumably the Sanskrit mss., contain several conflicts that are resolved by Conze – and in each case I have followed his example, but only after consulting some of the same sources (particularly the Chinese texts) and the secondary literature.[62] The last few lines are very confused and show a great deal of variation in both the syllable and the keyword, not to mention the fact that the number of syllables varies from 41 – 43, while the text itself later refers to 42 letters '*dvācatvāriṃśad akṣarāṇi*'.[63] Fragment five of the Bajaur Collection of birch bark manuscripts contains a series of verses in the order of the wisdom alphabet. This manuscript is still under study by Dr Ingo Strauch of the Free University of Berlin. A tantalising glimpse at the contents of this manuscript, probably dating from the first or second century, can be read in Dr Strauch's report: "*The Bajaur collection: A new collection of Kharoṣṭhī manuscripts. A preliminary catalogue and survey (in progress)*" - available on the Bajaur Collection Website.[64]

1.	A	the syllable *a* is an opening because of the primal quality of not arising (*anutpanna*) of all mental phenomena.
2.	RA	the syllable *ra* is an opening because of absence of impurity (*rajas*) of all mental phenomena.[65]
3.	PA	the syllable *pa* is an opening because it points to the highest truth (*paramārtha*) about all mental phenomena.[66]
4.	CA	the syllable *ca* is an opening because of the non-perception of the causes of falling (*cyavana*) of any mental phenomena.[67]

---

56 Xuánzàng translates three versions of the Large Perfection of Wisdom text: in 18,000 lines (T. 220 p489b), 25,000 lines (T. 220 p.81c), and 100,000 lines (T. 220 p.302b).

57 Transliteration of Chinese characters follows the Pinyin system.

58 Maitiu's comments are marked [MO] in this section.

59 Correctly cited in the text of his article, but incorrectly as T. 1909 in his bibliography.

60 The attribution is disputed by some scholars – see Chou (2004)

61 Broughs list of abbreviations (p. 94) suggests that he mainly relied on the *Śatasāhasrika* version (T.220 302b)

62 I am grateful to readers of my *Visible Mantra* Facebook page for clarification of some Chinese phrases, especially Khai Tong who provided me with his own translation of the Arapacana in T. 223, along with his analysis of the keywords.

63 Takayasu PSP_6-8:67-8. Though the Arapacana in Takayasu has only 41 syllables!

64 http://www.geschkult.fu-berlin.de/e/indologie/bajaur/publication/index.html#Strauch2007

65 Kumārajīva & Xuánzàng: 垢 'dirt' = S. *rajas*.

66 Kumārajīva (T. 1509): 第一義 = S. *paramārtha*.

67 Kumārajīva (T. 1509): 行 = S. *caryā* 'conduct'.

5. NA the syllable *na* is an opening because of the absence of names (*nāma*) of any mental phenomena.
6. LA the syllable *la* is an opening because of the state of having escaped from the world (*lokottīrṇa*) of the senses, and the destruction of the causes and conditions of the creeper of craving (*tṛṣṇālatā-hetu-pratyaya*) in all mental phenomena.
7. DA the syllable *da* is an opening because of the restraint, self-control, and circumspection (*dānta-damatha-paricchinna*) of all mental phenomena.
8. BA the syllable *ba* is an opening because of the bindings (*bandha*) of all mental phenomena are undone
9. ḌA the syllable *ḍa* is an opening because of the abscence of tumult (*ḍama*) in all mental phenomena.[68]
10. [ṢA] the syllable *ṣa* is an opening because of the absence of clinging (ṣaṃga) in all mental phenomena[69].
11. VA the syllable *va* is an opening because of the eradication of sounds suitable for speech (*vākpatha-ghoṣa*) from all mental phenomena.
12. TA the syllable *ta* is an opening because all mental phenomena don't deviate from Suchness (*tathatā*).
13. YA the syllable *ya* is an opening because of the non-arising of an essence (*yathāvat*) of all mental phenomena.[70]
14. [ṢṬA] the syllable *ṣṭa*[71] is an opening because no support (*stambha*) of all mental phenomena can be perceived.[72]
15. KA the syllable *ka* is an opening because no 'doing' (*kāraka*) is perceived in all mental phenomena.
16. SA the syllable *sa* is an opening because of non-apprehension of the sameness (*samatā*) of all mental phenomena.
17. MA the syllable *ma* is an opening because all mental phenomena lack a 'mine' maker (*mamakāra*).[73]
18. GA the syllable *ga* is an opening because we cannot apprehend the sky (*gagana*) of all mental phenomenon.[74]

---

[68] = Tibetan *dkrugs-pa* 'disturb, agitate', Conze (1967).

[69] Sankrit has SA and *saṃga*. Conze (1975b) has ṢA here and spells this *ṣaṅga*, which avoids the conflict at 16 where the key word is *samatā*. Kumārajīva (T. 223) transliterates the syllable with 沙 *shā* indicating he has an aspirated sibilant (*śa* or *ṣa*) in his original, and translates the keyword as 六自在王 = S. *ṣaḍāyatana* (the six sense faculties). "The commentary in T.1509 states that the syllable 沙 means six (沙秦言六)." [MO] Brough's Old LV. (1977) has 信 = G. *ṣaddhā*, S. *śraddhā*.

[70] Conze (1975b) translations *yathāvat* as 'fact'. Conze (1967) gives the Tibetan translation as *yang dag pa ji* 'as it really is, that which is as it really is'. C.f. *yang dag pa ji lta ba* = Sanskrit *yathābhūta-jñānadarśaṇa*; where *yang dag pa* = *bhūta* and *lta ba* = *dṛṣṭi*. The Tibetan and Chinese translations suggest that the word should by *yathābhūta* but the transcription in T.1509 suggests *yathāvat.*

[71] Sanskrit has STA, but Conze has ṢṬA and *ṣṭambha* avoiding the conflict with 26 STA below. Kumārajīva (T. 223) transliterates 咤 zhà which also occurs at 25. "In modern Mandarin this initial *zh-* is pronounced as a retroflex affricate but in middle Chinese this sound is usually reconstructed as a retroflex plosive (*ṭa* or *ṭha*) of some kind." [MO] Brough observes that Xuánzàng transliterates 瑟吒 *ṣṭa*; while Kumārajīva's commentary (T. 1509) implies *ṣṭambha* with his 吒婆 *ṭa(ṃ)bha* translated as 障礙 'obstruction' (p.89); T. 1509 also uses 吒 for *ṭha* in *akaniṣṭha* (阿迦尼吒). Finally 婆 is used by Kumārajīva (T. 223) to transliterate *ba*.

[72] From here on each phrase uses the verbal noun *upalabdhi* with the negative prefix *an–*, in the adjectival ablative: *anupalabdhitaḥ* 'because of non-recognition' or 'from not understanding'.

[73] This usually refers to the mental act of identifying *dharmas* as 'mine'; c.f. the oft repeated Pāli phrase 'this is mine, I am this, this is my self' (*etaṃ mama, eso'haṃasmi, eso me attā*) e.g. M. i.135, M i.233.

[74] Conze (1975b) follows Mokṣala (T.221) in reading *grahaṇa* 'seize'; other ms. including Tibetan have *gamana* 'going, moving'. Both Kumārajīva and Xuánzàng transliterate 伽 jiā; Kumārajīva's keyword is 去者 'that which goes; the leaver'; whereas Xuánzàng has 行動取: 行動 means 'move, moving' and 取 means 'grasp, hold, take'. "This phrase is somewhat obscure, given Xuanzang's usual translation methods it may be a translation of an unusual Sanskrit phrase. His translation suggests both the words *grahaṇa* and *gamana*." [MO] Brough's (1977) LV has 逝 'depart' (or 'die'!); the head word is absent from the explanation 於正法無憒亂 'going unperturbed in the saddharma'; and he notes Kumārajīva (T. 1509) explains as 伽陀 = S. *gata* – hence the Chinese versions probably represent a Sanskrit word from √*gam*.

19. STHA the syllable *stha* is an opening because we cannot comprehend the continued existence (*sthāna*) all mental phenomena.[75]
20. JA the syllable *ja* is an opening because the birth (*jāti*) of all mental phenomena is not recognised.
21. ŚVA the syllable *śva* is an opening because the 'breath' (*śvāsa* i.e. life) of all mental phenomena is not understood.
22. DHA the syllable *dha* is an opening because of the non-apprehension of the *dharmadhātu* of all mental phenomena.
23. ŚA the syllable *śa* is an opening because the serenity (*śamatha*) of all mental phenomenon is not cognised.
24. KHA the syllable *kha* is an opening because of the non-apprehension of the sameness of space (*kha-samata*) in all mental phenomena.[76]
25. KṢA the syllable *kṣa* is an opening because the destruction all mental phenomena is not perceived.
26. STA the syllable *sta* [means] all mental phenomena are openings because of not attaining 'and that'.[77]
27. JÑA the syllable *jña* [means] all mental phenomena are openings because omniscience (*sarvajña*) is unobtainable.
28. HA the syllable *ha* [means] all mental phenomena are openings because the cause (*hetu*) is not perceived.[78]
29. BHA [the syllable *bha* means all menta phenomena because breakdown (*bhaṅga*) is not perceived].[79]
30. [CHA] the syllable *cha* [means] all mental phenomena are openings because of the non-recognition of beauty (*chavi*).[80]
31. SMA the syllable *sma* [means] all mental phenomena are openings because of the non-recognition of recollection (*smaraṇa*).[81]

---

75 In Gāndhārī this was probably THA according to Salomon (1990). Both Kumārajīva and Xuánzàng have 他 *tā* = S. *tha* which Kumārajīva translates into 處 'place, location' = S. *sthāna*. Brough's (1977) LV has 止 *zhǐ* 'stop, stand' which also suggests S. *sthāna*.

76 Conze (1975b) notes that his Giligit ms. omits *samata*.

77 The Sanskrit in Takayasu is *tac cānupalabdhitaḥ* "because '*and that*' (*tat ca*) cannot be recognised" (?). Conze (1975b) follows Mokṣala who has *astitva* or *stabdha* 'fixed' and notes that Xuánzàng "agrees to some extent with it." What Xuánzàng says is: 入薩[多*頁]字門，悟一切法任持之性不可得故; roughly: 'The STA syllable is a gate because realising the nature of all dharmas he finds no support'. "任持 means basis or support (*upastambha, upastabdha*)." [MO] Kumārajīva's syllable is 哆 *duō* and his keyword 有 'be, exist' suggesting S. *bhava* cf comments on 29. BHA. The syntax of the Sanskrit changes from here with *mukhaḥ* changing to the plural *mukhāḥ*, and genitive plural *sarvadharnāṇāṃ* changing to the nominative plural *sarvadharmāḥ*. Since sandhi rules are applied the change is presumably is intended.

78 Takayasu and Dutt have HA. Conze (1975b) has RTA from *mārtya* here, and notes that Mokṣala has *artha*. Xuánzàng has 剌他 *là tā* (= RTHA?), and translates 義 = S. *artha*. Brough (1977) says that Kumārajīva explains with 阿他 '*attha*' = Skt *artha*. Salomon (1990) notes that RTHA, PHA and ITA also occur in this place (p.256). If not HA here, then it is absent altogether from the syllabary, but known to be used in Gāndhārī and all other Prakrits. Conze includes both RTA and HA giving 43 syllables in his syllabary. "The Tibetan has *rta* and gives the keyword *nyon mongs pa* which would usually translate *kleśa*, but here may be translating *ārta* 'afflicted, pained, suffering'." [MO]

79 Takaysu and Dutt omit this syllable. Conze (1975b) has BHA here deriving from *bhaṅga* 'breaking' at 30. Kumārajīva has the syllable 婆 (*pó*) and the keyword 破壞= S. *baṅga* (according to Brough 1977). Xuánzàng has 薄 Bá and 破壞 'destruction' but at position 30. Brough's Old LV (1977) translates the keyword as 有= S. *bhava* supporting the reading of BHA, but see comments on 26 STA. "The Tibetan keyword is *'jig pa med pa* '*abhaya*'." [MO]

80 Takayasu has *ccha* as the syllable. Conze (1975b) has CHA < *chaver api*; *chaveḥ* is ablative or genitive of *chavi* 'beauty'. Sandhi makes *sarvadharmāḥ chaveḥ api* > *sarvadharmāc cchaver apy*, hence perhaps the syllable is *ccha* in Sanskrit. Brough (1977) concludes that the Sanskrit mss. are corrupt. His Old LV has 棄 *qì* 'discard' corresponding to Prakrit *chaḍḍ-* which has the same sense. Brough notes that Mokṣala also has 棄, Dharmarakṣa (T.222) has 焚燒 'already burnt' [which is cryptic]; while at 31 Xuánzàng has 綽 *Chuò* as the syllable and 欲樂 'desire' [= S. *chanda*?]. Kumārajīva at position 30 has 車 *chē* as the syllable and 欲 'desire' as the keyword [= S. *chanda*?]. "The Tibetan has *mdog* "colour, appearance". *chanda* can mean appearance as well as "desire, pleasure"." [MO]

81 Salomon (1990) notes that in some mss. this syllable is SVA.

32. HVA the syllable *hva* [means] all mental phenomena are openings because of the non-recognition of the invocation (*āhvāna*).[82]
33. TSA the syllable *sa* [means] all mental phenomena are openings because of the unattainability of the strength (*utsāha*).[83]
34. GHA the syllable *gha* [means] all mental phenomena are openings because of the non-recognition of the killer (*ghana*).[84]
35. ṬHA the syllable *ṭha* [means] all mental phenomena are openings because of the non-recognition of the illusory creations (*viṭhapana*).[85]
36. ṆA the syllable *ṇa* [means] all mental phenomena are openings because of the cessation of pleasure/conflict (*raṇa*).[86]
37. PHA the syllable *pha* [means] all mental phenomena are openings because of the nonattaining of fruit (*phala*).
38. SKA the syllable *ska* [means] all mental phenomena are openings because of the nonrecognition of masses (*skandha*).[87]
39. [YSA] the syllable *ysa* [means] all mental phenomena are of the non-recognition of aging.[88]
40. [ŚCA] the syllable *śca* [means] all mental phenomena are openings because of the non-recognition of moral behaviour.[89]
41. ṬA the syllable *ṭa* [means] all mental phenomena are openings because of the nonrecognition of the syllable *ṭa*.[90]

---

[82] Conze translates *āhvāna* as 'true appellations', c.f. MW 'calling, invitation, invocation'. Kumārajīva has keyword 喚 'call to'. In position 33 Xuánzàng has 嗑縛 Kè fù (which is closer to the Sanskrit pronunciation of *hva* than it might look) and keyword 呼召 'calling, called to'.

[83] Takayasu has *sakāra* indicating SA, but Conze treats this as TSA without comment. Xuánzàng has 蹉 *cuō* which sounds similar to *tsa*, and Kumārajīva translierates 伽 *jiā*. Salomon (1990) says that *tsa* probably reflects an actual Gāndhārī phoneme. (p.268) Brough adopts 妬 (*dù*) from the Taisho footnote over 垢 (*gòu*) from the text of T. 186; he notes the explanation given by Kumārajīva is 末蹉羅 (*mò cuō luó*) = Skt *matsara* 'intoxicated, greedy' translated 慳 'stingy'; and says Xuánzàng has 勇健 (*yǒng jiàn*) 'strong, powerful' = S. *ṛddha*.

[84] Note there is a typo in Conze which prints BHA instead of GHA. Conze's keyword is *ghana*; though he translates it "things and persons are not apprehended each as one solid mass" (p.161), reading *ghana* as 'solid, compact'; in Conze (1967) he gives the Tibetan equivalent as *stug pa* 'thick, dense', however c.f. "The Tibetan reads *ghana* as meaning "harm, pain". [MO]. Kumārajīva and Xuánzàng translate the keyword as 厚 'thick'.

[85] BHSD lists this as an alternate spelling of *viṣṭhapana*. "The Tibetan translates *bsgrub pa* which usually means *sādhana*. *Viṭhapana* "fixation, establishment, creation, making" has a similar meaning to *sādhana* and fits the general meaning of *sgrub*." [MO]

[86] I.e. *raṇa-vigatatvāt*: *raṇa* is both pleasure and delight; *vigata* 'disappearance'. "The Tibetan also translates this *nyon mongs pa* which would normally mean *kleśa*. Xuanzang's translation of this phrase 喧諍 "noisy dispute" and the Tibetan translation suggest that it is the "war, fight, conflict" meaning of *raṇa* that is meant. The translations include a longer phrase at the end "…there is no going, coming, standing, sitting or reclining." [MO]

[87] Conze takes *skandha* here in its technical sense, what Hamilton calls "the apparatus of experience".

[88] Takayasu and Dutt both have JA, which conflicts with 20 JA. According to Salomon (1990) some mss. give this syllable as YSA. Cf Xuánzàng 逸娑 (*yì suō*). The explanation seems to be that *ysa* represents a Central Asian pronunciation of *ja* that was also used in the Kharoṣṭhī script to represent Persian *za* (c.f. Devanāgarī *ja* ज and *za* ज़). This identification and earlier conjectures are confirmed by Salomon (1990; p.257 and 269). Brough's old LV provides no help here (or in subsequent lines).

[89] Takayasu and Dutt have CA creating a conflict with 4 CA. Conze solves this by spelling the keyword *ścaraṇa*. As Conze notes this seems to be supported by Kumārajīva's 遮 zhē (c.f. 4 CA), and keyword 行 = *caryā*. "T.1509 suggests that the word would have been *carati* (遮羅地)". [MO] Salomon (1990) explains that in Gāndhārī *śca* is written using a modified *ca* (same character but with a horizontal bar above) which may explain the confusion. Conze's Tibetan ms. had *spyod-pa* = S. *caryā*. Xuánzàng on the other hand has 酌 (*zhuó*) also indicating an aspirated sibilant; with 足跡 'footprint'as keyword, which may also suggest S. *caryā* (or similar). Conze notes that his Giligit ms. simply has *caṃkārānupalabdhitaḥ* 'because the letter *ca* is not recognised'. The same pattern of saying that the letter isn't recognised is seen in the final two lines as well. This is intriguing since 42 is much too large a number of sounds for the Gāndhārī alphabet if we take thevowels as one (the Kharoṣṭhī script had only one character for initial vowels equivalent to 'a' and was modified with diacritics to indicate other vowels). Sanskrit would only require 34 syllables for instance, and Pāli 32.

[90] It is difficult to make sense of this. Takayasu "*ṭakāramukhāḥ sarvadharmāḥ ṣṭaṃkārānupalabdhitaḥ*" i.e. *ṭa* as the syllable and *ṣṭaṃkāṛa* (i.e. 'the letter *ṣṭa*') as his keyword; while Dutt has *ṭa* and *ṭhaṃkāra*. Here Conze (1975b) speculates that *ṭa* stands for *ṭalo* (= *sthala*?) and translates Kumārajīva as saying that "the other shore of Dharmas

42. ḌHA the syllable *ḍha* [means] all mental phenomena are openings because of the nonrecognition of the syllable ḍha (*ḍhaṃkāra*).[91]

does not exist" (邊竟處故不終不生 = literally: 'for the reason that the final place does not live'), however here he is citing Kumārajīva's entry for *ḍha*! Under *ṭa* Kumārajīva has the sound 咤 = *zhà* and the keyword 傴'bent over'; "while in T. 1509 he has 吒羅 and says it means 'bank' suggesting that it perhaps it should be read *ṭhala* (= Skt. *sthala*). Xuánzàng's translation uses 驅迫 (to drive, compel) in the phrase for *ṭa,* but it might make more sense for *ḍha* if *bāḍha* and the verb *bādh* are getting mixed up." [MO] Reading *ṣṭa* here would create a conflict with 14, which following Conze we read as ṢṬA. "The Tibetan gives the translation *sdug bsngal* "pain, suffering". It's not clear what word this is but perhaps it's a Prakrit form of *kaṣṭa, kliṣṭa, pīḍā* which all mean "pain, suffering". [MO]

[91] This is the most speculative of Conze's translations. He says the text cannot easily be reconstituted and each of his manuscripts appears to have something different. Kumārajīva has 荼 which he has used for 9 ḌA previously. See also the previous note on ṬA. "The commentary in T.1509 gives the keyword as *bāḍha*: strong, mighty; assuredly, certainly. However the main text gives "ḌHA the syllable ḍha [means] all mental phenomena are openings because of the nonattaining of the final sphere, because they do not end or arise". The Tibetan gives *g.yog pa* "to cover" which might be a translation of *gāḍha* "pressed together, tightly drawn, dense, strong, firm". The Chinese translations read something like "…because the ultimate abode of all dharmas cannot be obtained." It might be a form of *pari-bṛh* meaning strongest, supreme. The superlative forms are *parivraḍhiṣṭha* and *parivṛḍhatama.* [MO]

Background Reading.

In the following pages are a collection of essays on some aspects of mantra. They were written as standalone pieces and though I've edited them to some extent, they still tend to overlap. Some were written for the *Visible Mantra* website and some for my blog *Jayarava's Raves*. These are some aspects of mantra that have caught my attention from time to time and are not a comprehensive account of mantra in Buddhism. Such an account is still lacking though I hope to publish something with a broader scope before too long.

Essays

What is mantra?
On the Etymology of the Word 'Mantra'
Phonosemantics : the meaning of sounds.
Dhāraṇī: origins, meaning, and usage.
Non-lexical utterances, stobhas, and mantra
Mantra, Magic, and Interconnectedness.
Words in mantras that end in -e.
Tadyathā in the Heart Sūtra.

What is Mantra?

originally written for visiblemantra.org

WHAT IS A MANTRA? This is not an easy question to answer. In reading about mantra you will typically come across a confusion of Buddhist, Hindu, and New-age ideas couched in terms that seem to suggest that knowledge of mantras is so esoteric that nothing sensible can be said about it. Usually this means that no attempt is made to make the connection between mantra and Buddhist doctrine. Most serious teaching on the subject is purely pragmatic - "now, you chant this mantra in this way..." Often nothing at all is said about *why* you chant a mantra, or *how* a mantra achieves its goal. Compare this situation with meditation upon which dozens of books have been written over thousands of years spelling out in great detail what happens in the mind, why you do this and not that etc. Mantra begins to sound like rank superstition. I accept in the long run that awakening defies the intellect and words: but I do not accept that no rational account of Buddhist practice is possible.

After offering a very brief introduction to the history of mantra, I introduce a threefold classification of mantras based on use and context.

Beginnings

Mantra is an old word. It occurs in the *Ṛgveda* where it refers to the poetic hymns (*sukta*) to the wild chthonic forces of nature which we think of as the Vedic gods. Sanskritists tell us that the word refers to the instrumentality (*tra*) of the mind (*manas*). A later Tantric etymology suggests that it is something which protects the mind, since *–tra* can also mean 'protects'.[92] Clearly in this case neither etymology is very enlightening. Frits Staal - an eminent Sanskritist - goes so far as to suggest that Vedic mantras, especially the ones that most resemble Buddhist mantra, are not language at all. The reasons that Buddhists started to assign significance (if not meaning) to syllables such as *oṃ* or *hūṃ* remains obscure. However if we cannot understand immediately what the words mean, we can easily see how they are used.

Buddhist Mantra

The Pāli Canon forbids monks from chanting mantras or from putting the Dharma into Vedic style verses for chanting;[93] and the Buddha repeatedly mocks mantra chanting Brahmins. However at the same time there are a number of canonical protective chants (*paritta* [94]) for warding off misfortune. In the post-canonical literature, beginning with the *Milandapañha*, formalised ceremonies for the chanting of *paritta* are described. The *paritta* texts are frequently cited as precursors of Buddhist mantra, although they bear very little relationship (formally or doctrinally) to Tantric Buddhism and I am doubtful that they represent a continuity.

Around the 2nd century strings of words, often with no grammatical relationship to each other, began to appear in *sūtras* – either as a main element or as an interpolation in the body of a larger sūtra. This was the *dhāraṇī*. Sometimes, as in the Golden Light Sūtra these *dhāraṇī*

---

[92] See also *On the Etymology of the Word Mantra* (p.46).

[93] See especially vin ii.139 though the interpretation of the word chandaso is disputed it may mean 'Vedic language, verses as in the Vedas, or Sanskrit'.

[94] From *pari* (around) + *tta* (protection). 'A means of protection', or 'complete (i.e. all around) protection'. P. *–tta* is related to the S. verbal root √trā 'to rescue, to protect'. We see this in the S. *gotra* 'cowshed' ie that which protects cows, and figurative 'clan'. C.f. the Sanskrit verb *paritrāti* 'to rescue, save, protect'.

appear alongside apparently Hindu rituals which are not entirely assimilated to Buddhism.[95] The term may have first been used in reference to the Arapacana verses, the lines of which have keyuwords which are in the order of the *Gāndhārī* alphabet (aka the *Arapacana* or *Wisdom Alphabet*), and relate aspects of the nature of dharmas. *Dhāraṇī* means something like a memory aid, which it may have been originally, but actual *dhāraṇī* seldom have this function and are more often simply prophylactics.[96] The chanting of *dhāraṇī* became a very important practice in East Asian Buddhism as they functioned as magical protection for emperor and empire. Many scholars see *dhāraṇī* as a kind of proto-mantra and many *dhāraṇī* find their way into more clearly Tantric texts. However as in the case of paritta I am doubtful about interpreting this as evidence of continuity between *dhāraṇī* and Tantric Buddhism – as opposed to, for instance, the assimilation of the *dhāraṇī* tradition by Tantric Buddhism at a much later date. Compare the fact that chanting of Mahāyāna sūtras offers the chanter exactly the same kind of protection.

The final phase of development begins in the mid 7th century. Texts appear in which mantras are suddenly the main feature. These texts describe elaborate rituals of initiation and propitiation, the goal of which is to transform the practitioner into a Buddha. The emphasis has shifted away from ethics and *dhyāna* meditation, which are central to Śravakyāna and Mahāyāna Buddhism. These texts are not taught by Śākyamuni but come directly from the Dharmakāya Buddha. In the Tantric ritual each activity is marked, or even empowered, by a mantra. The fundamental ritual is the *abhiṣeka* or initiation. It was through the *abhiṣeka* that the Dharmakāya Buddha communicated his awakened state - via the triple medium of *mudrā*, *mantra*, and *maṇḍala* - and it was this ritual which was passed down via Vajrasattva, Nāgārjuna, Nāgabodhi, Vajrabodhi, Amoghavajra and Huiguo to Kūkai. The *abhiṣeka* ritual underlies all tantric *sādhana* and each step - establishing the *maṇḍala*, occupying the *maṇḍala*, invoking and summoning the deity, etc - has an associated mantra, although one mantra in particular, the *hṛdaya* (heart) mantra, is used by the deity to bestow their 'blessing' and transform the practitioner into a Buddha. This transformation is the point of tantric *sādhana* - as Kūkai was fond of saying "Awakening in this very life!" In general it is these *hṛdaya* mantras which feature in this book and the associated website.

Tantra incorporates many ideas about sound, words, and spoken language which come from the Vedic tradition (ie from texts like the *Ṛg* and *Atharva Vedas*, and the *Upaniṣads*); from the more metaphysical speculations of the Sanskrit grammarians; and from Hinduism, especially the Śaiva branches. These are assimilated into the Buddhist context, and various attempts are made to weld them together. However the emphasis in this context is definitely on practice - one 'understands' a mantra by chanting it 100,000 or a million times, not by thinking about it or puzzling over semantics. The question of what a mantra *means* is far less important than what it *does*, and what it does can only be discovered by using it.

There are three main contexts in which mantras are used in Buddhism: Tantric Ritual, devotional rituals, and non-ritual personal use.

Mantra in Tantric Ritual

Fundamental to the Tantric mantra is the old Vedic idea of the interpenetration of phenomena incorporated via the *Avataṃsaka Sūtra*. As Michel Foucault has noted the ancients saw

[95] c.f. Sangharakshita's comments in *Transforming Self and World* p.149ff.

[96] On the meaning of the word *dhāraṇī* see *Dhāraṇī – Origins, Meaning and Usage*, p.57.

knowledge not in terms of identity and difference, but in terms of relationship and similarity.[97] The Vedic priests sought to control wild nature (especially phenomena associated with the monsoons and the sun) by finding something similar on earth and manipulating it. Around this notion developed the elaborate ritual tradition of the Brahmins in which fire (personified as Agni) was the medium of communication between heaven and earth because it transformed things from a solid (corporial) state into smoke, which is like air and which rode up to heaven: Agni played the role of messenger which can be compared to Hermes in the Greek myths, or to angels in the Old Testament. The relationship gradually became more abstract so that one could manipulate the world via imagination alone. In Buddhist terms simply bringing the Buddha to mind was to be in the presence of the Buddha in a literal sense. The idea of the ritual presence was implicit in the *sādhana*, and explicit in the fire rituals (*homa*) imported directly from the Vedic tradition.

This is not a mystical explanation but it does rely on an episteme (a way of knowing) which is not popular in the West. An exception would be something like Homeopathy which operates on the same principles, and provided only that you believe in it, it does actually work![98] Tantra relies on the perceived correspondence between the microcosm of the individual and the macrocosmic universe. This idea comes from the Vedic religion but is tempered by Budhdist doctrine, and in particular the teachings about *śūnyatā*.

Kūkai used to say: “all sounds of the voice of the Dharmakāya preaching the Dharma”. I take this to mean that the nature of reality is explicit in every experience – it does not require a special experience in order to observe it, one simply has to observe. The elements of experience (*dharmas*) are marked by impermanence, unsatisfactoriness, and in-substantiality. Sounds are particularly well suited for contemplating the truth of this since they occupy a time frame which makes their arising and passing away, and our responses to them, more noticeable than is the case for thoughts or forms. Sound is naturally impermanent and insubstantial. Mantra here forms a focus for the contemplation of the central Buddhist insight into the nature of experience: pratītya-samutpāda or dependent arising.

The rules that pertain to this context are specific and localised. One must receive an initiation from a qualified master or you may chant the sounds and still not be chanting a mantra. One must chant the mantra at the appropriate place in a internalised ritual handed down from the Dharmakāya through generations of masters, accompanied by the appropriate *mudrā*, or else the mantra has no power. These rules are being relaxed to serve the needs of the Tibetan community in exile, and Western Disciples, but this causes some Buddhists a certain amount of disquiet. Part of the problem is that many mantra practitioners only have the Tantric paradigm with which to explain mantra, and yet there is a clear and traditional non-tantric explanation.

Devotional Mantras

In devotional rituals mantras are used to evoke a Buddha, and to expression devotional feelings and faith in the vow of the Buddha to save beings. The Buddha Amitābha is a frequent object of devotion, and features in Pure Land Buddhism which emphasises this style of practice. In the *Kāraṇḍavyūha Sūtra* the mantra of Avalokiteśvara (*oṃ maṇipadme hūṃ*) is intended to be used in this way, even though later it does become a fully tantric mantra. Mantra use in this context is essentially a form of nāmanusmṛti - recalling (*smṛti*) of the name (*nāma*) of (usually) Amitābha,

[97] See especial Foucault *The Order of Things*.

[98] The ‘placebo effect’ is gaining new credibility as medical researchers discover that it is a powerful healing force: as long as a person *believes* they are receiving an effective treatment they fair better than control groups who receive no treatment.

which activates his vow to ensure that any person who keeps in mind his name will be reborn in the Pure Land. There is also an element of an even older practice - *buddhānusmṛti* or bringing the Buddha to mind. By imaginatively bringing the Buddha to mind the practitioner can enhance feelings of inspiration to practise, and devotion.

An aspect of this style of practice is that the practitioner relies on 'other power'. We rely on Amitābha or the Buddha to rescue us. This may seem to run counter to some Buddhist doctrines which say that we are responsible for the consequences of our actions, the fruits of our *karma*. Sangharakshita encourages us to see this type of practice in terms of 'going for Refuge' (P. *saraṇa gamana*). It is the act of going for refuge which makes one a Buddhist, and this kind of mantra practice can be seen as orthodox in that one is expressing one's going for refuge to the Buddha. However going for refuge must also manifest in behaviour and it is not enough to have faith if that faith finds no expression in behaviour – we must allow our faith to transform us.

In addition to giving expression to feelings of devotion we can become very focussed and absorbed while chanting (c.f. *dhyāna* meditation), while medical research has shown rhythmic chanting or singing stimulates the release of endorphins which may account for the feeling of well being, and even ecstasy, which accompanies group chanting - a similar effect can be observed in secular choirs.

Informal Mantras

Finally many Buddhists use mantras informally outside of ritual contexts as expressions of devotion and faith, and also as a form of petitionary prayer to a Buddha. It is frequently noted that the words of the Avalokiteśvara mantra - *oṃ maṇipeme hūṃ*[99] - are always on the lips of ordinary Tibetans; and we can note that the landscape is dotted with 'mani stones', prayer wheels and prayer flags all of which have mantras written on them and are intended to invoke Avalokiteśvara as a protector. No rules seem to apply to mantra use in this context. Perhaps because of this decontextualisation and the lack of a coherent Buddhist account of mantra all manner of ideas are invoked to talk about informal mantras: in particular people seem to draw on Hindu ideas about 'vibrations' involved in chanting mantras – an idea which, as far as I am aware, is entirely absent from traditional Buddhist accounts of mantra.

Some practitioners swear that chanting a mantra has warded off particular misfortunes, and many simply feel a sense of comfort from chanting. Such applications can also be seen in terms of Going for Refuge, as expressions of an individual's faith. Outside of the ritual context, however, the use of a mantra seems to me to verge on superstition: if I chant a mantra in order to ask for help from a supernatural being then it begins to look like theism and there is not much to distinguish it from prayer to say a saint or the Virgin Mary. The crucial difference is in the Buddhist placing of responsibility for the results of actions in the individual and not in the supernatural being. There is no substitute for the practice of ethics and meditation.

Some observations on the form of mantras

Some authors, for instance Agehananda Bharati, attempt to classify mantras. There are also some traditional notes on what parts of mantras signify.[100] Conze erroneously declared that

[99] This spelling reflects the Tibetan pronunciation.

[100] In MAT (ii.80, Hodge, p.129) for instance it suggests that those with hūṃ and phaṭ are associated with the *Uṣṇīṣa*.

svāhā was only associated with mantras of feminine deities.[101] However over the years I have made some observations which I can offer here.

Firstly Buddhist mantras are almost composed of three parts.

1. A marker to show that this is a mantra, typically but not always *oṃ*.
2. The object of the mantra
3. A concluding part, typically one or more seed-syllables (*bījākṣara*)

Buddhists usually mark a phrase as a mantra by beginning with *oṃ.*[102] but in the *Mahāvairocana Abhisaṃbodhi Tantra* the mantras start with either *namaḥ samanta buddhānaṃ* or *namaḥ samanta vajrānaṃ* - homage to all the Buddhas, or homage to all of the Vajras. Another frequently used opening marker is namaḥ (or one of its *sandhi* variants *namo*, *namas* see p. 203). I have looked at various explanations of *oṃ* in mantras and concluded that it is entirely flexible in what it signifies – in fact the number of syllables in a mantra is often more significant than what those syllables are! *Oṃ* then, in Buddhist mantras, simply means "this is a mantra", and has an esoteric significance depending on which numbered list that the mantra is associated with: for example the Avalokiteśvara mantra of six syllables is associated with the six-realms of existence, the six elements, etc.

Something similar can be said about the third element. Very often this is a generic *hūṃ*, *phaṭ* or *svāhā*. Some mantras adopt the first syllable of the name of the object of the mantra: e.g. *paṃ* for Paṇḍāravāsinī. Others represent a quality: e.g. *dhīḥ* (visionary wisdom) for Mañjuśrī. Most seem either aribitray or the connection is not clear; perhaps this is because I lack the oral teachings.

The central 'object' is usually either the name of a *buddha* or *bodhisattva*, or some quality associated with the. Names can be played on see for instance the Green Tārā or Maitreya mantras. Mantras draw on quite a small pool of words: *caṇḍa, jvāla, padma, phala, vajra, ratna, roṣana, siddhi, sphoṭa.* These terms get recycled in mantras of deities with no apparent connection. Both names and attributes can be prefixed with *mahā* (great), or *vajra* (thunderbolt). Often they are given in a faux dative – simply adding a suffix *ya* or *ye*. The dative indicates to who or what an action is directed, and some Sanskrit nouns do form a dative with a suffix *–ya* or –ye, though most do not. This form seems to imitate mantras from the *Yajur Veda* in the form: 'to the deity *svāhā*'.

My suggestion is that once the three-part form is settled on, it ceases to have much interest or significance for Buddhists, who are more interested in finding the esoteric connections with numbered lists, or in linking the syllables to the Arapacana Alphabet to explore esoteric connections. Not everyone will agree with this rather prosaic approach, and indeed Lama Govinda goes to great lengths to draw out the significance of *oṃ* in part one of *Foundations of Tibetan Mysticism*. I could not help but notice, however, that in the process of his explanation he does not cite a Buddhist text, and indeed largely relies on the Upaniṣads.

Conclusions

The explanation of mantra, then, is dependent on the context. Each context requires its own explanation, and the rules of one may not apply in the other. In most accounts of mantra reference is only made to the Tantric context, but since this has specific requirements - such as

---

[101] Conze *Buddhist Wisdom Books* p.106

[102] Note that Buddhists never seem to use *auṃ*. For a discussion of *oṃ/auṃ* see p.185.

abhiṣeka, accompanying *mudrās* etc - it is seldom applicable outside the Tantric ritual. So outside of the Tantric context it is probably better to think of mantras as devotional in the sense I have set out. I think it will be helpful to have an account of mantra that explicitly applies to how it is used. My observation is that where ideas from, for example Hinduism, are employed to explain Buddhist mantra, the only serve to obscure our understanding. Not a great deal can be discovered from a detailed analysis of the mantras themselves – it is the connections they foster in the mind of the practitioner that are significant, not any inherent power (or worse 'vibration') that they possess. There is no substitute for knowing your mind.

On the Etymology of the Word 'Mantra'.
originally written for visiblemantra.org

ETYMOLOGY IS THE STUDY of what words mean. Broadly speaking there are two principles for constructing etymologies for words. The first looks at the historical progress of a word and tries to identify the 'original' meaning of a word, often creating putative roots in a theoretical language known as Proto-Indo-European. This is sometimes called scientific etymology as it is methodical, and employs as far as possible the principles of scientific inquiry; I prefer to call it historical etymology however since the focus is on the history of meaning. The second principle of etymology works on quite a different model. It is not concerned with meaning over time, but in the moment – linguistics label this method synchronic (with or in time), and the historical method diachronic (across time). In this second principle, the meaning of a word is brought out by comparing it with words that sound similar. Sometimes breaking the words into parts as small as a single syllable, and comparing the parts to similar sounding words or parts. This method can produce contradictory results, and sometimes words that sound similar are not related in meaning. The result is that exponents of historical etymology dismiss it, rather as some Western scholars dismiss mantras as 'meaningless'. Traditional Buddhist etymologies are all of this kind which is known as 'Nirukti etymology' after the 5th century BCE Indian linguistic text of that name by Yāska. The *Nirukti* systematised a principle that had been in use for centuries.

I want to dwell on this distinction for a little longer before giving any etymologies because without some idea of the principles behind them it will be easy to mistake the importance of their conclusions. In his book *The Order of Things* Michel Foucault makes a distinction between two kinds of epistemology. Epistemology it is concerned with theories of knowledge: with the study of what we know, and how we can know things. Modern theories of knowledge are rooted in ideas of difference. Something is a 'thing' if it can be clearly distinguished, if it is sufficiently different from other things. Traditional epistemology however works on a different principle. Something is knowable only through association. Knowledge relies on similarity and relationship. Now this traditional principle of association is a very important one in ancient Indian thought. The Vedic sages believed that the world was separated into two basic spheres – earth and 'heaven' – with an intervening space. Between heaven and earth was an infinite series of bonds (*bandhu*) or associations. The sages sought to control events in heaven, the realm of the gods who kept the cosmic order and performed such functions and raising the sun each day or bringing the monsoons in season. Such influence was wielded by manipulating the earthly counterpart of some heavenly body. Knowledge of the *bandhu* or associations was the chief knowledge of the Vedic sage.

So historical etymologies examine how a word has changed its meaning over time, trying to reveal an original meaning. Historical etymologies look for what is different and distinct about the word, trying to highlight those differences and spotlight the word. Traditional etymologies are only concerned with what a word means to a particular person at a particular time. Traditional etymologies are concerned to show how a word is similar to other words, how it relates to other similar words. Ironically we can get a better insight into a traditional etymology if we employ historical methods and place it in its historical context.

We need to know one more thing about the principle of association between words in traditional etymologies. The central principle of association is sound, or more specifically, pronunciation, or what linguists would call articulation (the way a sound is pronounced). Indian scholars were the first to come up with a systematic description of phonetics – around the time of the Buddha. In fact the modern 'science' of linguistics, and phonetics in particular, owes its existence to the discovery of Sanskrit by Western scholars, for example many of the important figures in the birth of modern linguistics studied the Sanskrit grammarians.

I believe that we need to pay attention to both kinds of etymologies when dealing with Buddhist technical terms. Scientific etymologies can give us information about the meaning of a word as it stands alone, but they are often somewhat remote from the way a technical term is used in Buddhist texts. The word Dharma, for instance, cannot be understood only in terms of its etymology, but must also be seen in context. However, historical etymologies can reveal things about a word which are lost to tradition.

Before we proceed I want to point out that mantra has two quite distinct uses. We will be concerned with the religious sounds and words chanted in a ritual way. However, mantra can also mean 'counsel, or advice'. Although it interesting to see how the same word can be used in these different ways I don't have space to deal with this second meaning in this essay. We are now ready to begin looking at etymologies of the word mantra.

Historical Etymology

All agree that *mantra* is made up of two parts: a root (*man-*) and a suffix (*-tra*). Agehananda Bharati confidently states in his book *The Tantric Tradition*:

> "There can be no doubt about the correct etymology of mantra. It combines the old Vedic (and Indo-European) root 'man' 'to think' with the element –tra, i.e. the kṛt- suffix indicating instrumentality."[103]

The meaning therefore is something like "what the mind does". A far longer and more considered examination of scholarly opinion on the etymology of mantra is provided by Jan Gonda (1963) in what is considered a seminal article on mantra. The verbal root *man-* is related to our English word 'mind'. Gonda draws out the range of references:

> Without entering into the linguistic details the root men- may therefore to be assumed to have expressed also such meanings as "emotional, moved, wilful, intentional, directed 'thought', experiencing impulses in heart and mind etc."[104]

Gonda says about the suffix tra-

> The Sanskrit words in *–tra* (= Indo-European *–tro*), when neuter, are generally speaking, names of instruments or sometimes names of the place where the process is performed. The former category may occasionally express also a faculty: Sanskrit *śrotram* "organ, act or faculty of hearing"; *jñātram* "the intellectual faculty"; or a "function": *hotram* "the function or office of a hotar priest".[105]

So again, we get a meaning of something like "mental/emotional functioning". This doesn't really tell us anything about mantra though. Another possibility occurs in Gonda: "As

[103] Bharati: p.103
[104] Gonda *Mantra*. p.250
[105] Gonda p.250

shown by Renou the verb *man-* has in Vedic usage also the sense of "evoking, calling up", and is then often associated with the noun *nāma* "name".[106]

The word *mantra* is quite rare in the Vedas, and then more common in the parts which are thought to be newer, chapters one and ten. Mantras in the Vedas were verses in praise of gods; later as the Vedic rituals were internalised mantra became more abstract – strings of sounds. Gonda explores the various ways the word is used and his definition of mantra is:

> "A mantra may therefore, etymologically speaking and judging from the usage prevailing in the oldest texts [ie in the Vedas], approximately be defined as follows: "word(s) believed to be of 'superhuman origin', received, fashioned and spoken by the 'inspired' seers, poets and reciters in order to evoke divine power(s) and especially conceived as a means to creating, conveying, concentrating and realizing intentional and efficient thought, and of coming into touch or identifying oneself with the essence of the divinity which is present in the mantra."[107]

This is a fair attempt at combining the etymological and usage meanings for Vedic mantra, though it is clear that he has had to work quite hard to make it come together. As a scholarly definition, it will probably also suffice for Buddhist mantra, though no doubt we would argue about the details.

Ellison Banks Findly draws attention to another etymological possibility, which echoes Gonda's reference to Renou. Findly quotes Sharma who argues that '*man*' actually comes from the root *mnā* (to rote, to utter) which would mean that mantra would mean "to speak, to utter".[108] This would lead to a simpler definition, and resolve the conflict between etymology and usage.

Traditional Etymology.

One folk etymology of *mantra* is it is that which saves (*trā-* "to save, rescue") the one "who, in thought, formulates it and meditates upon it" (*man-*).[109] This kind of protection is a theme especially in Mahayana Buddhist texts. Gonda is mostly interested in Vedic texts, and although he doesn't give a source for this etymology, he does footnote it to say that a similar folk etymology occurs in the *Chāndogya Upaniṣad* so that the idea is most likely pre-Buddhist. It reoccurs in the *Guhyasamāja Tantra* according to the Dalai Lama in his introduction to Tantra in Tibet.

An example of a Nirukti style etymology from the Visuddhimagga by Buddhaghosa says that:

> "the Buddha is blessed (*bhagavā*) because he has broken (*bhagga*) greed, hatred and delusion; he partakes or shares (*bhāgī*) in the gifts of lay devoted (*bhattavā*) followers such as alms and robes. He is possessed of blessings (*bhagī*) because he is a frequenter (*bhajī*)

---

[106] Gonda p.250
[107] Gonda p.255
[108] Sharma. B.R 1979. 'On mati in the Ṛgveda' cited in Findlay, E. B. 'Mántra kaviśasta: speech as a performative in the Ṛgveda.' in Alper, H. P. (ed) 1989. *Mantra* (Albany: State University of New York Press) p.25
[109] Gonda p.248

of places conducive to meditation. He has analysed (*vibhaji*) and classified (*paṭibhaji*) the Dharma Treasure. He is fortunate (*bhāgyavā*) and developed (*bhāvita*, *subbhāviatattno*).[110]

I haven't found a Nirukti etymology for mantra but it is easy enough to construct one on traditional models by collecting words that sound similar:

manā is devotion, atttachment, zeal.
manikṛ – to take to heart.
manu – wise, intelligent, thinking.
maṇ – sounds
maṇī is a jewel.
-tra indicates protection, and *trā* a protector
traṃs can mean "to speak" or "to shine".

From these we can say that: Mantra protects (*tra*) the mind (*man*) from confusion (*trap*) and so that one is not afraid (*tras*). A mantra tears (*tru*) the veil of illusion (*māyā*). Protection (*tra*) is born of the mind (*manoja*) because a well guarded mind protects on from all evil. A mantra is the function (*tra-*) of the intelligent mind (*manas*), it speaks (*traṃs*) intelligently (*manu*), it shines (*traṃs*) like a jewel (*maṇī*). In the final analysis wisdom (*manu*) is the best protector (*trā*), because all is mind (*manas*).

Paragraphs like this are very common in the Buddhist commentarial literature, if not the actual suttas themselves. You can see that the link between the words is poetic rather than literal; associative in a way that opens up possibilities rather than settling on certainties. Each word can be used in different ways.

There is a view in the West that ideally each word should stand for one thing or concept; and each thing or concept should have only one name. The consequences of this view are amusing at times and have lead to some quixotic adventures, some of which are chronicled in Umberto Eco's book *The Search for the Perfect Language*. The view is fuelled by the idea that everyone spoke only one language before God divided the languages – that is to say it is rooted in a literal reading of the Bible, and the story of the tower of Babel. The assumption that there can be a one to one relationship between language and what we might loosely call the world is entirely unscientific, is not at all practical or pragmatic, and is not a feature of natural language. Multiple meanings – polysemy – is the norm. Nirukti etymologies exploit polysemy in constructing a story about what a word means.

Ancient Indian linguists had a sophisticated understanding of polysemy, metaphor and metonym, and synonymy. It is true they also had views about ideal languages, and artificially changed Sanskrit to be closer to their ideal, but they did not, it seems, fall for a one-to-one correspondence ideal. Ideal in their case meant on the whole regular grammar and meter – which reach a very high degree in Sanskrit literature. Sanskrit is one of the few languages which can rival English for synonyms generally, and it gave rise to wonderful poetry.

Conclusions.

I believe that the question of "what is a mantra?" remains open to interpretation. In this essay, I have looked at the word mantra itself, drawing on a few key sources of scholarship. Amongst those who propose scientific etymologies there is not complete agreement on how to

[110] Condensed from Vism. VII.52-67; Ñānamoli p.224-230.

derive the word though at least one makes a claim to absolute certainty on the matter. Reconciling historical etymologies of the word mantra with actual usage, even in ancient texts, is not easy. The point of historical etymology is to remove as much ambiguity as possible, to make clear the 'original' meaning of a word. The urge to do this is more typical of Western approaches to language, which also spawned the search for the perfect language.

I found only one traditional etymology of mantra that was a fairly simple affair. But drawing on models in Buddhist commentarial literature I constructed what I hope is a plausible traditional etymology. It at last gives the flavour of how the traditional mind construed knowledge. The ancient etymologies hold more loosely to definition. What is important is to find a web of associations. The ancient Vedic principle of association meant that knowledge of associations gave one power over, or influence in, the heavens. This principle is still at the heart of mantra use, even in Buddhism.

Phonosemantics

originally written for visiblemantra.org

PHONOSEMANTICS IS A PORTMANTEAU WORD which suggests the meaning that comes from sounds. The idea that individual vocal sounds have meaning is not a new idea. You can find precedents in the Upaniṣads and in Plato. However it is not a popular idea amongst linguists who deny the possibility of such a relationship.

Try this. Get a dictionary of English and chose a consonant - but be aware that this experiment works on sounds so the hard /c/ and /k/ are the same sound. To eliminate the confusion I will refer to a phoneme. Phonemes are indicated by being placed between slashes. So c can be /c/ or /k/; and j or g can be either /j/ or /g/; but k is always /k/. Take each word which does not have a prefix or suffix, and put it into as many categories of meaning as you need to cover the basic senses. Words typically have more than one meaning. Work through all the words that start with that phoneme. At the end of the process most of the words will have fitted into a small number of reasonably well defined categories. Those that do not fit a category are typically concrete nouns - they are names for specific things. In /d/ daffodil is just a daffodil for instance, and has no other referent. This should take 60-90 minutes. Repeat for another sound and compare.

I can summarise the results you will find because I have done this experiment as suggested by Margo Magnus the person who first performed it as part of her doctoral research at Trondheim University, Norway.

- Firstly a very high percentage of words beginning with any phoneme, approaching 100%, which are not concrete nouns will fit into one of about a 10-20 broad categories of meaning. We call this effect clustering.
- Secondly comparing two different initial phonemes you will find only limited crossover of categories, and words beginning with one phoneme will not fit well into the categories associated with another phoneme.
- Thirdly more subtle patterns emerge when comparing similar phonemes such as /p/ an /b/ which are respectively the unvoiced and voiced bilabial stops. Taking a category - such as impacts - words beginning with different phonemes seem to emphasise different aspects of the referent. Impacts with /b/ are broad and blunt, stay on the surface; where /p/ words indicate precision, pin-points, and the impact will puncture the surface. This effect of the phoneme on the symbolism underlying a word we call iconism.

If you work through the whole dictionary you will find that, at least for the consonants, this pattern holds true for all the phonemes in English. Vowels appear to behave in a different manner.

Why should a pattern like this emerge? I know of three explanations.

1. Bounded Chance
2. Verbal roots
3. Sound symbolism

Bounded Chance

Chance is a slight misnomer. Contemporary linguists hold that the relationship between sounds and what they signify is arbitrary. If this were so it would predict a random distribution of meanings and sounds. As the simple experiment above shows there is not a random distribution. Linguists solve this problem by invoking social convention. Words that mean the same are given similar sounds because this has become conventional. The relationship is still fundamentally arbitrary because the sound itself carries no universal meaning, but it does have a relative value in each language. However this is a weak answer to the pervasive phenomenon of sound symbolism.

One way to disprove this hypothesis would be to demonstrate that clustering goes across languages. So far as I know a conclusive demonstration of this is wanting, but there are some results which are suggestive. For instance people have a better than random chance of guessing the meaning of a unfamiliar word in a language they do not speak. Also some phonemes, such as the compound /str/ do appear to cluster in a similar way across languages from different language families - the clustering in one language matches the clustering in another unrelated language for /str/.

Verbal Roots.

As far as I know the scholarly literature has not considered the idea that notional verbal roots underpin clustering. It occurred to me when studying Pāli and becoming familiar with Sanskrit words that verbal roots give rise to a range of words all starting (on the whole) with the same phoneme. These variations fill up dictionaries. However verbal roots are notional, which is to say that they were arrived at by considering similarities between words and working back to theoretical root entities - verbal roots do not exist in the wild.

It may be that verbal roots in fact offer a confirmation of a relationship of which clustering is a manifestation.

Sound Symbolism

The theory says that there is relationship between phonemes and meaning. That relationship is non-arbitrary, but also non-linear. We say that there is a degree of "motivation" behind the choice of phonemes in making a new word. A strong form of this theory would say that speakers have little freedom in choosing; while a weak version would say that speakers have much choice. But any theory of sound symbolism suggests that says that the sounds that make up words, the sounds themselves, carry information. One very simple experiment, now known from its result as "the bouba/kiki effect" shows that sounds can and do act as metaphors for forms in normal people.

The Bouba/Kiki effect

If you look at the image on the right you will see two letters from the "Martian" alphabet. One of the letters is called "bouba", and one "kiki". Which one is which?

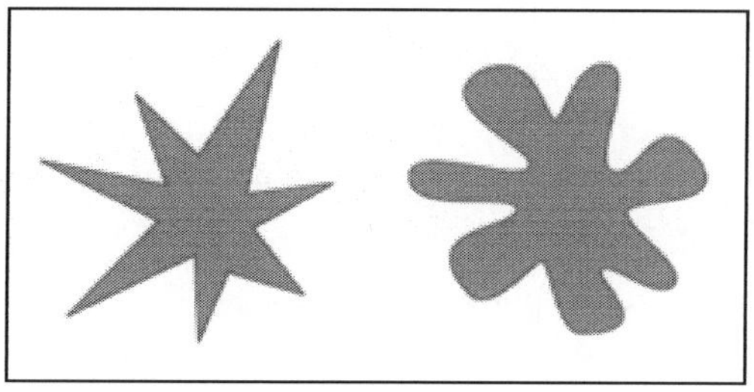

Irrespective of the language they speak around 95% - 98% of people will say that kiki is on the left (the spiky shape), and bouba is on the right (the rounded shape). This suggests that some sounds do indeed have an inherent symbolic "meaning". That meaning is metaphoric and fuzzy rather than literal and linear. The effect was first noted in 1929, but more recent studies have confirmed it. Interestingly children of 2.5 years, too young to read, also make this distinction.

Conventional linguistic theories cannot account for this result. If the relationship between sound and meaning is arbitrary then there is only a 50% chance of any two disparate people choosing the same label for each shape. However experimental results show that across language groups it is extremely unlikely that individuals will make a different choice.

Mechanisms

The mechanism of sound symbolism is as yet unknown. However one suggestion is that verbal gesture - the use of the lips and tongue - is an aspect of it. Margo Magnus for instance suggests that a large portion of words beginning with /b/ come under the headings "barriers, bulges, and bursting" because of the action of lips when creating the /b/ sound: viz they come together to form a barrier to the flow of air, resulting in a build up of pressure (and a bulge), and finally a burst of air and sound. Plato suggested that /r/ connoted movement and activity.

Another promising area is research into synaesthesia. Someone with synaesthesia interprets sensory experience in one mode via the language of another: they see music sounds as colours for instance, or experience words as taste sensations. Vilayanur S. Ramachandran has shown that not only are synaesthetes not faking it, but that there is a possible neurological explanation. His work is promising because it demonstrates how sounds might function as metaphorical images for us. Ramachandran thinks that cross activation between different areas of the brain explain not only synaesthesia, but the whole development of metaphorical thought, and language itself. In particular areas of the brain which process aural information are next door to those which process visual information. Cross linking between them gives rise, according to Ramachandran, sight-sound synaesthesia. Some cross linking is normal and it is this that allows us to perceive for instance sounds as dull or bright; or colours as loud or muted.

Problems with the Phonosemantic Hypothesis

The many languages/many words problem

The key objection from the mainstream is this: that different languages use different words for the same thing, therefore the relationship must be arbitrary. However this is a weak argument that involves a number of assumptions which are not legitimate. Listing the assumptions is useful.

The first assumption is that a single word refers to a single 'thing', and that there is a one to one correspondence between referents between languages. So for instance a "dog" is a single thing, and the word for that thing in French, say, *chien*, is a word for that same thing. This is an extremely naive assumption as anyone who has ever tried to translate from one language to another will know. Many words do not translate easily, and even when they do they may have both subtle and gross differences. Language is more frequently marked by ambiguity or multiplicity of reference (polysemy), than by singularity.

We might also ask whether a dog really is a simple phenomena? Well, obviously it is not. A dog has a general body plan and physical characteristics, and a set of behaviours which mark it out as a dog. The single word dog can take in chihuahua and great-dane; poodle and bloodhound. We know it is a dog because we are able to interact with it through our senses in a way which conforms to our previous experience of other dogs. Some dogs are closer to our mental picture of a dog, and some are much further away. Given that the dog is complex, and our relationship with it, would it then surprise us to find that there are many English words for a dog? Not really. So why would it surprise us to find that other languages, which often involve quite different patterns of thinking, use different words. If Swedes say "hund", might they not relating to the dog in a similar way to us when we choose to call a dog a hound?

Experience is not simple and linear. Experience is complex and non-linear. It is not just processing facts and churning out actions. Linguistics has a behaviouralist model of the relationship of people to their world as an unstated assumption. That assumption demonstrably is flawed and misleading.

The foundations of a new theory of the relationship may well be found in the work of George Lakoff and others working in the area of "linguistic categorization". Lakoff acknowledges the complexity of experience, the possibility of polysemy, and the importance of relationship in definition and the making of meaning. Lakoff emphasises the role of metaphor and metonym (where a part stands in for the whole) in creating meaning.

Comparing languages with radically different sound pallets

There is an unsolved problem with the phonosemantic hypothesis which is what happens when you compare two languages with very different sound pallets: Māori has 10 consonants, while Sanskrit has 34. Māori has at least one sound, /f/, that Sanskrit lacks. So far as I know there has been no research on this aspect of sound symbolism.

The vowels

The vowels do not have the same kind of symbolic associations. The initial phoneme /o/ shows the clustering, but the various sounds associated with the English vowel 'a' do not seem to. Research on the symbolism of vowels in words has shown a fairly consistent effect in regard to size - stressed high vowels (e, i) sound smaller, that rounded back vowels (o, u). Think minimum, medium, maximum (i,e,a). Also in sequences back vowels are later than front vowels: sang, sung. However no one has researched this in the comprehensive way that Magnus has done for the consonant sounds.

Applications to Mantra

A thorough application of the principles of phonosemantics to mantra has yet to be performed. But we can at least look at some general applications.

One of the features of aural experience is that we often take in and process sounds unconsciously. It is well known, for instance, that music evokes emotions without us making a conscious effort to "understand" the music. There is a good evolutionary biological explanation. Reacting to sounds has a positive survival value: we hear in 3 dimensions, and can typically pin-point the direction of a sound to about 1° of arc. This we hear some threat approaching and are launched into action often before we can think. Our aural systems is fine tuned for this survival: we have emotional responses to sounds. More than this however we are a social species and many of our interactions are conducted in the medium of vocal sounds. Anecdotally we say that only a very small percentage of the information in a conversation is down to the words we use. The bulk of what we are communicating is non-verbal. Included in this are factors such as intonation, and phrasing: features of language known collectively as prosody. Prosody gives us clues as to the attitudes and emotions of another person. It is prosody that allows us to completely change the meaning of a phrase through inflection (technically known as conversation implicature). I could say "I like your new hair cut" and convey many different messages by varying prosodic and gestural elements, even making it mean the complete opposite.

As a social species this kind of non-verbal information is vital to the healthy functioning of our group, and therefore once again we are highly attuned to it. We can tell simply from tone of voice for instance, if someone is angry with us, or genuinely pleased to see us. So on this level also we are attuned to sounds.

If we accept that vocal sounds are also gestures (in the broadest sense), or at least can symbolise a gesture, then we accept that a verbal sound may communicate information from other modes. This in a way is obvious, but I am drawing attention to it in the light of sound symbolism. If sounds are not arbitrary, then our choice of sounds conveys information. What I mean is that we convey information with a word, but that the choice of that word in particular, with those sounds, is a layer of non-verbal information.

Sound symbolism posits a symbolic link between sounds and meaning. The link is metaphoric or even poetic. Upon hearing a vocal sound we do not immediately leap to a concept. We may associate it with an image, or series of images; or we may simply respond emotionally. Linguistics on the whole tries to set aside this aspect of language, and to focus on trying to refine the meaning of words, or the structure of grammar and syntax. Anything which has no precise meaning, or which does not convey a concept is often dismissed out of hand. Linguists working within this paradigm come to conclusions which are a variation on "mantras are meaningless". The exemplar of this is Frits Staal who uses the tools of Structuralism and Semantics to try to understand ritual and mantra. Ritual according to Staal is a set of rules with no meaning, and mantra is not a form of language but a relic of a time before language, a persistence of pre-human animal sounds into the human arena. Neither of these theories are very attractive, nor do they offer much in the way of insight into the effects of mantra, or why they are such potent symbols. Staal is a more sophisticated version of the Victorian scholars of Buddhism who frequently concluded that if they did not understand something, then it was incomprehensible to all.

However linguists working within the paradigm of Pragmatics often find more meaning in mantras. They see for instance poetic devices such as repetition, alliteration, and rhyming in some mantras. Despite the lack of proper words, a mantra can be using the effects of language to create an image.

Phonosemantics goes even further. It says that vocal sounds, even single syllables, have meaning. That meaning is imprecise and metaphoric. If we accept the phonosemantic hypothesis then we need not conclude that the sounds of mantras have no meaning. Mantras can be meaningful in the sense that phonemes communicate in images and feelings. Compare this idea with research that shows that the inarticulate noises we make during conversations – *hmm*, *uh*, *uhuh*, *mmm*, etc. – are packed with meaning.[111]

My understanding of mantra in Tantric Buddhism is that its purpose is to give us an experience. That experience should help us to transform ourselves in line with the Buddhist teachings. We are highly attuned to sounds, and vocal sounds in particular, and they are able to

[111] See for instance: http://www.nigelward.com/egrunts/

produce a physical/emotional response in us without involving conscious cognition. Sounds can indeed evoke an involuntarily response in us, that is, they can give us an experience. What is communicated is non-verbal and non-linear; it is metaphorical and symbolic. What's more, by choosing specific syllables, that have built up associations by use, and may even have inherent meanings, we may be able to direct that experience. Anecdotally, practitioners often report that different mantras have a different "feel" to them.

A lot of what I am saying here is speculative, and based on an admittedly limited understanding of linguistics, but I think it is plausible. In this essay I have not appealed to any mystical entity or process. This is not metaphysics, although a metaphysical explanation may be more satisfying to some people. Personally I want to understand the process to better apply it. If I know how the average person might respond to a given combination of sounds, for instance, then it will be possible to create new mantras designed to evoke a particular kind of experience. If however mantras are a kind of divine revelation that we mustn't tamper with or investigate then we are stuck. Perhaps Sanskrit mantras do not work so well for Westerners? What if one or other of the sounds in English which are not in Sanskrit (/f/ for instance) might work better for me? What if, having grown up with no retroflex consonants, they merely confuse my aural processing facility?

A lot of work remains to be done, and there are few people to do it. If you want to follow up this thread then the place to start is Margaret Magnus's website: The Magic Letter Page.[112] There is a lot of info here, and links to other material.

I also recommend:

Lakoff, G. and Johnson, M. 1981 *Metaphors we live.* Chicago University Press. (a very interesting introduction to the pervasiveness of metaphor in communication and language).

The 2003 BBC Reith Lectures by V.S. Ramachandran included a talk, *Purple Numbers and Sharp Cheese*, on his ideas about how synaesthesia might provide an account of metaphor more generally, and also insights into the development of language.[113]

---

[112] http://www.trismegistos.com/MagicalLetterPage/
[113] http://www.bbc.co.uk/radio4/reith2003/lecture4.shtml

Dhāraṇī - origins, meaning, and usage.

originally written for Jayarava's Raves 11 July 2008

THE WORD *DHĀRAṆĪ* is a characteristically Buddhist term, at times synonymous with mantra and at others seeming to have its own special significance. In this short essay I want to examine the word, and the main ways it is used.

The word *dhāraṇī* according to Edgerton's dictionary of Buddhist Hybrid Sanskrit does not occur outside of texts written in BHS. This point is sometimes summarised as "does not occur outside of Buddhist texts", but Edgerton's point is more specific and that specificity has some possible consequences. We need to be aware here of the shifting and uncertain nature of BHS. BHS is in fact a Prakrit language that was in the process of being Sanskritised. By which we mean a vernacular North Indian dialect was being regularised in its grammar to conform to the ideals of linguistic form represented by Classical Sanskrit.[114] As such BHS shows considerable variation in grammar and spelling especially in the area of inflections - the suffixes added to words to indicate the grammatical relationship between them.

Buddhist texts cover a spectrum:

- Texts written in relatively pure Prakrits (the Gāndhārī texts for instance),
- Texts written in Pāli, a somewhat artificial "church language" constructed from several Prakrits.
- Texts in which the Prakrit has begun to be Sanskritised
- Texts in which the process of Sanskritisation is well advanced
- Texts in more or less pure Classical Sanskrit (e.g. Aśvaghoṣa's *Buddhacarita*)

In fact there is a word in Sanskrit - *dhāraṇa*. It means, according to Monier-Williams:

> "holding, bearing, keeping (in remembrance), retention, preserving, protecting, , maintaining, possessing, having".

This is so close to the uses of our word that I am somewhat surprised that the literature supplies no argument for distinguishing the two terms. In Tibetan the word is frequently translated, again according to Edgerton, as "*gzuṅs*, literally, "hold, support". This supports the supposition that the Tibetans understood *dhāraṇī* to by synonymous with *dhāraṇa*. I'm not aware of any publications which directly address this issue.

Jan Nattier suggests that the earliest use of the term *dhāraṇī* occurs in relation to the Arapacana Alphabet (Nattier: 292) - now known to be the alphabet of the Gāndhārī Prakrit. This alphabet, uniquely in India, was used as a mnemonic device, a kind of acrostic where each letter stood for a keyword, which then became the subject of a phrase. By the time of the *Pañcaviṃśatisāhasrikā Prajñāpāramitā Sūtra* (ca. 2nd century) this technique was being used as a memory aid for a meditation on aspects of *śūnyatā*. From this usage we find the word *dhāraṇī* associated with mnemonic devices - many writers insist the *dhāraṇī* is always a mnemonic device. However a glance over some of the many *dhāraṇī* preserved in, or as, texts will quickly make this identity much less certain. Most *dhāraṇī* apparently have no mnemonic features, i.e. they do not appear to stand for other things. They do employ many of the prosodic

[114] Where I do not qualify it the word *Sanskrit* will specifically refer to Classical Sanskrit from now on.

features of poetry in order perhaps to help them be memorable, but they do not seem to, as some authors would have us believe, "summarise the text to which they are attached". More often a *dhāraṇī* bears no apparent relationship to a text, even when it is strongly associated with a text - as in the very prominent case of the *Heart Sūtra* where interpretations of what the mantra means are as numerous as are commentaries on the text. That there is no consistent exegetical tradition associated with any of these dhāraṇī only serves to confirm this impression.

Like mantras *dhāraṇī* come in a variety of forms. In early Buddhist texts markers at the beginning such as '*oṃ*' or '*namaḥ samanta buddhāṇāṃ*' are missing. *Dhāraṇī* can be strings of words, frequently all with the same grammatical ending (usually the feminine vocative). An example from the *Saddharmapuṇḍarīka Sūtra* is:

> *anye manye mane mamane citte carite same samitā viśānte mukte muktatame same aviṣame samasame jaye kṣaye akṣaye akṣiṇe śānte samite dhāraṇi ālokabhāṣe pratyavekṣaṇi nidhiru abhyantaraniviṣṭe abhyantarapāriśuddhimutkule araḍe paraḍe sukāṅkṣi asamasame buddhavilokite dharmaparīkṣite saṃghanirghoṣaṇi nirghoṇi bhayābhayaviśodhani mantre mantrākṣayate rute rutakauśalye akṣaye akṣayavanatāye vakkule valoḍra amanyanatāye svāhā* || [115]

Such strings make frequently use of poetic devices such as alliteration, repetition, and often make use of phonetic variations on a theme. These are clearly visible in the first line of the dhāraṇī above. Alternatively they may be strings of syllables which do not make words. Again from the *Saddharmapuṇḍarīka*:

> *iti me iti me iti me iti me iti me* | *nime nime nime nime nime* | *ruhe ruhe ruhe ruhe ruhe* | *stuhe stuhe stuhe stuhe stuhe svāhā* || [116]

Here the effect is of repeated sounds, which to my ear suggests some kind of sound symbolism. On a Buddhist online forum one member suggested that they represent coded coordinates for some object like a stūpa, but as far as I know this is pure speculation. Though the argument is similar to ones made by Subhash Kak about codes in the *Ṛgveda*.[117]

Another kind of *dhāraṇī* reads like a poem or prayer to a particular deity. These are more like the Vedic mantra in literary character - here we could translate *dhāraṇī* as "hymn" just as many Vedic scholars do for mantra. These *dhāraṇī* are part of an extant Buddhist tradition which is rooted in Pure Land ideas: chanting the *dhāraṇī* invokes the saving power (or vow) of the Buddha or Bodhisattva, delivering the chanter either from some immediate misfortune, or ultimately from the suffering of *saṃsara* altogether.

One oddity of the way the word *dhāraṇī* is used is that it can be both the means to the goal, and the goal itself. One chants a *dhāraṇī* in order to be protected or gain insights; however some texts talk about the acquisition of *dhāraṇī* as one of the results of the Bodhisattva's practice. The *Saddharmapuṇḍarīka* deities offer *dhāraṇī* to be memorised and chanted for protection, while the *Pañcaviṃśatisāhasrikā* has the Bodhisattva attaining *dhāraṇī*: in this case *dhāraṇī* almost seems to be synonymous with *samādhi*, and note that this is sometimes how the word *dhāraṇa* is used in the Upaniṣads (see for example Deussen: p. 389f)

---

115 Vaidya (1960) p.234.
116 Vaidya (1960) p.235.
117 See for instance: Kak, Subhash. 2000. *The Astronomical Code of the Ṛgveda.*

It is frequently assumed that *dhāraṇī*, and the Pāli *paritta* texts, are simply precursors to mantra. However I'm not convinced that there is continuity here. Some of the popular *dhāraṇī* texts did end up being considered to be *kriyā tantra* by later Tibetan exegetes, but there is nothing in the content of these *dhāraṇī*, nor in the context in which they occur, to suggest that they function like mantras in the Tantric sense. This identification has led some scholars, for instance Robert Thurman, to argue for very early dates for Tantric texts, when other evidence makes it seem very unlikely.

A more thorough exploration by a qualified scholar is eagerly awaited, although I am not presently aware that any scholar of Buddhism is taking an interest. I speculate that a closer analysis of the evidence will reveal a more subtle interplay of religious ideas and impulses at work, and make it clear that *dhāraṇī* and *paritta* are not in origin at least, simply mantra by another name. The word *dhāraṇī* came into play in a time and place of innovation: in the 1st-2nd centuries in Gāndhāra, under foreign rulers (the Kuṣans), during which period also the first images of the Buddha were made, and the *Mahāyāna* began to be mainstream. However it was quickly taken up by the Buddhist world - new ideas appear to have spread quickly at this time, perhaps due to extensive trading networks. The term then appears to have undergone a process of evolution over several centuries until the advent of Buddhist mantra proper, probably in the 7th century, when it was subsumed under that rubric. Traditional explanations of what makes *dhāraṇī* distinctive lack this historical perspective, while contemporary accounts have jumped too quickly to the conclusion that similarity equals sameness.

Non-lexical utterances, stobhas, and mantra

originally written for Jayarava's Raves 4 July 2008

IN RESEARCHING THE BACKGROUND to Buddhist mantra I inevitably began to read about Vedic mantra. There is a lot more research on Vedic mantra and on the whole it is more interesting than research on Buddhist mantra, so far. Reading up on the Vedic tradition has given me an appreciation of the Vedic literature which is of surpassing beauty and profundity at times. I think we Buddhists tend to write off the other Indian scriptures but that is our loss. The Vedic tradition stands in relation to Indian culture rather like the Ancient Greeks do to Europe.

If you do read up on Vedic mantras you will find that mantra originally meant one of the hymns to the gods as exemplified and recorded in the *Ṛgveda*. The date of this text is disputed rather vigorously and sometimes hotly, but it seems likely that it was compiled around 1500-1200 BCE, probably out of an already existing oral literature. As the verses (or *ṛk* [118]) began to be used ritually two things happened. Firstly an exegetic literature began to be composed to explain how, where, and when to use the verses in the rituals; and secondly the verses themselves were reframed. The *Sāmaveda* reframes the *Ṛgveda* verses by setting them to music. Verses sung or chanted to these rhythms and tunes as called *sāman*.

One of the key features of *sāmans* is the insertion of syllables to alter the metre of the original. These syllables are called *stobha*. *Stobha* can be one or two syllables. One list of *stobha* is:

> *ā (e)re hā-u is phat as hā hṃ iṭ pnya auhovā hahas ho-i kāhvau um bhā hai hum kit up dada hā-i hup mṛ vava (e)bṛ ham hvau nam vo-I (e)rā has ihi om.*[119]

Recently I was revisiting some websites about the sounds that people make during conversations - which the researchers call "non-lexical utterances" or "conversational grunts". The interest in these sounds came out of research into human-computer interfaces. Here is a list of non-lexical utterances from one website:

> ai, hh-aaaah, iiyeah, okay, nuuuuu, ukay, uam, uumm, yeahh, am, hhh, m-hm, okay-hh, nyaa-haao, um, uh, uun, yeahuuh, neeu, ao, hhh-uuuh, mm, ooa, nyeah, um-hm-uh-hm, uh-hn, uuuh, yegh, nuu, aoo, hhn, mm-hm, ookay, o-w, umm, uh-hn-uh-hn, uuuuuuu, yeh-yeah, ohh, aum, hmm, mm-mm, oooh, oa, ummum, uh-huh, wow, yei, yeah, eah, hmmmmm, mmm, ooooh, oh, unkay, uh-mm, yah-yeah, yo, ehh, hn, myeah, oop-ep-oop, oh-eh, ununun u, uh-uh, ye, yyeah, achh, h-nmm, hn-hn, nn-hn, u-kay, oh-kay, uu, uh-uhmmm, yeah, ah, haah, huh, nn-nnn, u-uh, oh-okay, uuh, uhh, yeah-okay, ahh, hh, i, nu, u-uun, oh-yeah, uum, uhhh, yeah-yeah.[120]

The list could be supplemented from popular music (think James Brown for instance!), or for that matter from serious vocal music, which also use non-lexical syllables to pad sentences or verses to fit a metre. These non-lexical sounds function as feedback to the speaker, and are uttered in concert with the speaker in order to let them know that they are being heard and understood. A lot (but not all) of the information conveyed by these non-lexical sounds is

[118] The stem is *ṛc* which in the nominative is *ṛk*, and when followed by a voiced consonant (such as *va*) it becomes *ṛg*. These changes are due to sandhi rules. (See Glossary)
[119] Staal *Vedic Mantras* p.61
[120] *Responsive Systems Project* website.

contained in the prosodic aspects of speech – tone of voice, inflection – along with non-verbal signals such as facial expression, hand gestures, and body posture. These can indicate the attitude of the listener to what is being said, and how they feel about it.

While we cannot confirm this, it seems reasonable to surmise that *stobha* were drawn from non-lexical sounds amongst Vedic speakers at the time. This further suggests that stobhas not only help a verse to conform to a metre or rhythm, but may also have served another pragmatic function when chanted in *sāman*. They may have been imitating prosodic elements of speakers of the time, incorporating information about responses to the sāman within it. It may be possible for a suitably qualified person to test this idea.

It is the conclusion of some researchers into mantra, Frits Staal being the leading light, that because mantra contain non-lexical sounds, that they are 'meaningless'. We would have to agree that sounds like *oṃ*, *āḥ* and *hūṃ* do not have dictionary definitions, and so they do not refer to any 'thing'. However it's clear that Staal et al have been too narrowly focussed on semantics. Languistics may be focussed on words, but human communication involves very much more, and a great deal of communication may take place without any words at all. We can even make words mean the opposite of their dictionary meanin: I can say "I like your new haircut", while implying the exact opposite in an unequivocal way through the use of facial expression and vocal inflection for instance. (This is known technically as conversational implicature)

After the *Ṛgvedic* period mantras began to make more use of non-lexical sounds. Staal sees this as a persistence of primitive pre-linguistic sounds into the present: they are like bird song, animal noises, or the burbling of infants, and quite meaningless. They are the caveman grunts of popular imagination, retained by Indian religious leaders for ritual purposes. If we for a moment accept Staal's hypothesis, his analysis of those kinds of sounds is grossly oversimplified since all three of these phenomena are far from meaningless if one knows how to listen. Worse still Staal appears to be making some unfortunate, rather 'orientalist', implications about the subjects of his studies. This inelegant hypothesis is untestable, and does not open the way to further research. It certainly does not chime with the experience of mantra. Kūkai goes to the other extreme and counts every mantric syllable as being infinitely meaningful, and being the starting point for elucidating all knowledge and experience. In this he is adopting a world view which has its basis in the *Avataṃsaka Sūtra*. A full explanation of Kūkai idea deserves its own essay, and goes beyond what I am suggesting here. Not that I disagree, but I am looking for intermediate steps that make sense in a contemporary context.

Stobha used in *sāman* may well have been the model for the use of non-lexical syllables in mantra although this would be difficult to prove. They do bear a resemblance to non-lexical sounds used meaningfully in conversation by contemporary English speakers (and others). But even if they did not, what it suggests to me is that we can look for meaning in ways that might not be obvious, and still not have to stray into metaphysics and mysticism. It may be that no explanation in these terms can fully comprehend mantra. That is not a problem. But in attempting such an explanation I think we can shed a lot more light on this subject, and make it more accessible in the process. The 'mantras are meaningless' mantra is a dead end as far as research goes, and do not explain the persistence of mantra over several millennia in Indian religious contexts.

Mantra, Magic, and Interconnectedness.

originally written for Jayarava's Raves 27 June 2008

At the heart of the practice of mantra is the idea that everything is interconnected. Although the idea is not apparent in early Buddhist teachings it is strongly associated with the *Avataṃsaka Sūtra*, and with the Buddhism that centres on it, often known by the Chinese equivalent: *Huayen*. The *Avataṃsaka* coalesced in the 3rd century though it is thought to be a composite work that accumulated parts over time. However the idea that everything is interconnected was not new to India at the time, but goes back to the earliest religious text: the *Ṛgveda*.

In the Vedas the cosmos is divided into three realms: human, god, and intermediate or sky. The earliest gods were personifications of the awesome forces of nature: the sun, storms, and fire, etc. The ancients believed, for instance, that a single principle linked all things which were hot or bright: the sun, fire, digestion, and even the spark of imagination. This particular principle was called Agni – sometimes referred to as the 'god' of fire. Even in our technologically advanced times we are still subject to nature (think global warming!): how much more so were our ancient forebears! They desired control over the sun and the monsoons, and developed a kind of magic technology for doing so. The very early Vedic poets acted as shamans who were directly in contact with the gods and the Vedic hymns are records of their conversations with the gods, or their prayers to them. They became the keepers of the the sacred fire. The Agni was the hermetic messenger and fire was an exchange medium: sacrifices were transformed by the fire into smoke, and this was carried upwards to the gods who could consume it in that form. In return the gods were compelled to respond favourably.

The key to effective rituals was the *bandhu* or connection between this world and the god realm. By manipulating the *bandhu* at this end, changes could be wrought at the other end. The priests were masters of the *bandhu*, and a great deal of the vast exegetical literature on the Vedas is devoted to listing or explaining *bandhu*. As with many ancient cultures knowledge at this time was based on resemblance and relationship; our own approach to knowledge relies on difference and isolation. A *bandhu* worked because something in this world resembled something in the other world. It can be difficult for us moderns to understand this, as we are attuned to seeing differences. To the ancients a metaphor might have seemed far more substantial for instance: they would never have said, as we might, that it's "just a metaphor". They understood the concept of metaphor, but took the relationship to be far more substantial than we do.

The late Vedic period saw the internalisation of the rituals, which were then carried out in imagination – thereby inventing meditation. The Buddha was born into this time, and studied for a time with Late Vedic sages, known as *śramaṇas*. The Buddha explicitly rejected the various forms of Vedic ritual, both external and internal, and substituted his own practices which emphasise a balance of blissful tranquillity and penetrating insight. Although he taught that all experiences arise from causes, he did not make the link between all experiences to explicitly talk about interconnectedness.

By the 3rd century some Buddhists were using the kinds of images of interconnectedness that have become familiar - Indra's net of jewels which each reflect all of the others for instance. In the 6th century a great synthesis of religious ideas occurred, partly in response to a breakdown in social and political order as the Gupta Empire was smashed by the Huns. Many of the old Vedic ideas were assimilated into Buddhism and key amongst these was the idea of bandhu. One sees this, for instance, in the Tantric explanation of the Avalokiteśvara mantra. The syllables are not considered as linguistic units, but as representing the six realms of existence, and the six manifestations of the Bodhisattva in those realms, etc.

It can be difficult for us to see how this medieval Indian idea makes sense. In *The End of Magic* Ariel Glucklich describes his research amongst the Tantric magicians of present day Benares. Working through the various Western ideological explanations of magic he rejects them all in favour of an explanation which relies on a sense of interconnectedness. Having done field work amongst Tantric healers in Banares, Glucklich concludes that:

> "Magic is based on a unique type of consciousness: the awareness of the interrelatedness of all things in the world by means of simple but refined sense perception... magical actions... constitute a direct, ritual way of restoring the experience of relatedness in cases where that experience has been broken by disease, drought, war, or any number of other events."[121]

I think that Glucklich has had a penetrating insight in this statement and one that we can relate back to Tantric Buddhism generally. Crucially to my mind he insists that what he calls the magical experience is neither a mystical nor a metaphysical concept.

> "It is a natural phenomenon, the product of our evolution as a human species and an acquired ability for adapting to various ecological and social environments."[122]

Some work remains to be done to adapt Glucklich's work to the Buddhist context: we need to see it in the light of Buddhist psychology for instance, and the Buddhist view of reality and experience; and we also need to make clear how mantra works in this framework. I am confident that it can be done because at the heart of the matter is interrelatedness.

---

[121] Glucklich *The End Of Magic*, p.12
[122] Glucklich *The End Of Magic*, p.12

Words in mantras that end in –e

originally written for Jayarava's Raves 6 March 2009

Anyone familiar with Buddhist mantras will be familiar with the number of words that end in '*e*'. They constitute something of a mystery as they don't make sense grammatically or semantically, and explanations of them are obviously ad hoc (i.e. made up on the spot). For instance the Heart Sūtra mantra:

> *gate gate paragate parasaṃgate bodhi svāhā*

Compare to this to the dhāraṇī offered by the Medicine King Bodhisattva in the *Saddharmapuṇḍarīka Sūtra*:

> *anye manye mane mamane citte carite same samitā viśānte mukte muktatame same aviṣame samasame jaye kṣaye akṣaye akṣiṇe śānte samite dhāraṇi ālokabhāṣe pratyavekṣaṇi nidhiru abhyantaraniviṣṭe abhyantarapāriśuddhimutkule araḍe paraḍe sukāṅkṣi asamasame buddhavilokite dharmaparīkṣite saṃghanirghoṣaṇi nirghoṇi bhayābhayaviśodhani mantre mantrākṣayate rute rutakauśalye akṣaye akṣayavanatāye vakkule valoḍra amanyanatāye svāhā* ||[123]

Note how many of these words have the -e ending. Kern, the first person to translate the *Saddharmapuṇḍarīka* into English, in 1884, links many of these names to the Great Mother Goddess.

> "All of these words are, or ought to be, feminine words in the vocative. I take them to be epithets of the Great Mother, Nature or Earth, differently called Aditi, Prajñā, Māyā, Bhavānī, Durgā. Anyā may be identified with the Vedic *anyā*, inexhaustible, and synonymous with *aditi*. More of the other terms may be explained as synonymous with *prajñā* (e.g. *pratyaveksaṭi*), with nature (*kṣāye akṣāye*), with earth (*dhāraṇī*)."[124]

For the uninitiated perhaps a brief explanation about inflected languages is in order. Where in English we use prepositions such as "of, for, to, by, with, on, in, from" etc. to indicate the relationship between words in a sentence, inflected languages add different endings to the words. The easiest way will be to show. Let's take a word that has a stem in -a: buddha. (It's actually a past-participle meaning awoken or understood). So somewhat simplistically we could show the (singular) endings and their 'meaning':

> *buddhaḥ* – nominative – the Buddha.
> *buddhaṃ* – accusative – the Buddha as the patient of a verb: e.g. I saw the Buddha.
> *buddhena* – instrumental – by means of, or with the Buddha.
> *buddhāya* – dative – to or for the Buddha. e.g. namo Buddhāya – homage to the Buddha.
> *buddhāt* – ablative – from the Buddha
> *buddhasya* – genitive – of the Buddha; the Buddha's... (possessive)
> *buddhe* – locative – in or on the Buddha
> *buddha* – vocative – O Buddha. (address or invocation)

[123] Vaidya 1960: p.233
[124] Kern p.371, note 3

There are many paradigms like this in Sanskrit. Each noun has dual forms in addition to singular and plural. Masculine, feminine and neuter nouns vary slightly, and stems can end in any monophthong vowel or certain consonants - meaning that there are very many different forms to remember! The *-e* ending is typically associated with three grammatical forms. In the case of the word *gata*, which is a part-participle and declined like a noun, the possibilities are:

feminine vocative
masculine or neuter locative

Gaté therefore most likely means something like "O she who is gone", i.e. it is in the vocative case. This is what Edward Conze thought. The other possibilities are open, but the subject of the *Heart Sūtra* is Prajñāpāramitā - who is feminine both in gender and grammatically. But when all the words in a mantra, as above, are in the feminine vocative, the string of words is not grammatically sensible, that is, they do not make a sentence. The usual explanation is some variation on the idea that these are strings of invocations to deities or qualities. Kern obviously thought something like this and expected feminine vocatives - but note that he is expecting Hindu goddesses in a Buddhist text. To some extent they do appear, but he may not, in 1884, had a very clear idea of the differences between Buddhism and Hinduism

An unspoken assumption here is that the mantras are written in Classical Sanskrit. This is the language which was formalised and polished (i.e. *saṃskṛta* - literally "made complete") in about the 4th century BCE, and became the standard language for literary and religious compositions in India. Given that some of the texts, the *Heart Sūtra* for one, are written in Classical Sanskrit this seems at first glance a reasonable assumption. However we know that Buddhists before the Gupta Empire (4th – 6th centuries CE) wrote in a Sanskritised version of the Prakrit, or spoken dialect, locally spoken. This literary language which is now known as Buddhist Hybrid Sanskrit actually shows massive variations over time and place. The name Buddhist Hybrid Sanskrit (BHS) was coined by Frank Edgerton who wrote a grammar and dictionary for it. Many well known *sūtras* were written in BHS including the *Mahāvastu*, *Saddharmapuṇḍarīka*, *Suvarnabhasottama*, *Gaṇḍhavyūha*, *laṅkāvatāra*, *Sukhāvatīvyūha* (larger and smaller), *Pañcaviṃśatisāhasrikā Prajñāpāramitā*, and the *Vajracchedikā*. Śantideva's *Śikṣāsamuccaya* which is made up of quotes from many *Mahāyāna* sutras is almost entirely in BHS. In addition, notably, Buddhists reverted to BHS during the Tantric period after the 6th century.

BHS is full of irregularities particularly in the grammatical endings. For Classical Sanskrit nouns with stems ending in –a, the nominative singular is -aḥ (e.g. *devaḥ*, the god, or the king), whereas is Pāli it is -o, (e.g. *devo*), while in Māgadhī the nominative singular is -e (*deve*). The variety of BHS nominative singular endings for nouns with -a stems found in extant manuscripts includes: -o, -u, -ū, -a, -ā, -aṃ, and -e.[125] The -e ending is also used for the vocative singular as in Sanskrit. In the case of the Gāndhārī Prakrit, at least in written form, the variety of nominative singular case endings has been described as "bewildering", and it seems as though final vowels may have been de-emphasised to the point of almost disappearing in speech, which caused confusion amongst scribes.[126]

If the mantras were written in Prakrit or perhaps BHS then we might suspect that they were simply words in the nominative singular. It might better explain the long lists of words such as the Lotus Sūtra example quoted above, although the Heart Sūtra mantra might still best

[125] Edgerton, Vol. 1, p.49-50.
[126] Salomon *Indian Epigraphy* p.130-131

be seen as an invocation. If one is stringing together words then the most basic form is usually the nominative singular.

But why would Sanskrit texts preserve a form that is aberrant from the point of view of Classical Sanskrit grammar? To answer this I cite the example of a Prakrit feature that is preserved in many Sanskrit texts, over quite a long period of time and including in indirect borrowings.

The Arapacana alphabet is the alphabet of the Gāndhārī prakrit. We know that at least from the first couple of centuries of the common era it was used as a mnemonic device, where each letter stands for a key word that is used in a line of verse of a poem. Most extant examples are either obviously a practical reminder about a meditation practice, or derive from one of these. Having been composed in Gāndhārī, perhaps as a stand alone poem,[127] it was imported into Sanskrit texts such as the Lalitavistara Sūtra and the Large Perfection of Wisdom Sūtra.[128] In the case of the Lalitavistara a version exists which was fully Sanskritised, but there is also a version in Chinese translation which retains the Gāndhārī order (see Brough *The arapacana syllabary* 1977). In the Large Perfection of Wisdom Sūtra all known versions retain the Gāndhārī order. In the *Gaṇḍhavyūha Sūtra* the Gāndhārī order is retained but the phonetic connection between the alphabet and the keywords is lost. In the *Mahāvairocana Abhisaṃbodhi Tantra* (MAT) the alphabet is Sanskrit, but the vowels except 'a' are left off in imitation of the Gāndhārī alphabet (which only uses one sign for initial vowels, which is then modified by diacritics to make all the other vowels). It's reasonably obvious that the source for the alphabet in the MAT is the Large Perfection of Wisdom Sūtra, which means that it is twice removed from Gāndhārī, a language not spoken in India for several centuries by the time the MAT was composed! Perhaps not surprisingly there was a streak of conservatism by Buddhists when composing texts, especially with regard to mantra.

So there is a possibility here: if the mantras were in fact composed in Māgadhī or Buddhist Hybrid Sanskrit, or some other dialect where a nom sg. in -e was used, then it is likely that the original form of the mantra would have been retained even as the text itself was Sanskritised. It might even have stayed in that form when borrowed by other texts. This means that the form in the mantras could be nominative and strings of words in nom sg., or at least intended to be. Perhaps a closer examination of the words, without the assumption of Classical Sanskrit might lead to a better understanding. For the moment the puzzle remains, and my conjecture though plausible is not a final answer to the problem - if anything I may have muddied the waters!

---

[127] We're still waiting for a full translation and analysis of a fragment of manuscript containing the earliest known version of the Arapacana. See the publications page of the Bajaur Collection of Buddhist Kharoṣṭhī Manuscripts for a preliminary report.

[128] The Large Perfection of Wisdom Sūtra has versions in 18,000, 25,000 and 100,000 lines which are distinguished chiefly by the number of repetitions and the thoroughness of spelling out variations on a theme. The chief feature of the version in 100,000 lines is the lack of the use of "etc" or "and so on". Conze has published an English translation largely based on the 25,000 line version, but which draws freely on the others due to the "execrable state" of the manuscripts. See also *The Wisdom Alphabet* (p.27ff)

Tadyathā in the Heart Sūtra

Originally written for Jayarava's Raves 13 Novemeber 2009

The word *tadyathā* is often found at the beginning of mantras and is often included in the actual chant. *Tadyathā* is an adverbial compound consisting of *tad* 'that' and *yathā* 'as like, according to, in that way'. So *tadyathā* means 'like this' or 'this way'. The mantra in the *Heart Sūtra* is being introduced this way:

> *Tasmāj jñātavyaṃ prajñāpāramitāyām ukto mantraḥ tadyathā: gate gate pāragate pārasaṃgate bodhi svāhā.*
>
> In the 'wisdom gone beyond' the mantra is spoken like this: *gate gate pāragate pārasaṃgate bodhi svāhā.*

If we follow Conze's punctuation in Buddhist Wisdom Books (p.101)[129] the passage is pretty confusing, because the breaks seem to come at the wrong place, and interestingly his English is in fact punctuated quite differently from his Sanskrit (c.f. for instance the colon after *tasmaj jñātavyam* but not after "Therefore one should know"). In Vaida's Sanskrit editions the punctuation is minimal – the only traditional punctuation is the *daṇḍa* or vertical stroke.[130] Vaida has a *daṇḍa* between *mantraḥ* and *tadyathā*. I'm not convinced by this, and as I will show below it is more natural to take *prajñāpāramitāyām ukto mantraḥ tadyathā* as a single (well formed) sentence. So let us examine the grammar of this phrase.

The verb is *ukto* from √*vac* 'to speak'.[131] Grammatically it is a passive past-participle, so it means 'spoken' or 'said', and functions something like an adjective describing something that is done. It is in the nominative singular form, *uktaḥ*, and *sandhi* dictates that the *-aḥ* ending changes to *-o* when followed by *ma*: hence we spell it *ukto*.

Mantraḥ is also in the nominative case so we can deduce that *ukto* is describing *mantraḥ*, and the phrase *ukto mantraḥ* means 'the mantra is spoken'. Note that word order is not important in Sanskrit so it could equally be *mantra uktaḥ*.[132]

Now despite the fact that both Conze and Vaida take *tadyathā* as a standalone word - separating it out with punctuation - it seems to me that *tadyathā* can quite naturally be seen to be an adverb modifying the verb *ukto*: 'spoken like this'. Separating *tadyathā* out seems to make for both poor Sanskrit and poor English: ...*ukto mantraḥ. Tadyathā* - 'The mantra is spoken. Like this.' Sometimes a preconceived idea can blind us to the obvious, and perhaps this is what has happened in this case. So the phrase *ukto mantraḥ tadyathā* means 'the mantra is spoken like this'.

Prajñāpāramitāyām is a locative singular so I don't follow Conze's translation of it as an instrumental '*by* the *prajñāpāramitā*'. In *Perfect Wisdom* (p.140) Conze aims for a more literal reading and has "In the Prajñāpāramitā has this spell been uttered".[133] Later in *Perfect Wisdom*

---

[129] Sanskrit texts for both versions of the Heart Sūtra can be found at the *Digital Sanskrit Buddhist Canon Website*. From the texts edited by Vaidya, P.L. Vaidya's punctuation is minimal. A *daṇḍa* before *tasmaj jñātavyam* which begins the series of epithets of the mantra, and another after *mantraḥ* in both.

[130] A *daṇḍa* | is used to mark the end of a line, and the double *daṇḍa* || marks the end of a verse.

[131] Via some tortuous internal sandhi: vac + -to > vakto (with samprasāraṇa va > u) > ukto.

[132] in this case *-aḥ* followed by *u > a*)

[133] Several prominent scholars of the early to mid 20th century including Conze and Snellgrove insisted on translating mantra as 'spell'. I think this is unhelpful and Snellgrove's justification of it in Indo-Tibetan Buddhism seems disingenuous. It is one of those words with no exact equivalent in English, and though there is some cross-over under some circumstances, 'spell' gives entirely the wrong impression in most cases.

(p.143), however, he repeats the version from *Buddhist Wisdom Books* 'by the *prajñāpāramitā*'. The locative is used to indicate where the action of a verb takes place - in space or time. I think there are three ways to interpret this:

1. In (the state of) perfect wisdom
2. In the system of practice known as perfect wisdom
3. In this perfection of wisdom text

Option one suggests that the mantra is spoken like this in the state of perfect wisdom, or by someone in that state. It may also refer to the point of view of perfect wisdom. Option two acknowledges that perfection of wisdom is also the name of a system of practice - we might say something like: 'in the perfection of wisdom school the mantra is said like this...' Option three allows for the possibility that the mantra is the one found in this text. Conze insists the mantra is not found in the any of the large *prajñāpāramitā* texts.[134] However compare Jan Nattier's note of McRae and Fukui's discovery that "some or all of the mantra found in the Heart Sūtra also occurs in at least three other texts contained in the Chinese Buddhist canon".[135] I think Conze is opting for option one by translating *prajñāpāramitāyām* as "by the perfection of wisdom" – that is he is taking *Prajñāpāramitā* to be the personification of perfect wisdom. My feeling is that option one is the most likely but I'm unsure exactly how to translate it. I'm reluctant to follow Conze's translation, because it mangles the grammar, even though I take his meaning.

It seems to me that *tadyathā* was not intended to be included in the mantra, although in many traditions it is. This essay was sparked by someone asking about the mantra of the Medicine Buddha, as given to him by the Dalai Lama, which also has *tadyathā* included in the recitation. In the locus classicus for that mantra: Sūtra of the Medicine Buddha[136] *tadyathā* is preceded *namo* followed by a number of epithets for the Buddha all in the dative form, then *tadyathā* is followed by the mantra: "homage to [the Medicine Buddha] like this: *oṃ bhaiṣajye bhaiṣajye mahābhaiṣajya-samudgate svāhā*". The grammar is quite different and suggests that this mantra is being presented as a way of paying homage to the Medicine Buddha. Here again though *tadyathā* forms a natural part of the introduction, but not the mantra.

Compare Frits Staal's comments on the incorporation of 'stage directions' during the recitation of Vedic mantras in *Discovering the Vedas* (p.115):

> Stage directions should not slip into the recitation. Once I recorded a mantra recited by a priest when he gave a stick (*daṇḍa*) to a boy. The recitation included the final words of a rule: *iti daṇḍaṃ dadhyāt*, 'thus he should give the stick'.

The inclusion of *tadyathā* is a similar case which probably occurred amongst people who recited texts in Sanskrit without knowing the language. Interestingly from what I can tell, the practice occurs in both Tibetan, and in Far Eastern lineages. The inclusion of the *tadyathā*, though technically an error, is actively being passed on by living, authoritative teachers such as the Dalai Lama. Sometimes convention trumps philology.

---

[134] Conze (1975b) p.106.
[135] Nattier (1992) p.177. The references are given in footnote no.52: McRae (1988) identifies T. no.901, 18.785a-897b, esp. p.807b20-21. See also T. 18.8071b19-c9; and T. 18.804c-807b.
[136] http://www.buddhanet.net/pdf_file/medbudsutra.pdf = Taisho XIV, 450.

Buddhas

There are three sets of Buddhas in this section. The first three are not a natural set except that they are Buddhas and not part of the other sets: Śākyamuni, the historical or *nirmāṇakāya* Buddha; Vajrasattva, representing the *ādibuddha* or *dharmakāya*; and finally Bhaiṣajyarāja or the Medicine Buddha. Different schools of Buddhism represent the *dharmakāya* through different Buddhas: Vajrasattva, Mahāvairocana, Vajradhara, Samantabhadra; and these names apply to other aspects of the Buddhist system when they are not representing the *dharmakāya*. The variation is a sign of the life of the tradition, the extraordinary vigour and variety expressed in the development over many centuries of Buddhist 'theology'. We can think of them as being like different dialects, with different words for the same thing. What is meant by the symbol is not different.

The second set is variously known as the *Five Buddha Maṇḍala*, or the *Maṇḍala of the Jinas*. The term *Dhyāni Buddhas* is also used in some older works. It seems that this term and it's companion *dhyāni bodhisattva* were first used in the *Dharmakośasaṅgraha*. This Sanskrit text was compiled in 1826 by the Nepalese *paṇḍita* and *vajrācārya* Amṛtānanda at the request of Brian Houghton Hodgson, the British Resident in Nepal. Hodgson sought out Amṛtānanda in order to find Buddhist manuscripts and later he became Hodgson's informant on Buddhism. The text of the *Dharmakośasaṅgraha* consists of the written answers to Hodgson's questions. Much of the material concerns iconography and a substantial proportion of that deals with the five buddha *maṇḍala*. It seems that as Amṛtānanda's work was one of the first available in the West some of his terminology has taken root even though it may have been idiosyncratic.[137]

The Buddhas are arranged at the points of the compass with one in the middle – creating a beautifully balanced figure. The *maṇḍala* emerged gradually over perhaps two centuries with Buddhas changing their positions and names – and several new Buddhas had to manifest to fill the spaces. The form we generally use is first found in the *Sarvatathāgata-tattvasaṃgraha*, a tantric text from the late 7th or early 8th century. The general plan of the *maṇḍala* is more or less settled afterwards, except that later tantras have Vairocana and Akṣobhya exchange places.

The third set is one that existed in tradition only as the counterpart of the Five Buddha Maṇḍala, but has begun to take on a life of its own in the Triratna Buddhist Order. These are the five female counterparts of the five Jinas – traditionally seen only in sexual embrace (*yab-yum*) with the Jinas in higher tantra maṇḍalas. Here they are presented as individual figures with mantras and *bījas* from *sādhana* composed by Dharmacārī Vessantara.

[137] Maitiu O'Ceileachair [personal communication, 2011].

Śākyamuni

Japanese: *Shakamuni* 釋迦牟尼[138]; Tibetan: *Sangyé Shakya Tuppa* (སངས་རྒྱས་ཤཱ་ཀྱ་ཐུབ་པ་)

IN EARLY TEXTS THE BUDDHA is most often referred to as *bhagavat* 'the Blessed One' or as *Gautama* (Pāli *Gotama*) his family name.[139] He refers to himself mostly as *Tathāgata* (see notes below). The word *buddha* is the past-participle of the verb *budh* ('to understand, to awaken') and thus is usually said to mean 'awakened'. We refer to him as *the* Buddha – the one who has awoken.

In Sanskrit texts he is commonly referred to as Śākyamuni – the sage of the Śākyas - and this is the name used in the mantra of the historical Buddha. *Śākya* is the name of the clan which the historical Buddha was born into. In the *trikāya* doctrine Śākyamuni is the *nirmana-kāya* aspect of the Buddha.

It is said that the historical Buddha grew up in a life of luxury but after seeing that everyone would grow old, become ill, and die, he abandoned his home and joined a group of ascetics seeking the way beyond death. Subsequently he abandoned severe asceticism as well and pursued a middle way between hedonism and asceticism that enabled him to make a decisive breakthrough known as *bodhi* (also from the verb *budh*). He spent the rest of his life teaching others how they could also awaken.

Seed Syllable

Śākyamuni's seed syllable in Tibetan traditions is 'a'. The letter 'a' is also known as the source of all the other letters, the source of all mantras. (See 'a' as a seed-syllable p. 180)

Siddhaṃ

Tibetan Uchen

Lantsa

Devanāgarī

[138] Also known in Japanese as *Shaka Nyorai* (釈迦如来) 'Shakya Tathāgata'. 釈 is the Japanese variant of 釋 and is not used in Chinese.

[139] Strangely 'Gautama' is a distinctively Brahmin surname. See: 'What was the Buddha's Name?' *Jayarava's Raves*. http://jayarava.blogspot.com/2009/11/what-was-buddhas-name.html.

Siddhaṃ

ༀ་མུ་ནི་མུ་ནི་མ་ཧཱ་མུ་ནི་ཤཱ་ཀྱ་མུ་ནི་སྭཱ་ཧཱ།

Tibetan – Uchen

ओं मुनि मुनि महामुनि शाक्यमुनि स्वाहा

Devanāgarī

Lantsa

Transliteration

oṃ mu ni mu ni ma hā mu ni śā kya mu ni svā hā

oṃ muni muni mahāmuni śākyamuni svāhā

Alternate Tibetan Mantra

ༀ་མུ་ནི་མུ་ནི་མ་ཧཱ་མུ་ནི་ཡེ་སྭཱ་ཧཱ།

oṃ muni muni mahāmuniye svāhā

Notes

The alternate mantra uses the dative form of the word *mahāmuni,* indicated by adding the *–ye* suffix and meaning 'to or for the great sage'. You may also sometimes see the *–ye* suffix added to Śākyamuni in the standard version. The correct dative of *muni* would be *munaye*.

Buddhists most often understand *tathāgata* to mean 'thus-gone', taking *-gata* to be the past-participle of √*gam* 'to go' – similarly *sugata* is translated as 'well-gone'. This is not entirely wrong, but when *-gata* is used in compounds of this type, it loses its primary meaning in both Pāli and Sanskrit and means 'being, being in'.[140] *Tathāgata* should properly mean 'being thus' or someone 'in that state'.

Shingon

Bija

In the Shingon School the seed-syllable of Śākyamuni is *bhaḥ*. This comes from the first letter of the most common way of addressing or referring to the Buddha – *bhagavat* – with the *visarga* (*ḥ*). The *visarga* is a common indicator of a *bīja* in early tantra, but is eclipsed by *anusvāra* (*ṃ*) in later traditions.

bhagavat in Siddhaṃ

mantra

na maḥ sa ma nta bu ddhā nāṃ bhaḥ

namaḥ samantabuddhānāṃ bhaḥ

Notes

This mantra is found in the *Mahāvairocana Abhisaṃbodhi Tantra.* It can be rendered as: 'homage to all the Buddhas *bhaḥ*'

[140] See for instance: Macdonell, A.A. *A Sanskrit* Grammar *for Students*. (3rd ed.) 1926. D.K. Printworld Ltd, 2008. p.171, n.4; and Gair, J.W. and Karunatillake, W.S. *A New Course in Reading Pāli*. Motilal Banarsidass. 1998. p.25.

Vajrasattva

Japanese: *Kongōsatta* (金剛薩埵); Tibetan: *Dorje Sempa* (རྡོ་རྗེ་སེམས་དཔའ་)

VAJRASATTVA IS PURE WHITE in colour and is sometimes known as the Prince of Purity. His name means "Adamantine Being", or more poetically "Embodying Reality". He is a member of the Vajra family of Akṣobhya which also includes Vajrapāṇi.

He is depicted as a young man in the prime of life, with all the silks and jewels of a wealthy prince. In his right hand he delicately balances a vajra at his heart. In his left had he holds a bell at his waist. The vajra represents Reality, and Compassion; while the bell represents Wisdom.

In some mandalas Vajrasattva represents the *ādibuddha* or the Primordial Principle of Buddhahood; in others he changes places with Akṣobhya in the East. In Shingon Buddhism it is Vajrasattva that passes on the initiation of the Dharmakāya Buddha Mahāvairocana to Nāgārjuna, thereby creating the Vajrayāna lineage.

In the *mūla-yogas* the practitioner carries out a set of four practices 100,000 times. One of these is visualisation of Vajrasattva and repeating his 100 syllable mantra 100,000 times which helps to purify the karma of the person intending to go on to the *tantra* proper. Completing these practices is seen as essential prior to receiving initiations or ordination in some Tibetan lineages.

Seed Syllable

The seed syllable *hūṃ* is shared by a number of Buddhas and Bodhisattvas, especially those associated with the Vajra family of which Vajrasattva is the epitome. Other members are Vajrapāṇi, and Akṣobhya

Siddhaṃ

Tibetan Uchen

Lantsa

Devanāgarī

Mantras

Vajrasattva is associated with the hundred syllable mantra, the chanting of which is used in rituals of purification especially funerals (see below). There is also a short version of the Vajrasattva mantra. We'll start with the short mantra.

The short Vajrasattva mantra

Siddhaṃ

ཨོཾ་བཛྲ་སཏྭ་ཧཱུྃ།

Tibetan Uchen

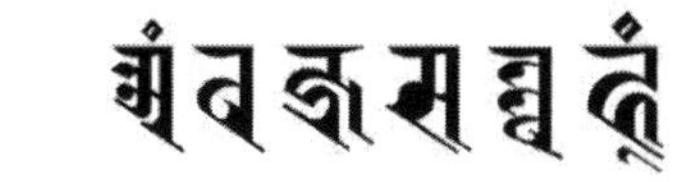

Lantsa

ओं वज्रसत्त्व हूं

Devanāgarī

Transliteration

oṃ va jra sa ttva hūṃ

oṃ vajrasattva hūṃ

A strict transliteration of the Tibetan would be: *oṃ badzra satva hūṃ*, which is actually pronounced *oṃ benza satva hūṃ*.

The 100 syllable Vajrasattva mantra

This mantra is well known from its use in purifying negative karma. The text of the mantra exists in several recensions in several languages with some variation between them. The Tibetan version has clearly garbled the original Sanskrit and unless it was translated from a different original text has also slight rearranged the phrases. I go into detail below. The Sanskrit text here is the one found in the *Triratna Pūjā Book*.[141]

[141] See my article: 2010 'The Hundred Syllable Vajrasattva Mantra.' *Western Buddhist Review*. 5.

Transliteration

oṃ va jra sa ttva sa ma ya ma nu
pā la ya va jra sa ttva tve no pa
ti ṣṭha dṛ ḍho me bha va su to ṣyo
me bha va su po ṣyo me bha va a
nu ra kto me bha va sa rva si ddhiṃ
me pra ya ccha sa rva ka rma su ca
me ci ttaṃ śre yaḥ ku ru hūṃ ha ha
ha ha hoḥ bha ga van sa rva ta thā
ga ta va jra mā me mu ñca va jrī
bha va ma hā sa ma ya sa ttva aḥ
(hūṃ pha ṭ)

oṃ vajrasattva samayam anupālaya
vajrasattvatvenopatiṣṭha
dṛḍho me bhava sutoṣyo me bhava supoṣyo me bhava
anurakto me bhava sarvasiddhiṃ me prayaccha
sarvakarmasu ca me cittaṃ śreyaḥ kuru hūṃ
ha ha ha ha hoḥ bhagavan sarvatathāgatavajra mā me muñca
vajrī bhava mahāsamayasattva āḥ
(hūṃ phaṭ)

Tibetan – Uchen

༄༅། ཨོཾ་བཛྲ་སཏྭ་ས་མ་ཡ། མ་ནུ་པཱ་ལ་ཡ། བཛྲ་ས་ཏྭ་ཏྭེ་ནོ་པ། ཏི་ཥྛ་དྲྀ་ཌྷོ་མེ་བྷ་བ།
སུ་ཏོ་ཥྱོ་མེ་བྷ་བ། ཨ་ནུ་ར་ཀྟོ་མེ་བྷ་བ། སུ་པོ་ཥྱོ་མེ་བྷ་བ། སརྦ་སི་དྡྷི་མྨེ་པྲ་ཡ་ཙྪ།
སརྦ་ཀརྨ་སུ་ཙ་མེ་ཙིཏྟཾ་ཤྲེ་ཡཿ་ཀུ་རུ་ཧཱུྃ། ཧ་ཧ་ཧ་ཧ་ཧོཿ། བྷ་ག་ཝཱན། སརྦ་ཏ་ཐཱ་ག་ཏ། བཛྲ་
མཱ་མེ་མུཉྩ་བཛྲཱི་བྷ་བ་མ་ཧཱ་ས་མ་ཡ་སཏྭ་ཨཱཿ། ཧཱུྃ་ཕཊ། །

The Tibetan pronunciation and orthography have diverged somewhat from the Sanskrit and there are a variety of ways of writing this mantra in Tibetan script. With so many variations in the orthography of the Tibetan, especially in Romanised form, I opted to use the version of the mantra as it is written in the *Sarvatathāgata-tattvasaṃgraha* in the Derge edition of the *Tibetan Tripiṭaka*.[142] Apologies if this one is not the one that you are familiar with.

Devanāgarī

ओं वज्रसत्त्वसमयमनुपालय वज्रसत्त्वत्वेनोपतिष्ठ दृढो मे भव
सुतोष्यो मे भव सुपोष्यो मे भव अनुरक्तो मे भव सर्वसिद्धिं मे
प्रयच्छ सर्वकर्मसु च मे चित्तं श्रेयः कुरु हूं ह ह ह ह होः
भगवन्सर्वतथागतवज्र मा मे मुञ्च वज्रीभव महासमयसत्त्व
आः । हूं फट् ॥

Notes

The Vajrasattva originally occurs in the *Sarvatathāgata-tattvasaṃgraha*, a tantra of the late 7th or early 8th century.[143] This important text established many of the conventions of Tantric Buddhism such as the Five Buddha Maṇḍala with the Buddhas that I discuss in this book. The Vajrasattva mantra occurs towards the end of Chapter Two with some accompanying text which tells us that the mantra enabled one to make spiritual progress despite having committed all

142 *De-bshin-gśegs-pa thams-cad-kyi de-kho-na-ñid bsdusp-pa shes-bya-ba theg-pa chen-poḥi mdo* (*Sarvatathāgata-tattvasaṃgraha-nāma-mahāyāna Sūtra*) *Derge*. vol. p.192.

143 Maitiu O'Ceileachair and I have established that the earliest occurance of the mantra in the Chinese Canon is in this text.

sorts of negative acts. The following commentary was previously published in the *Western Buddhist Review* (Jayarava. 2010)

The first thing to notice is that the mantra is in Sanskrit and unlike most mantras contains a series of well-formed grammatical sentences. The *vajra* was the weapon of Indra who, like the Greek Zeus, hurled thunderbolts at his enemies and was sometimes called Vajrapāṇi (thunderbolt wielder). The word (as Pāli *vajira*) is not unknown in this sense in early Buddhist texts but in Tantra it is very prominent, and by this time also means 'diamond', and metaphorically 'reality'.[144] It's difficult to translate vajra in a way that conveys what is intended and for that reason it's often left untranslated.

Sattva is an abstract noun from the present-participle *sat* 'to be true or real' (from √*as* 'to be' [145]). *Sattva* then is trueness/truth or realness/reality. In use it is very close in meaning to our word 'being', as in 'a state of being', or 'a being'. Vajrasattva then is the 'adamantine-being', 'the thunderbolt reality', or the personification or embodiment of the true nature of experience.

In Buddhist mantras *oṃ* is there chiefly to signal that this is a mantra, or that the mantra starts here. Lama Govinda's eloquent speculations aside, *oṃ* does not seem to have any fixed esoteric associations in Buddhist exegesis.[146] As with the speculations of the earlier Upaniṣads the symbolism varies with the context, often depending more on the number of syllables in the mantra rather than what the syllables are. As Donald Lopez suggests: "... the Tibetan concern is generally with establishing a wide range of homologies between the six syllables of the mantra... and other sets of six in Buddhist doctrine." [147]

Taking the mantra one line at a time we find that when written in Devanāgarī it contains an ambiguity in the first line because of a sandhi phenomenon. The line is conventionally written as *vajrasattvasamayamanupālaya* leaving us to find the word breaks with our knowledge of Sanskrit grammar! Vajrasattva is most likely a vocative singular, meaning the mantra is addressed to Vajrasattva: 'O Vajrasattva'. [148]

The phrase *samayamanupālaya* could be either *samaya manupālaya* or *samayam anupālaya*. Both are commonly seen and the former is a traditional Tibetan approach, but *samayam anupālaya* is a natural Sanskrit sentence with *samayam* (in the accusative case) being the object of the verb *anupālaya. Anu* + √*pāl* means 'preserve' and *anupālaya* is the second person singular imperative. *Samayam* means 'coming together' or 'meeting' and is used in the sense of 'coming to an agreement'. As a technical term in Tantric Buddhism it specifically refers to agreements the practitioner takes on when receiving *abhiṣeka*. These agreements are sometimes referred to as a vow or pledge.[149] To preserve an agreement is to honour it, so

---

[144] By the time Tantric Buddhism adopted this symbol – circa 7th century CE – Indra was no longer prominent in India religion. He does occur in Buddhist texts however where he is known as Śakra (P. Sakka) – for instance he makes regular appearances in the Pāli *Jātaka* tales and is a prominent figure in the *Aṣṭasāhasrikā Prajñāpāramitā Sūtra* (The Perfection of Wisdom in 8000 Lines).

[145] √ indicates a verbal root. Sanskrit grammarians analysed verbs into roots, stems, and suffixes indicating conjugation. The monosyllabic root or dhātu is notional but carries the primary meaning of the word, which can be modified with prefixes. Dictionaries, particularly the popular Monier-Williams Sanskrit-English Dictionary, are often organised according to roots.

[146] *Foundations of Tibetan Mysticism* is a popular book, however in his explanations of mantra generally and of *oṃ* in particular Lama Govinda cites only *Hindu* texts - which I have always found puzzling. He is viewed with some suspicion by some: see for instance comments in Lopez (1998).

[147] See Lopez (1998). 150.

[148] In Tibetan Sadhanas one frequently sees a version of this mantra where the word *vajra* is substituted by *padma* to form the Padmasattva mantra; in a version to Heruka Vajrasattva where we find Vajra Heruka instead of Vajrasattva.

[149] Snellgrove explains that the word means 'a sacrament' when used in a ritual context, but regularly translates it as 'pledge' (2002), p.165. C.f. the word *saṃvara* a 'bond' or 'restraint' which is used in the sense of taking on rules of behaviour.

vajrasattva samayam anupālaya means: 'O Vajrasattva honour the agreement', or 'preserve the coming together' – the coming together of Buddha and disciple, or of guru and cela.

Vajrasattvatvenopatiṣṭha is again two words: *vajrasattvatvena upatiṣṭha* (*a* followed by *u* coalesces to *o*). *Vajrasattvatvena* is the instrumental singular of the abstract noun formed from the name Vajrasattva. *Vajrasattva-tva* could be rendered as 'vajrasattva-ness', the quality of being a vajra-being. The instrumental case usually indicates how the action of a verb is carried out, though Sthiramati points out that with abstract nouns the instrumental case is used to indicate in what *capacity* someone acts so that it means something like '*as* Vajrasattva'. The verb here is *upatiṣṭha* a passive past-participle from *upa* + √*sthā* 'stood near, was present, approached, supported, worshipped; revealed oneself or appeared'. So the phrase means 'manifest as Vajrasattva'.

Things get simpler for a bit as we meet a series of phrases with the verb *bhava* which is the second person singular imperative of √*bhū* 'to be'. They also contain the particle *me* which in this case is the abbreviated form of the 1st person pronoun in the dative 'for me'. The form then is 'be X for me'. First we have 'be *dṛḍhaḥ'* 'firm, steady, strong'. The sandhi rule is that an ending with *aḥ* changes to *o* when followed by *bha*: so *dṛḍhaḥ* > *dṛḍho*. *Dṛḍho me bhava* means "be steadfast for me".

Sutoṣyaḥ is a compound of the prefix *su-* meaning 'well, good, complete' and *toṣya* from √*tuṣ* 'satisfaction, contentment, pleasure, joy'. *Sutoṣyo me bhava* is therefore 'be completely satisfied with me', or 'be very pleased for me'.

Supoṣyaḥ is again *su-* but combined with *poṣya* from √*puṣ* 'to thrive, to prosper, nourish, foster'. *Sutoṣyo me bhava* is then 'be fully nourishing for me'. Sthiramati suggests "Deeply nourish me".

Anuraktaḥ is *anu* + *rakta*. *Rakta* is a past-participle from √*rañj* and the dictionary gives 'fond of, attached, pleased'. [150] In his seminar on the mantra Sangharakshita suggests 'passionate' and this seems to fit better with √*rañj* which literally means 'to glow red, or to redden'.[151] We can translate *anurakto me bhava* as 'be passionate for me', or as Sthiramati suggests 'love me passionately'.

Now comes: *sarvasiddhiṃ me prayaccha. Prayaccha* is a verb from the root √*iṣ* 'to desire, to wish' and means 'to grant'. (√*iṣ* forms a stem *iccha*; and *pra* + *iccha* > *prayaccha* - which is also the second person singular imperative). *Sarva* is a pronoun meaning 'all, every, universal' and *siddhi* is a multivalent term which can mean 'magical powers, perfection, success, attainment'. So *sarvasiddhiṃ me prayaccha* must mean 'grant me every success' or 'give me success in all things'. Note that *sarvasiddhiṃ* is an accusative singular so it can't mean 'all the attainments' (plural).

The next line is somewhat longer and more complex: *sarvakarmasu ca me cittaṃ śreyaḥ kuru*. *Ca* is the connector 'and', which indicates that we should take this phrase with the previous line. *Sarvakarmasu* is a locative plural. The locative case is being used to indicate where in time and space the action takes place. *Sarva* we saw just above and *karma* means action - so this word means 'in all actions'. *Me* here is a genitive 'my'. *Cittaṃ* is mind and is in the accusative case, so it is the object of the verb *kuru* which is the second person singular imperative of √*kṛ* 'to do, to make'. *Śreyah* is from *śrī* which has a wide range of connotations: 'light, lustre, radiance; prosperity, welfare, good fortune, success, auspiciousness; high rank, royalty'. I think 'lucid' would be a good choice in this case. It is the comparative so it means

---

[150] Note the root is not √*rakṣ* 'to protect' which would give *rakṣita* 'protected' as a past-participle, though this interpretation is encountered in some Tibetan exegesis.

[151] The same root gives us the word *rāga* – emotion, feeling, passion.

'more *śrī*'. Putting all this together we find that *sarvakarmasu ca me cittaṃ śreyaḥ kuru hūṃ* means 'and in all actions make my mind more lucid!'[152]

In Sthiramati's version (and in most others) *hūṃ* is tagged on to this line, however I'm inclined to separate it and leave it as a stand-alone statement; note that the three syllables *oṃ āḥ hūṃ* are used in the mantra, though not in that order. In any case *hūṃ* is untranslatable. Kūkai sees it as representing all teaching, all practices and all attainments, so perhaps we could see this as Vajrasattva's contribution to the conversation.[153]

The string of syllables *ha ha ha ha hoḥ* won't detain us long since it is untranslatable and generally understood to be laughter. Sometimes it is said that each syllable represents one of the five *Jina*. We could see this either as *our* response to the *hūṃ* of Vajrasattva; or as Vajrasattva's response to us.

Then we come to: *bhagavan sarvatathāgatavajra mā me muñca*. Although these are sometimes broken up into separate lines, we put them together because there is one verb *muñca* (again in the second person singular imperative). *Bhagavan* 'Blessed One' is a vocative singular; this is how his disciples addressed the Buddha, although I think we are still addressing Vajrasattva here. The phrase then is addressed to the Blessed One. *Sarvatathāgata* on its own would also be a vocative singular, but this presents some difficulties since *sarva* is 'all' but *Tathāgata* is singular. Sthiramati suggests that this can be resolved by taking *sarvatathāgatavajra* as a single compound (allowing us to read *tathāgata* as a plural) meaning 'O vajra of all the Tathāgatas'. Buddhists most often understand *tathāgata* to mean 'thus-gone', taking *-gata* to be the past-participle of √*gam* 'to go' – similarly *sugata* is translated as 'well-gone'. This is not entirely wrong, but when *-gata* is used in compounds of this type, it loses its primary meaning in both Pāli and Sanskrit and means 'being, being in'.[154] On this basis I agree with Richard Gombrich's suggestion that *Tathāgata* would make more sense if we read it as 'being thus' or someone 'in that state' – that is as the Buddha referring to his being awakened.[155]. *Mā* is the negative particle 'don't'', and the verb, as I have said, is *muñca* from √*muc* 'to abandon'. So *bhagavan sarvatathāgatavajra mā me muñca means*: 'O Blessed One, vajra of all the Tathāgatas, do not abandon me!'

In the final phrase *Vajrībhava mahāsamayasattva*, *vajrībhava* is an example of a factitive verbal compound. The noun *vajra* is compounded with the verb √*bhū*, the final *a* changes to *ī*, and the sense of the word is causative, implying transformation: 'become a vajra'. Again the conjugation is 2nd person singular imperative - so it's saying 'you should become a vajra'. In his seminar Sangharakshita coins the word '*vajric*' which Sthiramati does not like, but I can see what Sangharakshita might have meant: someone who becomes the *vajra*, in the sense of personifying it, might be described as *vajric*. Note that there is another way of interpreting *vajrībhava* which is to take *vajrī* as the nominative singular of *vajrin* – a form of possessive. *Vajrī bhava,* then (with a word break), might be taken to mean 'be the *vajra-bearer*'. This is how Sthiramati understood the phrase, and it fits the pattern of the other phrases. Either reading is possible. *Mahāsamayasattva* is once again a vocative, and a compound of three words. I think here that *mahā* 'great' qualifies *samayasattva, which is* a technical term in Tantric Buddhism – 'agreement-being' - meaning the image of the deity generated in meditation which becomes the

---

[152] Most Tibetan traditions seem to take this as *sarva karma suca me* but this is much more difficult to resolve as sensible Sanskrit. Tradition takes it to mean 'purify all my karma' seemingly taking *suca* to be related to √*śuc* although this cannot be the case. However this tradition is very important as it relates to the purifying function of the mantra – and purification is not otherwise mentioned even indirectly. I discuss this below.

[153] For Kūkai's exegesis of *hūṃ* see 'The Meanings of the Word Hūṃ (Ungi gi)' in Hakeda (1972), p.246ff.

[154] See for instance: Macdonell (1926) p.171, n.4; and Gair and Karunatillake (1998), p.25.

[155] C.f. Gombrich (2009) p.151. Gombrich points out that the traditional Buddhist attempts to etymologise the term are "fanciful". I would also argue that though "thus-gone" has become familiar, it is poor English, and in fact quite meaningless.

meeting place (*samaya*) for the practitioner and the *Dharmakāya*. In a sense this is our contact with 'reality' or '*śūnyatā*' and we want it to go from being imagined to being genuine, so that we are transformed into a Buddha ourselves. *Vajrībhava Mahāsamayasattva* then means 'O great agreement-being become real!'

The Hundredth syllable is *āḥ*. In Classical Sanskrit *āḥ* is an exclamation of either joy or indignation – similar to the way we might use the same sound in English. However in this context it is untranslatable. Note that the mantra as a whole contains *oṃ āḥ* and *hūṃ* - the symbols of body, speech and mind, and the corresponding aspects of the Dharmakāya.

Hūṃ and *phaṭ* are traditionally added under specific circumstances: *hūṃ* when the mantra is recited for the benefit of the deceased; and *phaṭ* when the mantra is recited to subdue demons.[156] In the Triratna Order they are routinely included. See also the section on *phaṭ* (p.198) for more. So my full translation goes:

> *oṃ*
> O Vajrasattva honour the agreement!
> Reveal yourself as the vajra-being!
> Be steadfast for me!
> Be very pleased for me!
> Be fully nourishing for me!
> Be passionate for me!
> Grant me all success and attainment!
> and in all actions make my mind more lucid!
> *hūṃ*
> ha ha ha ha hoḥ
> O Blessed One, diamond of all those in that state, do not abandon me!
> O being of the great contract be a vajra bearer!
> *āḥ*

In Tibetan sadhanas one frequently sees a version of this mantra where the word *vajra* is substituted by *padma* which is then known as the Padmasattva mantra.

---

[156] Incidentally *phaṭ* is pronounced 'p-hut' not 'fat'. Sanskrit doesn't have an 'f' sound – ph is 'p' followed by a puff of air similar to the sounds in the word 'to*ph*at'.

Bhaiṣajyaguru - the Medicine Buddha

Japanese: *Yakushi Nyorai* (薬師如来); Tibetan: *Sangyé Menla* (སངས་རྒྱས་སྨན་བླ་)

BHAIṢAJYAGURU, THE MEDICINE BUDDHA, also known more fully as *Bhaiṣajyaguru-vaiḍūrya-prabharāja* is a somewhat enigmatic figure. His mythology goes back to early Buddhism where the historical Buddha is described as a physician (P. *bhisakka*; S *bhiṣaj*) come to cure the ills of the world. However the actual origins of the Medicine Buddha are unclear, and to date no Indian image of him has been found. Bhaiṣajyarāja and Bhaiṣajyasamudgata are the names of two bodhisattvas in the White Lotus or *Saddharma-puṇḍarīka Sūtra* who may form antecedents, though there is no direct association with healing in that text.

The common feature in all the Sanskrit names is *bhaiṣajya*, which can mean: "curativeness, healing efficacy; a ceremony performed as a remedy for sickness; any remedy, drug or medicine; the administering of medicines." '*Guru*' is teacher, so the name means Medicinal teacher. For other names see notes below.

He is depicted as deep blue in colour, dressed in *bhikṣu's* robes, holding his begging bowl in his left hand and with his right hand making the *varada mudrā*. *Varada* means 'granting wishes, conferring a boon, ready to fulfil requests or answer prayers'. Sometimes, especially in East Asian iconography, the begging bowl is replaced by a medicine jar; in Tibetan images a *myrobalan* plant (*Terminalia chebula*), thought to be a panacea, grows out of the bowl. His Buddha-field is called *Vaiḍuryanirbhāsa*.

Seed Syllable

Bhaiṣajyaguru's *bīja* is the first syllable of his name: *bhai*

Siddhaṃ | Tibetan | Uchen Lantsa | Devanāgarī

The Syllable *bhai* unusually looks very different in each of the scripts.

Mantra

Siddhaṃ

ཨོཾ་བྷཻ་ཥ་ཛྱེ་བྷཻ་ཥ་ཛྱེ་མ་ཧཱ་བྷཻ་ཥ་ཛྱ་ས་མུ་དྒ་ཏེ་སྭཱ་ཧཱ།

Tibetan Uchen

Lantsa

ओं भैषज्ये भैषज्ये महाभैषज्यसमुद्गते स्वाहा

Devanāgarī

Transliteration

oṃ bhai ṣa jye bhai ṣa jye ma hā bhai ṣa jya sa mu dga te svā hā

oṃ bhaiṣajye bhaiṣajye mahābhaiṣajya samudgate svāhā

Tibetan Pronunciation

om beh ka dze-yah beh ka dze-yah ma ha

beh ka dze-yah la dza sah mo kyah deh sowa ha

This mantra can be found the *Bhaiṣajyaguru Sūtra* where it is described as "a great *dhāraṇī*". [157] In the *sūtra* the mantra is introduced by the words:

> *namo bhagavate bhaiṣajyaguruvaiḍūryaprabharājāya tathāgatāya arhate samyaksam-buddhāya tadyathā: oṃ bhaiṣajye bhaiṣajye mahābhaiṣajya samudgate svāhā.*

> homage to the blessed medicinal teacher king with jewel-like radiance, to the one who is like that, the worthy, the fully awakened one, thus: *oṃ bhaiṣajye bhaiṣajye mahābhaiṣajya samudgate svāhā.*

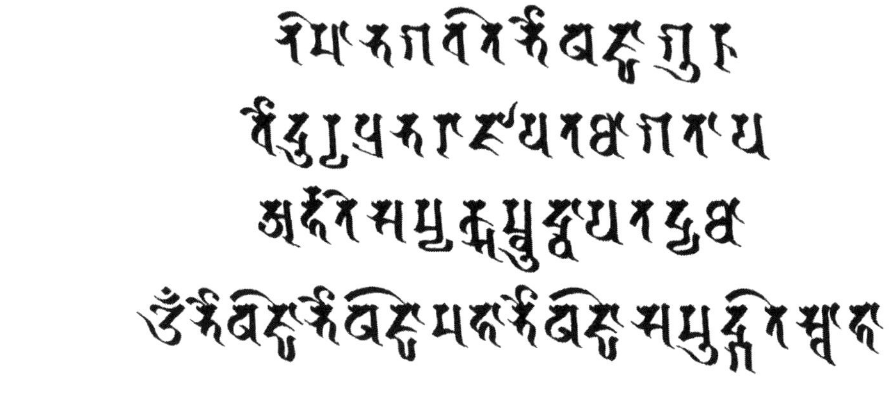

नमो भगवते भैषज्यगुरु
वैडूर्यप्रभराजाय तथागताय
अर्हते सम्यक्सम्बुद्धाय तद्यथा
ओं भैषज्ये भैषज्ये महाभैषज्यसमुद्गते स्वाहा

namo bhagavate bhaiṣajyaguru-
vaiḍūryaprabharājāya tathāgatāya
arhate samyaksambuddhāya tadyathā
oṃ bhaiṣajye bhaiṣajye mahābhaiṣajya samudgate svāhā

Notes

Of the alternative and antecedent names mentioned above *Bhaiṣajya-guru-vaiḍūrya-prabha-rāja* means 'medicinal teacher king with jewel-like radiance'; Bhaiṣajyarāja means 'Medicinal King', and Bhaiṣajyasamudgata means 'Manifested Medicines'.

There are many variations on this mantra, and some other mantra and *dhāraṇī* associated with Bhaiṣajyaguru. The mantra uses the Buddha's name *bhaiṣajye* with the –e ending. Opinions are divided on the significance of this. My theory is that the mantra was composed not

---

[157] Thành, Minh and Leigh, P.D. *Sūtra of the Medicine Buddha* (Taisho XIV, 450). North Hills, CA.: International Buddhist Monastic Institute, 2001. Online: http://www.buddhanet.net/pdf_file/medbudsutra.pdf [checked link 1.9.2010]

in Classical Sanskrit, but in Buddhist Hybrid Sanskrit or a Prakrit and the –e ending is simply a masculine nominative singular.[158] The word *samudgate*: *sam* + *ut* + *gata* means 'manifest, arisen, appeared'. Again the –e ending is probably a nominative singular. *Svāhā* comes from Vedic ritual, see the section on *svāhā* (p.199).

A Sanskrit manuscript of the *Bhaiṣajyaguruvaidūryaprabharāja Sūtra* found at Gilgit does not contain the *dhāraṇī*.[159] Subsequent texts especially the *Saptathāgatapūrvapraṇidhāna-viśeṣavistara Sūtra* contain more *dhāraṇī* and elaborate the iconography of Bhaiṣajyaguru into a set of seven healing Buddhas. This is typical of how a Mahāyāna text passes into Tantric usage. The *Saptathāgata* forms the basis of Tibetan Medicine Buddha lore. In both Japan and Tibet, rituals involving Bhaiṣajyaguru were performed for the health of the ruler and the nation.

---

[158] See my essay *Words in Mantras that End in –e* (p.64).

[159] Vaidya, P.L. *Mahāyāna-sūtra-saṁgrahaḥ* (part 1). Buddhist Sanskrit Texts No. 17. Darbhanga: The Mithila Institute of Post-Graduate Studies and Research in Sanskrit Learning, 1961. Online: http://dsbc.uwest.edu/node/6329

Vairocana

Japanese: *Dainich Nyorai* (大日如来); Tibetan: *Nampa Nangdzé* (རྣམ་པར་སྣང་མཛད་)

VAIROCANA IS THE WHITE BUDDHA at the centre of the Five Buddha *Maṇḍala*. In the Shingon School he is considered to be a personification of the *Dharmakāya* and is usually referred to as Mahāvairocana - a name which comes from the *Mahāvairocana Abhisaṃbodhi Tantra* (also known as the *Mahāvairocana Sūtra*). Tantric discourses are traditionally said to be have been taught by Mahāvairocana rather than the historical Buddha Śākyamuni.

The image shown is a kind of generic Vairocana depicted in *bhikṣu* robes with his hands in the *cakravartin*, or wheel turning *mudrā* - which alludes to his teaching of the Dharma which is poetically referred to as 'turning the wheel of the Dharma'. Vairocana has two main forms: in the *Garbhadhatu maṇḍala* he has one face and displays the *dhyāna mudrā* with a golden *dharmacakra* sitting in his hands. In the *Vajradhātu maṇḍala* he has four faces and displays the *bodhyagrī* or 'fist of wisdom' *mudrā* (Japanese: *Chiken-in*) where the index finder of the left hand is grasped in the fist of his right hand.

Vairocana is associated with the *śāntikakarman*, the White Rite of Pacification.

Maṇḍala of the Jinas

Position in maṇḍala	centre	
Colour	white	
Mudrā	wheel-turning	
Wisdom	reality	*dharmadhātujñāna*
Emblem	*dharmacakra*	
Consort/*prajñā*	Ākāśadhātvīśvarī	

Seed Syllables

The seed syllable of Vairocana is the short *a*.

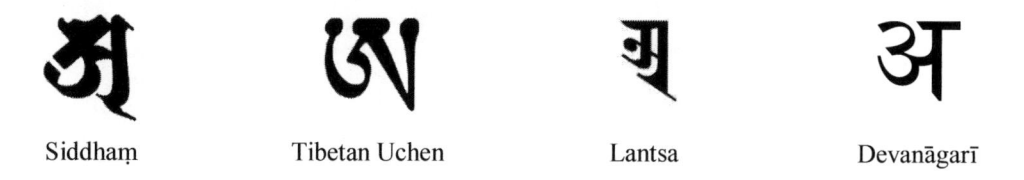

Siddhaṃ | Tibetan Uchen | Lantsa | Devanāgarī

Mahāvairocana in the Garbhadhatu Mandala associated with the Mahāvairocana Sūtra has the seed syllable of the short *a*, but sometimes this is elaborated into *āṃḥ*.

Siddhaṃ | Tibetan Uchen | Lantsa | Devanāgarī

The form *āṃḥ* combines the four forms of *a* – *a ā ṃ ḥ* - which has particular significance in the *Mahāvairocana Sūtra* – see also the section on the *bīja a.*

Mahāvairocana in the *Vajradhātu Maṇḍala,* associated with the *Vajraśekhara Sūtra* has the seed syllable *vaṃ*

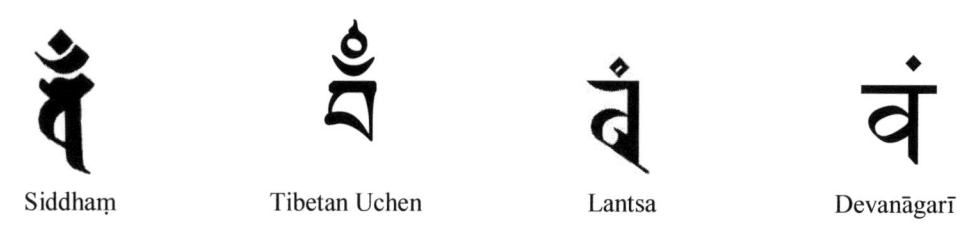

Siddhaṃ | Tibetan Uchen | Lantsa | Devanāgarī

The vaṃ syllable is also elaborated on the model of āṃḥ, *vāṃḥ*

Siddhaṃ | Tibetan Uchen | Lantsa | Devanāgarī

Note that Tibetans often (as here) substitute *ba* for *va* when writing Sanskrit.

Mantra

Siddhaṃ

ཨོཾ་བཻ་རོ་ཙ་ན་ཧཱུྃ

Tibetan – Uchen

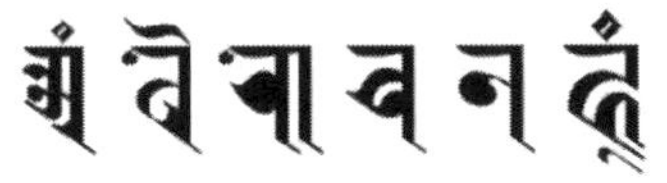

Lantsa

ओं वैरोचन हूं

Devanāgarī

Transliteration

oṃ vai ro ca na hūṃ

oṃ vairocana hūṃ

Avira Mantra

In Shingon there is another important Vairocana mantra:

a vi ra hūṃ kha

In the *Mahāvairocana Abhisaṃbodhi Tantra* (MAT) the full mantra is *namaḥ samantabuddhānāṃ a vi ra hūṃ kha.*[160] This mantra links Mahāvairocana to the six elements - the five letters here representing the four material elements and space, while Mahāvairocana himself represents the element of consciousness. The idea is that the whole of the universe is a

[160] MAT: Chp vi, 'The True Nature of Siddhi Accomplishment.' Hodge (trans), p.185

manifestation of Mahāvairocana - all forms are the body of Mahāvairocana; all sounds are the voice of Mahāvairocana; and all mental activity is the mind of Mahāvairocana.

space	*kha*
air	*ha*
fire	*ra*
water	*va*
earth	*a*

One often sees these syllables painted on Japanese funeral markers, sometimes with a *vaṃ* at the top representing Mahāvairocana. Sometimes the syllables have an anusvāra added, i.e. *a vaṃ raṃ haṃ khaṃ*. There are two different schemes linking these syllables to the five Buddhas, one by Śubhākarasiṃha and one by Amoghavajra, both of whom were pivotal in transmitting Vajrayāna from India to China.

The Mantra of Light

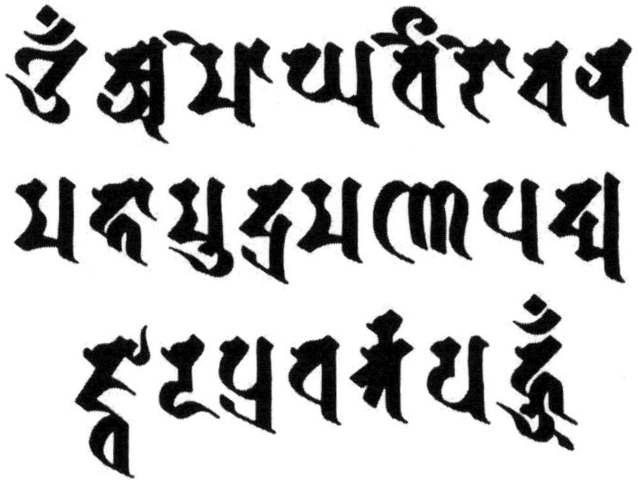

A late Shingon mantra associated with Vairocana is known as the Mantra of Light or in Japanese as *kōmyō shingon* (光明真言). It features in the *Amoghapāśakalparāja-sūtra* and is often written in a circle.

Transliteration

oṃ a mo gha vai ro ca na

ma hā mu dra ma ṇi pa dma

jvā la pra va rtta ya hūṃ

oṃ amogha vairocana mahāmudra maṇipadma jvāla pravarttaya hūṃ

ओं अमोघ वैरोचन महामुद्र मणिपद्म ज्वाल प्रवर्त्तय हूं

Notes

The Mantra has been translated as:

> Praise be to the flawless, all-pervasive illumination of the great mudra (the seal of the Buddha). Turn over to me the jewel, lotus, and radiant light
> - according to Mark Unno
>
> Infallible brilliance of the great mudra! Creating the radiance of the Jewel and the Lotus
> - according to John Stevens

Literally the words, which all appear to be undeclined, translate as:

> oṃ unfailing illuminating great-seal jewelled-lotus blazing evolve (?) *hūṃ.*

Pravarttaya is unclear (turn around? creating? evolve?) and I'm not sure of the root. The dictionary has several possibilities. *Pravartya* = to be excited to activity. *Pravṛtta* = round, rotund; circulated; issued from, resulted, arisen; come back, returned; acting proceeding, etc. Mark Unno seems to derive it from *parivarta* (revolving, revolution) but this seems less likely to me. Shingon Buddhist International has "evolve" and given they represent the tradition I have adopted their translation.[161]

[161] http://www.shingon.org/ritual/daily.html

Akṣobhya

Japanese: *Ashuku nyorai* (阿閦如来); Tibetan: *Mikyöpa* (མི་བསྐྱོད་པ་)

AKṢOBHYA IS THE BLUE BUDDHA who sits in the eastern quarter of the five Buddha *maṇḍala*. The name Akṣobhya means immovable or imperturbable. His mudrā is the *bhūmisparśa* or earth touching *mudrā*. His emblem is the *vajra*, which sits balanced in his left hand; he is the head of the Vajra family.

Akṣobhya is associated with the Tantric rite of subduing or overcoming. In the set of four rites it is known as the Black Rite, the Rite of Destruction or the Fierce Rite (*raudrakarman*).

Akṣobhya was probably the earliest of the Jinas to emerge as a distinct figure. The *Akṣobhyavyūha Sūtra* describes his pureland Abhirati which translates as "delightful". Getting into Abhirati requires assiduous practice, unlike Amitabha's pureland which merely requires faith in Amitabha's vow to save all beings.

Mandala of the Jinas

Position in mandala	east	
Colour	blue	
Family	vajra	
Mudra	earth touching	*bhūmisparśa*
Wisdom	mirrorlike wisdom	*ādarṣajñāna*
Emblem	vajra	
Consort/prajñā	Locanā	

Seed Syllable

Siddhaṃ

Tibetan Uchen

Lantsa

Devanāgarī

The seed syllable hūṃ is shared by a number of Buddhas and Bodhisattvas, especially those associated with the Vajra family of which Vajrasattva is the epitome. Other members are Vajrapāṇi, and Akṣobhya.

Mantra

There are several variations of the Akṣobhya mantra. The main one used in the Triratna Buddhist Order is this one:

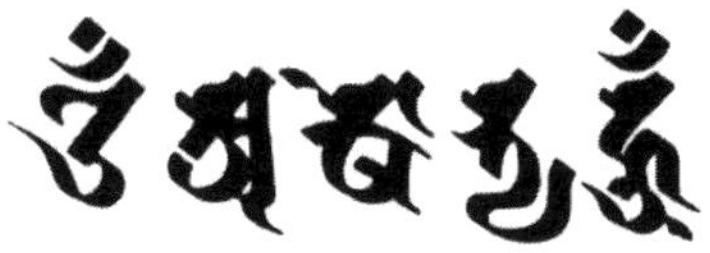

Siddhaṃ

Tibetan – Uchen

Lantsa

ओं अक्षोभ्य हुं

Devanāgarī

Transliteration

oṃ a kṣo bhya hūṃ

oṃ akṣobhya hūṃ

Alternate Akṣobhya mantra

We sometimes see the mantra with 'vajra' inserted before Akṣobhya's name: *oṃ vajrākṣobhya hūṃ*.

Siddhaṃ

ཨོཾ་བཛྲ་ཨ་ཀྵོ་བྷྱ་ཧཱུྃ།

Tibetan – Uchen

Lantsa

ओं वज्राक्षोभ्या हूँ

Devanāgarī

Transliteration

oṃ va jrā kṣo bhya hūṃ

oṃ vajrākṣobhya hūṃ

Ratnasambhava

Japanese: Hōshō Nyorai (宝生如来); Tibetan: Rinchen Jungné (རིན་ཆེན་འབྱུང་གནས་)

RATNASAMBHAVA is the yellow Buddha of the southern quarter of the five Buddha maṇḍala. His name means "jewel born". His emblem is the *ratna* jewel, symbolising *bodhicitta*, the mind of awakening, the highest value of the Buddhist. His mudra is *dana* or generosity, the most fundamental Buddhist virtue. He represents, therefore, the values and virtues of Buddhism.

He is also associated with the *puṣṭikarman*, the Tantric rite of increase and with prosperity generally. To prosper according to Buddhism one must embody these values and practise these virtues.

Ratnasambhava first appears, along with Amoghasiddhi, in the *Sarvatathāgata Tattvasaṃgraha Tantra* in the late 7th or early 8th century, and from that time onwards occupies the southern direction in Buddhist mandalas.

Mandala of the Jinas

Position in mandala	south	
Colour	yellow	
Family	ratna	
Mudra	giving	
Wisdom	wisdom of sameness	*samatājñāna*
Emblem	jewel	
Consort/prajñā	Māmakī	

Seed Syllables

Ratnasambhava's seed syllable is *traṃ*.

Siddhaṃ

Tibetan Uchen

Lantsa

Devanāgarī

Mantra

Siddhaṃ script

ཨོཾ་ར་ཏྣ་སཾ་བྷ་ཝ་ཏྲཾ།

Tibetan - Uchen

Lantsa

ओं रत्नसंभव त्रं

Devanāgarī

Transliteration

oṃ ra tna saṃ bha va traṃ

oṃ ratnasambhava traṃ

Notes

The correct spelling is most likely *sambhava* (सम्भव) but Sanskrit allows for the use of the *anusvāra,* i.e. *saṃbhava* (संभव) in this case.[162] When Tantrikas write mantras they seem to make use of the *anusvāra* whenever they can – perhaps because they were using Buddhist Hybrid Sanskrit rather than Classical Sanskrit?

[162] See the section on Sanskrit for more information on the *anusvāra*

Amitābha and Amitāyus

Japanese: *Amida Nyorai* (阿弥陀如来); Tibetan: *Öpamé* (འོད་དཔག་མེད་)

AMITĀBHA IS THE RED BUDDHA of the Western quarter of the Five Buddha Maṇḍala. His name means "infinite light" - *amita* (unmeasured, boundless, infinite) + *ābha* (splendour, light; colour, appearance, beauty).

He is usually depicted as a *bhikṣu* with his hands in the *dhyāna mudrā*. He is deep red in colour. Another form common in the Western Buddhist Order shows him with his right hand holding up a full red lotus, while his left hand remains in his lap. Amitābha is associated with the *vaśyakarman*, the red Tantric rite of fascination or subjection to one's will.

Amitābha dwells in his pureland called *Sukhāvatī* - the happy realm which is described in the large and small *Sukhāvatīvyūha Sūtras*. Amitābha is closely related to Amitāyus - infinite life - who is sometimes described as his 'reflex'.[163] A mantra for Amitāyus is included below. A visualisation meditation on Amitāyus is described in the *Amitāyurdhyāna Sūtra*. These three sūtras are collectively described as the 'Pureland Scriptures'. The *Sukhāvatīvyūha Sūtras* belong to the earliest strata of *Mahāyāna* texts, and the *Amitāyurdhyāna,* although this is often considered part of a set with them is now believed to be a Chinese apocryphal text.

Amitābha's special quality is Compassion, which is balanced in the Five Buddha Maṇḍala by Akṣobhya the Buddha of Wisdom in the East. Amitābha is the head of the Padma, or Lotus family.

Mandala of the Jinas

Position in mandala	west	
Colour	red	
Family	lotus	
Mudra	meditation	
Wisdom	discriminating wisdom	*pratyavekṣanajñāna*
Emblem	lotus	
Consort/prajñā	Pāṇḍaravāsinī	

[163] I've never been quite sure what this means.

Seed Syllable

Amitābha's *bīja* mantra is *hrīḥ*

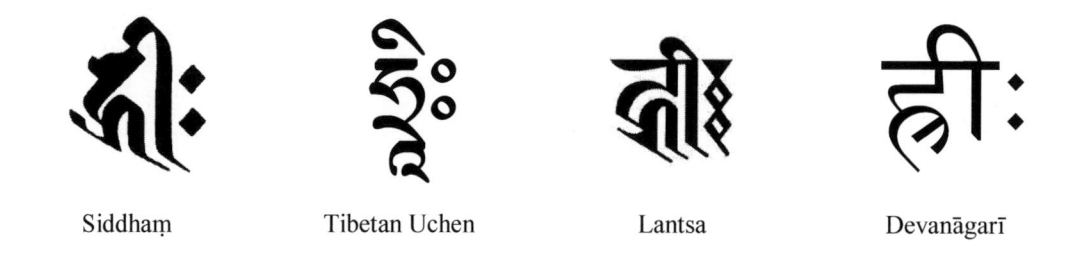

Siddhaṃ

ཧྲཱིཿ

Tibetan Uchen

Lantsa

ह्रीः

Devanāgarī

Mantra

There are a number of Amitābha mantras. This one is the main one used in the Tibetan traditions, but below are two other mantras used in two different Japanese traditions.

Siddhaṃ

ཨོཾ་ཨ་མི་དེ་ཝ་ཧྲཱིཿ།

Tibetan – Uchen

Lantsa

ओं अमिदेव ह्रीः

Devanāgarī

Transliteration

oṃ a mi de va hrīḥ

oṃ amideva hrīḥ

Notes

The word *amideva* is not as it would seem 'undying god', but is due to a Tibetan mispronunciation of Amitābha's name.[164] Compare the Tibetan transliteration of *vajra* as *badzra*. I have also seen Tibetan explanations which say that *dewa* (the Tibetan spelling) is

[164] This was pointed out to me by David Leskowitz [personal communication], and is also mentioned by Sangharakshita (1981) p.111.

short for *dewachen* the name of *Sukhāvatī* in Tibetan, *dewa* being the Tibetan translation of *sukha*.

Shingon Amitābha Mantra

The Shingon school uses a rather different mantra for Amitābha or as they call him *Amida Nyorai*. Nyorai is the Japanese word for Tathāgata.

oṃ a mṛ ta te je ha ra hūṃ

oṃ amṛta tejehara hūṃ

Amṛta means deathless; *tejehara* is possibly a compound of *tejas* - sharp, bright, brilliant; and *hara* - bringing, bearing, wearing etc: so *tejehara* is probably something like "bearing brilliance". (Note that this would be very similar in meaning to the name Lucifer in Latin, the name of the Morning Star and later erroneously associated with the Christian Devil [165]). Interestingly in Shingon they still use *hrīḥ* as his seed-syllable, despite having *hūṃ* in the mantra.

Pureland Amitābha Mantra aka the "Nembutsu"

Amitābha is the focus of the Pure Land schools of Buddhism which are very popular in Japan. Japanese Pure Land Buddhists will often be heard to chant the *nembutsu*: *namu amida butsu* (Japanese: 南無阿弥陀仏 ; Sanskrit: *namo 'mitābhāya buddhāya*). We can easily use Siddhaṃ to write Japanese - a fact which may have led to the development of the Japanese *kana* scripts after the study of Siddham was introduced to Japan by Kūkai in the 9th century.

Japanese

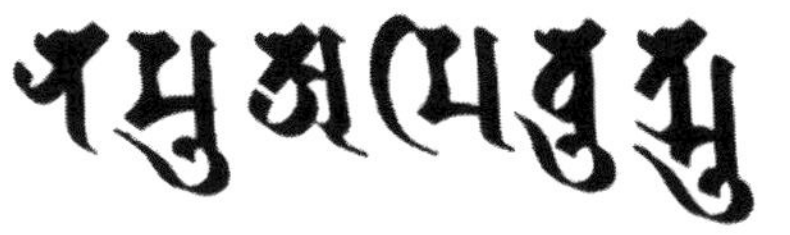

na mu a mi da bu tsu

南 無 阿 弥 陀 仏

Sanskrit

[165] The misidentification is based on a reading of Isaiah (14:12) first by Origen and then Augustine, the latter being the decisive influence. See for instance: Link, L. *The Devil : The Archfiend in Art*. London: Harry R. Abrams, 1995.

Siddhaṃ

नमो ऽमिताभाय बुद्धाय

Devanāgarī

na mo ‘mi tā bhā ya bu ddhā ya

namo ‘mitābhāya buddhāya

Note that the last syllable in Japanese, 仏, is pronounced ‘butsu’. The Nembutsu literally means ‘homage to Amitābha Buddha’, although it is common to see translations such as “I have faith in Amitābha” cited as “the literal meaning” of the words. *Namo* is from namaḥ which undergoes a sandhi change so that *namaḥ amitābha* becomes *namo ‘mitābha* and in Devanāgarī the *avagraha* ‘ऽ’ is used to show this. It can also be written as *namomitabha* नमोमिताभ leaving the reader to figure it out. *Namaḥ* is also found in the word *namaste* which means “homage to you” (*namaḥ te* - with a sandhi change to *namas* before the dental consonant).

The Nembutsu comes from the *Amitāyur-Dhyāna Sūtra* which details six meditations on the Buddha, known technically as *Buddhānusmṛti* or recollection of the Buddha, in Japanese: *nembutsu* (念仏) The Nembutsu is the sixth meditation which is designed for a person who has never considered the consequences of their actions and is on their death bed. They can be saved from a sojourn in the Hell Realms by reciting the name of Amitābha.

Amitāyus Mantra

Amitāyus means “Infinite Life”, or immortality. Amitāyus takes the place of Amitābha in the *Garbhadhātu Maṇḍala* of the *Mahāvairocana Abhisaṃbodhi Tantra*. This mantra is popular in Tibetan Buddhism. I have yet to find a Sanskrit version but have tried to reconstruct it from the Tibetan.

ཨོཾ་ཨཱ་མ་ར་ཎི་ཛཱི་ཝན་ཏེ་ཡེ་སྭཱ་ཧཱ།

Transliteration:

The transliteration often given is *om amarani jivantaye svaha* though the actual Tibetan letters are:

oṃ ā ma ra ṇi dzi wan te ye svā hā

oṃ āmaraṇi dziwanteye svāhā

Lacking a Sanskrit source I’ve done my best to reconstruct a plausible Sanskrit version of the mantra – my reasoning is given below.

Siddhaṃ

ओं अमरणि जीवन्तये स्वाहा

Devanāgarī

oṃ a ma ra ṇi ji va nta ye svā hā.

oṃ amaraṇi jīvantaye svāhā.

This mantra is frequently seen on Tibetan *mani stones* along with the mantras of Amitābha and Avalokiteśvara.

Notes

The Tibetan has *āmaraṇi* which *is* a Sanskrit word – meaning 'till death' – however, I think the context requires us to read this as *amaraṇi* with a short 'a'. *Amaraṇi* will be an action noun/adjective from the verbal root √mṛ 'to die' and so mean 'undying' or 'immortal'.

Jīvantaye is clearly from the verbal root √*jīv* means 'to live, to exist'. Through the addition of the possessive *–vant* suffix we come to *jīvanta* an adjective meaning 'long lived' in fact we can see *jīvanta* as a synonym of *amaraṇi*. The suffix *–ye* is, I think, intended to be a dative case ending so *jīvantaye* means 'to the one who possesses life' – i.e. to him who lives [forever]. However this is not entirely good Classical Sanskrit grammar. The dative singular of *jīvanta* is *jīvantāya*, plural *jīvantebhyaḥ*. The *–ye* suffix is a generic dative and, though this is common in mantras, is not used correctly in these cases. In the Pāli canon the common people said "*jīvatu*" (the same verb in the imperative mood 'may you live') when someone sneezed, equivalent of 'bless you' or '*gesundheit*'.[166]

We could, then, read *amaraṇi jīvantaye* as 'to the undying immortal'.

[166] See Vin ii.139, where the Buddha forbids bhikkhus from saying *jīvatu* because it is superstitious.

Amoghasiddhi

Japanese: *Fukūjōju Nyorai* (不空成就如来); Tibetan: *Dönyö Drubpa* (དོན་ཡོད་གྲུབ་པ་)

AMOGHASIDDHI OCCUPIES THE NORTHERN quarter of the Five Buddha Maṇḍala. He is depicted as a *bhikṣu*, and is deep green in colour. His name means infallible (*amogha*) success (*siddhi*). Amoghasiddhi is the head of the *karma* or action family in the Five Buddha Maṇḍala. Like his counterpart Ratnasambhava, Amoghasiddhi first appears in the *Sarvatathāgata-tattvasaṃgraha Tantra* in the late 7th or early 8th century.

Amoghasiddhi's emblem is the double vajra, a mysterious symbol which is two five pointed vajras arranged in a cross. His *mudrā* is *abhaya* or fearlessness. This is reminiscent of the story of the Buddha stopping a stampeding bull elephant by holding is hand palm outwards and radiating mettā towards it. The elephant is often depicted is art as bowing at the Buddha's feet. *Abhaya* can also mean "no danger".

Amoghasiddhi is associated with the Tantric Rite of Fearlessness (*abhayakarma*). The siddhis or accomplishments were the often magical powers attained by yogins (also known as siddhas). The greatest siddhi is, of course, *samyak-sambodhi* or full and perfect enlightenment.

Mandala of the Jinas

position in mandala	north
Colour	green
Family	karma
Mudra	fearlessness
Wisdom	All accomplishing Wisdom
Emblem	crossed vajra
Consort/prajñā	Tārā

Seed Syllable

Amoghasiddhi's mantra is *āḥ* - the long *ā* plus the *visarga* or aspiration. There is a alternate form in Siddhaṃ.

Siddhaṃ and alternate form

Tibetan Uchen

Lantsa

Devanāgarī

Mantra

Siddhaṃ

ཨོཾ་ཨ་མོ་གྷ་སི་དྡྷི་ཨཱཿ་ཧཱུྃ།

Tibetan – Uchen

Lantsa

ओं अमोघसिद्धि आः हूं

Devanāgarī

Transliteration

oṃ a mo gha si ddhi āḥ hūṃ

oṃ amoghasiddhi āḥ hūṃ

Notes

The Chinese translation of *amogha* 不空 means 'not empty', while the Tibetan དོན་ཡོད་ (*don yod*) means 'worthwhile, meaningful'. Maitiu O'Ceileachair says "this suggests to me that the Chinese and Tibetan translators interpreted the etymology of *amogha* as 'not fruitless, not unprofitable'."[167] From this is seems the translators had in mind the root word *mogha* 'vain, fruitless'.

[167] Personal Communication.

Ākāśadhātvīśvarī

Tibetan: *Namkha Ying Kyi Wangchukma* (ནམ་མཁའ་དབྱིངས་ཀྱི་དབང་ཕྱུག་མ་)

ĀKĀŚADHĀTVĪŚVARĪ IS WHITE in colour, and her name means 'The Sovereign Lady (*īśvarī*) of the Sphere (*dhātu*) of Infinite Space (*ākāśa*)'. She is sometimes also referred to as Dhātvīśvarī or Vajradhātvīśvarī. Ākāśadhātvīśvarī is the consort or *prajñā* of Vairocana.

Her mudrā is the *cakravartin* or wheel turning *mudrā* which is associated with the Buddha's first teaching, referred to as the first turning of the wheel of the Dharma. In each hand she holds a lotus which blooms at the shoulder. On the right shoulder is a *dharmacakra*, and on the left is the vajra-bell.

This *bīja* and mantra are from a *sādhana* and accompanying *pūjā* composed by Dharmacārī Vessantara.

Seed Syllable

The seed syllable of Ākāśadhātvīśvarī is *aṃ* (pronounced like: *ung*).

Siddhaṃ

ཨཾ

Tibetan Uchen

Lantsa

अं

Devanāgarī

Mantra

Siddhaṃ

ཨོཾ་སརྦ་བུདྡྷ་ཌྷ་ན་ཨཾ་སྭཱ་ཧཱ།

Tibetan – Uchen

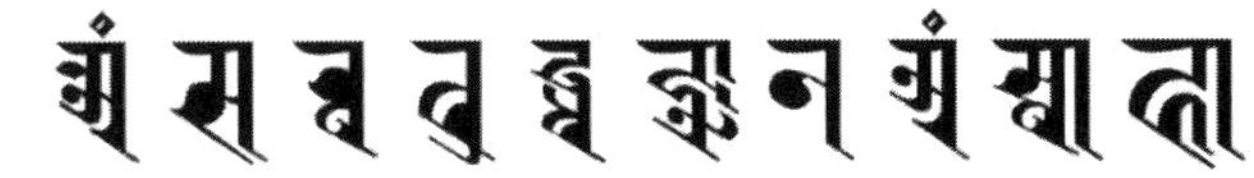

Lantsa

ओं सर्वबुद्धज्ञान अं स्वाहा

Devanāgarī

Transliteration

oṃ sa rva bu ddha jñā na aṃ svā hā

oṃ sarvabuddhajñāna aṃ svāhā

Notes

None of the words in the mantra have case endings, and in mantras it is permissible to treat them as three separate terms, but there is a certain logic here which suggests we take them as compound. The word *sarvabuddhajñāna* means 'the gnosis (*jñāna*) of all (*sarva*) the Buddhas'.

There are a couple of incorrect variations on the spelling of the name Ākāśadhātvīśvarī. One sees, for instance, the spelling Ākāśadhātīśvarī which may be down to Lama Govinda as he uses that spelling in his *Foundations of Tibetan Mysticism*. One may also see Ākāśadhāteśvarī and this may be an attempt to model it on the name Avalokiteśvara but it is erroneous. Ākāśadhātvīśvarī is a (*tatpuruṣa*) compound of *ākāśa* + *dhātu* + *īśvarī*. When combining the last two words in a compound Sanskrit sandhi rules dictate that *u* + *ī* combine to give *vī*.

Locanā

Tibetan: *Sangyé chenma* (སངས་རྒྱས་སྤྱན་མ་)

LOCANĀ IS PALE BLUE in colour and her name means "The One with the Eye", or the "Clear Visioned One". Her name derives from the root √*loc* 'to see' or 'to shine', which is etymologically related our word 'lucid' (and to the name Lucy). There is also a connection to the root √*lok* which is related to our word 'look'. So we could also render her name as 'lucidity'. She is also known as Buddhalocanā (the Tibetan form of her name above).

She is associated with pure awareness, and represents the pure, simple, direct awareness of things as they are. Her left hand is in the *dhyāna mudrā* and holds a vajra-bell, while her right hand is in the *bhūmisparśa mudrā* and holds a five pointed vajra. Locanā is the consort or *prajñā* of Akṣobhya.

This *bīja* and mantra are from a *sādhana* and accompanying *pūjā* composed by Dharmacārī Vessantara

Seed Syllable

The seed syllable of Locanā is *loṃ*.

Siddhaṃ

ལོཾ

Tibetan Uchen

Lantsa

लों

Devanāgarī

Mantra

Siddhaṃ

ཨོཾ་བཛྲ་ལོ་ཙ་ནེ་ལོཾ་སྭཱ་ཧཱ།

Tibetan – Uchen

Lantsa

ओं वज्रलोचने लों स्वाहा

Devanāgarī

Transliteration

oṃ va jra lo ca ne loṃ svā hā

oṃ vajralocane loṃ svāhā

Notes

The Tibetan text varies slightly due to the demands of Tibetan orthography and pronunciation. *Vajra*, following the Tibetan practice is actually written *badzra*; and the *ca* in Locanā is transcribed *tsa*. *Locane* is the vocative form of Locana's name and therefore means "O Locana".

Svāhā is an ancient Vedic word that was used to mark the making of oblations to the sacred fire. (see *svāhā*, p. 206)

Her seed syllable is simply the first syllable of her name with *anusvāra*.

Māmakī

Japanese: *Mōmōkei* (忙忙鷄)[168]; Tibetan: *Māmakī* (མ་མ་ཀཱི)

MĀMAKĪ IS YELLOW IN COLOUR, and her name means "Mine-maker" from the genitive singular pronoun *māma* meaning 'my' or 'mine'. She identifies with everything and everyone as "mine": she makes no distinctions. Her right hand is in the *varada mudrā* on which rests a jewel (*ratna*), and her left hand holds a lotus, on which rests a *vajra* bell. Māmakī is the consort or *prajñā* of Ratnasambhava

This *bīja* and mantra are from a *sādhana* and accompanying *pūjā* composed by Dharmacārī Vessantara.

Seed Syllable

Seed Syllable of Māmakī is *māṃ* the first syllable of her name with the *anusvāra*.

Siddhaṃ | Tibetan Uchen | Lantsa | Devanāgarī

Mantra

Siddhaṃ

[168] Some dictionaries give the Japanese pronunciation as Mamakei. The name is also spelt 麼麼雞 = Mamakei. These are transliterations of the sounds, not translations.

ཨོཾ་རཏྣེ་སུ་རཏྣེ་མཱཾ་སྭཱ་ཧཱ།

Tibetan – Uchen

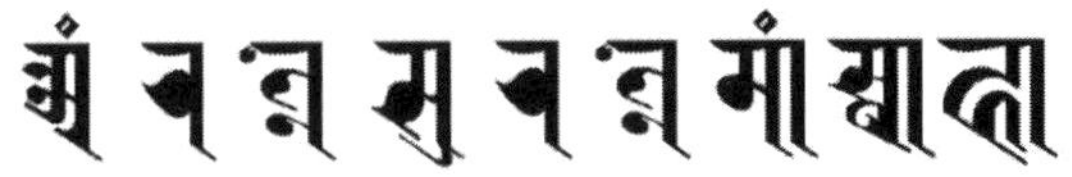

Lantsa

ओं रत्ने सुरत्ने मां स्वाहा

Devanāgarī

Transliteration

oṃ ra tne su ra tne māṃ svā hā

oṃ ratne suratne māṃ svāhā

Notes

Ratna is the Sanskrit word for jewel, and *ratne* is (probably intended to be) the vocative form – 'O jewel'. The prefix *su-* means 'well, good, virtuous'. *Svāhā* is an ancient Vedic word that was used to mark the making of oblations to the sacred fire.

For the Tibetan script I have transliterated: *rat ne su rat ne* because this would be more natural for Tibetan pronunciation.

Pāṇḍaravāsinī

Japnese: *Handarabashini* (伴陀羅縛子尼)[169]; Tibetan: *Gökarmo* (གོས་དཀར་མོ་).

PĀṆḌARAVĀSINĪ is light red in colour, and her name means 'robed (*vāsinī*) in white (*pāṇḍara*)' suggesting that she is vested with purity. Pāṇḍaravāsinī is the consort or *prajñā* of Amitābha. She holds her hands together at her breast in the *añjali mudrā*, and is clasping the stems of two lotuses. Upon the lotus at her left shoulder rests a vajra bell (*vajraghaṇṭā*), and on the lotus at her right shoulder rests a vase of immortality.

Sangharakshita likens Pāṇḍaravāsinī to the image of the Buddha in the fourth *dhyana*: it is like the experience of someone who on a hot and dusty day, takes a bath in a beautiful pond and, having bathed, emerges and wraps themselves in a clean white sheet.

This *bīja* and mantra are from a *sādhana* and accompanying *pūjā* composed by Dharmacārī Vessantara.

Seed Syllable

Seed Syllable of Pāṇḍaravāsinī is *paṃ*.

Siddhaṃ

Tibetan Uchen

Lantsa

Devanāgarī

Mantra

Siddhaṃ

[169] Alternatively 半拏囉嚩悉寧 (*Handarabashinei*); or 白衣觀音 (*Byakue Kannon*) which inclues the Chinese name for Avalokiteśvara and in East Asian Buddhism this White Robed female form of Avalokiteśvara is one of the most commonly seen Buddhist images.

ཨོཾ་པད་མ་དེ་ཝཱི་པུ་ཥྤ་དེ་ཝཱི་པཾ་སྭཱ་ཧཱ།

Tibetan – Uchen

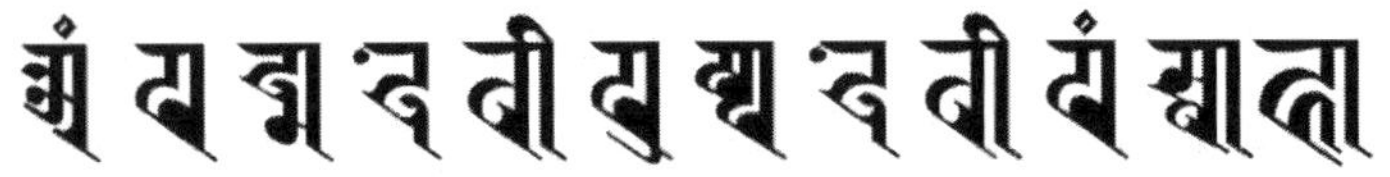

Lantsa

ओं पद्मदेवी पुष्पदेवी पं स्वाहा

Devanāgarī

Transliteration

oṃ pa dma de vī pu ṣpa de vī paṃ svā hā

oṃ padmadevī puṣpadevī paṃ svāhā

Notes

In the mantra *Padma* means 'lotus' and *puṣpa* means 'flower'. *Devī* usually means a goddess, however kings and queens were often referred to as *deva* or *devī* in India, just as we might say Your Majesty. Vessantara says that 'queen' applies here.[170] So the (translatable) words in the mantra mean 'queen of lotuses, queen of flowers'.

I've transliterated the Tibetan as *pad ma de vī puṣ pa de vī* because it would be more natural for Tibetan pronunciation.

[170] Vessantara. *The Five Female Buddhas*. Private edition, 2004. p.44. Online: http://vessantara.net/wp-content/uploads/five-female-buddhas.pdf

Bodhisattvas and other mythic beings

Most of the figures in this section are bodhisattvas – from *bodhi* (awakening, understanding) and *sattva* (being) – see below for a more in-depth discussion of the word. The original *bodhisattva* (P. *Bodhisatta,* J. *Bosatsu* 菩薩) was Gautama, the historical Buddha, before his experience of *bodhi*. Subsequently assiduous practitioners took on to become Buddhas in this life (they identified with being a bodhisattva), and at around the same time archetypal bodhisattvas began to appear in texts (images other than Maitreya came much later). The Bodhisattvas here are mythic or archetypal figures who do not have historical counterparts.

Other types of figures the Four Great Kings (*Caturmahārāja*) who are devas that appear in the earliest Buddhist scriptures. Another term for the four is *lokapāla* 'world-protector'. Another kind of deva, the *yakṣa*, is represented by Vajrapāṇi but in the form that we meet him his origins as a *yakṣa* are not obvious. Vajrayoginī is a *ḍākiṇī* – a kind of chthonic spirit that entered the Buddhist pantheon very late in its development on Indian soil. Acala may be a development from the *lokapāla*, he is a wrathful figure – externally angry – and this kind of figure is sometimes known as a *dharmapāla* 'dharma-protector'.

A note on the word Bodhisattva

The typical explanation of this word tells us that *sattva* is the Sanskrit word for 'being', an abstract noun from *sat* 'true, real', ultimately from the verbal root √*as* 'to be' (cognate with English 'is'). Sanskrit used the notion of 'being' in much the same way we do in English: being 'a state of existence (or realness) and; a being 'a living entity'. *Sat* (and its derivative *satya*) was a very important term in Vedic metaphysics, and is still important in contemporary Hindu metaphysics. Adding the *-tva* suffix gives 'truth' or 'reality'.

It's plausible enough, however, the Pāli commentaries take the Pāli equivalent *satta* as related to either *sakta* 'intent on' (the past-participle of the verb √*sañj* 'clinging'); or from *śakta* meaning 'capable of' (past-participle of √*śak* 'strong, capable, able'). The suggestion then is that *sattva* is a hyper-Sanskritisation. In this case Sanskrit *satka*, *śakta* and *sattva* all become *satta* in Pāli and other Prakrits. The option of 'intent on' (*satka*) would fit the way 'bodhisattva' practitioners are described in very early Mahāyāna sūtras (e.g. the *Ugraparipṛccha* - see Jan Nattier. *A Few Good Men*).

A bodhisattva, then, is 'intent on bodhi' and perhaps should be spelt *bodhisakta* (though centuries of tradition weigh against such a correction). The word is an adjective used in the sense of someone aspiring to, or about to, attain bodhi and become a Buddha. Both *buddha* and *bodhi* derive from the same root √*budh* 'to understand, to wake up to' - *buddha* is the past-participle meaning 'awoken', while bodhi is verbal noun meaning 'knowledge' (c.f. *buddhi* 'intelligence').

Note the spelling '*satva*' (with a single 't') seems to have begun as a scribal error - inadvertently leaving off the extra 't'. There is a word *satvan* which is literally 'one who possesses *sat'*, and which is used to mean 'living, breathing' and 'powerful, strong, a warrior'. The nominative singular is *satvā*, and it is purposefully used in some cases to describe the Buddhas and Bodhisattvas - they are described as *mahāsatvā* 'great heros' in the *Sarvatathāgata-tattvasaṃgraha* for instance. Cf the use of *mahāsattva* 'great-being' which is commonly used in Mahāyāna sūtras.

Acala Vidyārāja

Japanese: *Fudō myōō* (不動明王); Tibetan: *Migyowa*. (མི་གཡོ་བ་)

ACALA-VIDYĀRĀJA is a wrathful figure associated with Vairocana. He is frequently described as a messenger, but his main function in the *Mahāvairocana Abhisaṃbodhi Tantra* (MAT) is as a destroyer of obstacles.

Acala means 'immovable'. *Vidyā* can mean knowledge, but is also a synonym for mantra and is frequently used to refer to magic. It can be taken to mean something like esoteric knowledge. *Rājā* means 'king'. He is also known simply as Acala (J. Fudō, 不動).

He is depicted as a robust and powerful young man wreathed in flames, his hair is plaited into bangs, one of his eyes squints and his visage is angry. He holds a sword in his right hand and a noose in his left. The flames in his aura are the flames which transmute mundane anger into the Mirror-like Wisdom. See the notes for more on his wrathful aspect.

Fudō is also part of a group of five Vidyārājas in Shingon iconography.

Seed Syllables

Fudō's seed syallble is *hāṃ*.

Siddhaṃ

Tibetan Uchen

Lantsa

Devanāgarī

Another seed syllable associated with Acala is *hāmmāṃ*, which is a combination of the two final bīja - *hāṃ* and *māṃ* - from his mantra.

Mantra

Siddhaṃ

Tibetan – Uchen

Lantsa

नमः समन्त वज्रानां चण्ड महारोषण स्फोटय हुं त्रट् हां मां

Devanāgarī

Transliteration

na maḥ sa ma nta va jrā nāṃ ca ṇḍa ma hā ro ṣa ṇa spho ṭa ya hūṃ traṭ hāṃ māṃ

namaḥ samanta vajrānāṃ caṇḍa mahāroṣaṇa sphoṭaya hūṃ traṭ hāṃ māṃ

Notes

The mantra comes from the *Mahāvairocana Abhisaṃbodhi Tantra*. It occurs in the chapter General Mantra Treasury.[171] Acala is one of only three wrathful figures in the MAT along with Trailokyavijaya and Hayagrīva.

This is a wrathful mantra which includes words which must be understood in the context of Tantric Buddhism. For instance *caṇḍa* means 'violent', *mahāroṣaṇa* means 'great wrath', and *sphoṭaya* means 'destroy'. Anger is associated with, and transformed through Tantric practices into, the mirror-like wisdom (*ādarṣajñāna*) of Akṣobhya that sees perfectly clearly. The energy of the anger is directed towards breaking through to Buddhahood: it breaks through spiritual ignorance. There is no sense in which this justifies expressing mundane anger towards people, as the anger of the Bodhisattva arises out of Compassion for their suffering, and is rooted in Perfect Wisdom. The MAT insists that the mantra is to be recited while keeping *bodhicitta* in mind.[172] It is the obstacles to awakening that Acala destroys.

---

[171] Chapter four in the Tibetan recensions: see Hodge *The Mahāvairocana Abhisaṃbodhi Tantra* p. 161

[172] MAT III.4. Hodge p.154.

In later texts there is a distinct figure called Caṇḍa Mahāroṣaṇa. As well as destroying obstacles, the Acala mantra can be used for occupying the ground where a mandala is being created. Tantric texts seem to assume that creating a mandala is something that one does on an actual plot of land, although this could of course be symbolic.

Note that the MAT is no longer extant in Sanskrit. Hodges' translation from the Tibetan is far superior to those from Chinese by Yamamoto or Giebal.

Ākāśagarbha

Japanese: *Kokūzo Bosatsu* (虚空蔵 菩薩); Tibetan: *Namkhé Nyingpo* (ནམ་མཁའི་སྙིང་པོ་)

ĀKĀŚAGARBHA is an important figure in far eastern Buddhism. His emblems are the sword and *cintāmani* (translated as 'wish fulling jewel', though literally 'thought-jewel') portrayed here, as it often is, as the three jewels. He is sometimes shown as here, and sometimes with his right hand in the *varada*, or giving, *mudrā*. He is one of the set of eight great bodhisattvas.

Ākāśagarbha is very important in the life story of Kūkai. As a teenager he met a Buddhist priest who taught him a mantra of Ākāśagarbha known as the Morning Star Mantra (J. *Gumonji-hō*. See below). It was in repeating this mantra millions of times that he had some decisive spiritual experiences, including many powerful visions of Ākāśagarbha.

Seed Syllable

The seed syllable of Ākāśagarbha is *trāḥ*.

Siddhaṃ

ཏྲཱཿ

Tibetan Uchen

Lantsa

त्राः

Devanāgarī

Mantra

Siddhaṃ

ཨོཾ་བཛྲ་རཏྣ་ཨོཾ་ཏྲཱཿ་སྭཱ་ཧཱ།

Tibetan – Uchen

Lantsa

ओं वज्ररत्न ओं त्राः स्वाहा

Devanāgarī

Transliteration

oṃ va jra ra tna oṃ trāḥ svā hā

oṃ vajraratna oṃ trāḥ svāhā

The Japanese pronunciation of this mantra is:

om bazara aratanno om taraku sowaka

Morning Star Mantra

This mantra is very important in Shingon Buddhism and comes from a text known in Japanese as *Kokūzō bosatsu nō man shogan saishō shin darani gumonji hō* (虚空藏菩薩能滿諸願最勝心陀羅尼求聞持法: T. 20.1145). Repeated one million times according to the requisite rituals, in a certain time period, one gains the ability to remember and understand any text.

Siddhaṃ

नमो आकाशगर्भय ओं आर्यकमरिमौलि स्वाहा

Devanāgarī

Transliteration

na mo ā kā śa ga rbha ya oṃ ā rya ka ma ri mau li svā hā

namo ākāśagarbhaya oṃ ārya kamari mauli svāhā

The Japanese pronunciation of this mantra is:

nōbō akyasha kyarabaya on ari kyamari bori sowaka

Notes

This mantra has been translated as: "Homage to the great space-bearer who holds a flower and wears a garland and a jewelled crown svāhā".[173] I'm a bit doubtful about this. *Namo ākāśagarbhaya* is 'homage to Ākāśagarbha'. *Ārya* should be familiar and means 'noble'. *Kamari* is not in my Sanskrit dictionary and the translation above appears to be taking *kamari* as *kamala* 'lotus' (*kamali* may be a feaux feminine). The *kanji* used to transliterate the mantra is 利 (advantage, profit) which is pronounced /ri/ in Japanese. *Kamara* means desirous, lustful and can hardly have been intended! *Mauli* is the top-knot of the Bodhisattva indicating his princely status clearly visible in many depictions of *bodhisattvas* – it was this that the Buddha-to-be is said to have cut off on leaving home. However 'crown' or 'turban' are also potential translations. (The word may also be familiar in its Pāli form from the name of the well known translator Ñāṇamoli – which means something like 'crowned with gnosis'). I think we should read this as *āryakamalamauli* (a *bahuvrīhi* compound) – 'having a noble lotus top-knot'.

[173] Eidson. *Shingon Esoteric Buddhism* p.68.

Avalokiteśvara / Guānyīn

Japanese: *Kannon Bosatsu* (観音菩薩); Tibetan: *Chenrezig* (སྤྱན་རས་གཟིགས་)

AVALOKITEŚVARA is associated with the quality of *karuṇā* or compassion. His name means 'Lord (*īśvara*) who beholds (*avalokita*)'[174], and is said to relate to his looking upon the earth and its suffering beings with compassion.

In China, where Avalokiteśvara was very popular, he underwent a change and became Guānyīn (觀音[175]; also transliterated Kwan Yin etc.) a female Bodhisattva. Guānyīn actually translates an earlier version of the name of this bodhisattva: Avalokitasvara. *Svara* means sounds and the name Avalokitasvara means 'regarder of sounds or cries' which is how the name often appears in English translations of the Chinese *Saddharmapuṇḍarīka Sūtra*. The name changed as the bodhisattva absorbed some of the qualities of Śiva, the Hindu Īśvara or Lord: *svara* became *īśvara*, and *-eśvara* in combination. In Chinese Avalokiteśvara would be Guānzìzài (觀自在).

Avalokiteśvara appears in many forms. There are a number of two armed forms, and a form with one thousand arms and eleven heads! This image of his four armed form is known as *Ṣaḍakṣarī* (six syllabled) Avalokiteśvara, because of the association with the popular mantra *oṃ maṇipadme hūṃ*. He holds a *cintāmani* or wish fulfilling jewel to his heart and in his upper left hand a lotus in full bloom, and in his upper right hand a *mālā* for counting mantras.

Avalokiteśvara is a member of the Lotus family which is headed by Amitābha.

Seed Syllable

Siddhaṃ | Tibetan Uchen | Lantsa | Devanāgarī

[174] A technicality here: *avalokita* is a past-participle and so means 'observed': the name strictly speaking means 'observed by the lord', but I give the traditional interpretation above.

[175] The Japanese form of the name – 観音 (pronounced Kannon) – uses the character 観 which is one of the Japanese simplified characters (*shinjitai*) that was introduced after the Second World War. The character already existed as a 'vulgar' variant of 觀 but it's not used in modern Chinese or the Taishō Edition of the Tripiṭaka. In simplified Chinese the name is written 观音.

Mantra

Siddhaṃ

ཨོཾ་མ་ཎི་པ་དྨེ་ཧཱུྃ

Tibetan – Uchen

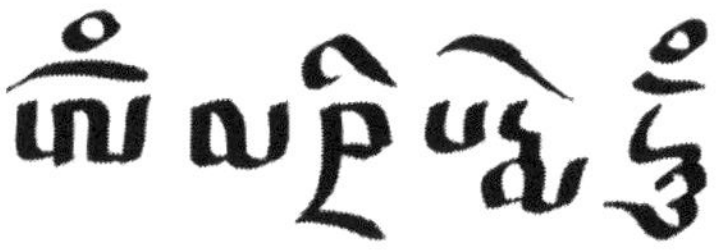

Tibetan – Ume

Lantsa

ओं मणिपद्मे हूं

Devanāgarī

Transliteration

oṃ ma ṇi pa dme hūṃ

oṃ maṇipadme hūṃ

Mani Stones

Stones carved with the Avalokiteśvara mantra – *mani* stones - are, like prayer flags, a feature of the Tibetan landscape. The stones are piled up into cairns, or made into walls on all major routes, and in significant places such as mountain summits.

In Tibet near a place called Yushu, someone carved the Avalokiteśvara mantra into a frozen lake that can be seen on Google Maps (coordinates: N 32.909982, E 97.04612).[176] The tallest letters are a bit over 50 meters high.

Notes on the Avalokiteśvara Mantra

The earliest known text containing this mantra is the *Kāraṇḍavyūha Sūtra*. The *Kāraṇḍavyūha* has not been translated into English but is the subject of an in-depth study in Alexander Studholme's book *The Origins of Oṃ Maṇipadme Hūṃ: a Study of the Kāraṇḍavyūha Sūtra*. The *Kāraṇḍavyūha*, which Studholme dates to the fourth century, contains elements which are later equated with Tantric Buddhism, though it is not a tantric text. In this sūtra the mantra is presented in terms very similar to Pureland Buddhism: the mantra is for instance an example of *nāmānusmṛti* or 'calling to mind the name [of the Buddha]' which is an important practice in the *Saddharmapuṇḍarīka Sūtra*, and in the *Sukhāvatīvyūha Sūtra*. Reciting the mantra is said to fulfil the six perfections and to protect the reciter against misfortune.

The six syllable mantra is frequently translated as 'oṃ *the jewel in the lotus* hūṃ', *maṇi* being a jewel and *padma* a lotus, but this is probably incorrect. In the book *Prisoners of Shangrila* Donald Lopez argues that it is more likely that *maṇipadmā* is the name of a feminine Bodhisattva, and the *-e* ending is the feminine vocative so that *maṇipadme* would mean: "O Jeweled Lotus!"[177] An early Tibetan text, dated to the 9th century, on Sanskrit grammar favours this reading of the mantra.[178] Alexander Studholme however suggests that *maṇipadme* is a masculine or neuter locative so that it would mean "in the jewel lotus" and refer to the way in which beings are 'born' in Sukhāvatī (the 'pureland' of Amitābha). Despite the fact that the grammar of *maṇipadme* cannot be interpreted as meaning "the jewel in the lotus", this is not to say that explanations which employ the image are doctrinally incorrect.

A typical Tibetan exegesis relates each of the six syllables to the six realms of conditioned existence, and various other sets of six. Avalokiteśvara appears in each realm offering what the inhabitants need in order to awaken from that state. Often when the mantra is written in Tibetan, each of the letters is coloured to match the colour of Avalokiteśvara's manifestation in that realm.

---

[176] Satellite photos are replaced from time to time. This one was still visible on 09/09/09.

[177] Lopez Prisoners of Shangrila p.114ff. I discuss the possibilities of the *–e* ending in a separate essay (see p.64).

[178] Verhagen, P.C. 'The mantra oṃ maṇi-padme hūṃ in an early Tibetan Grammatical Treatise,' *Journal of the International Association of Buddhist Studies*. 13 (2) 1990. p.134-5. I have omitted Tibetan equivalents, and parentheses indicating interpolations in the translation

Syllable	Realm	Colour
oṃ	devas	white
ma	asuras	green
ṇi	human	yellow
pa	animal	blue
dme	hungry ghosts	red
hūṃ	hells	black

The mantra then is seen as activating the quality in the universe which liberates beings, whichever realm they are in, and this is far more important than the dictionary definitions of the words which make it up. The fact that there are six syllables is probably more important for its associations than the sounds of those syllables.

Other Scripts – just for fun

Anglo Saxon Runes

Elvish [179]

Klingon

Egyptian Hieroglyphs[180]

[179] Tengwar script in the Quenya mode.
[180] According to Jim Loy's Heiroglyph font. http://www.jimloy.com/hiero/font.htm

Caturmahārāja: The Four Great Kings

Japanese: *Shitennō* (四天王); Tibetan: *Gyalchen Dezhi* (རྒྱལ་ཆེན་སྡེ་བཞི་)

The Four Great Kings are devas in the Indian pantheon, where they occupy the lowest of the devalokas (god realms). They feature in some of the earliest Buddhist scriptures, representing a strand of Indian religous thought which was being adopted and adapted by Buddhists, probably in the first few centuries after the death of the Buddha. Each one presides over one of the four directions of space, and is associated with a particular type of non-human being.

Mantras of the Four Great Kings

Dhṛtarāṣṭra

Japanese: *Jikoku-ten* (持国天) Tibetan: *Yülkhorsung* (ཡུལ་འཁོར་བསྲུང་)

King of the East. White in colour, holding a lute. King of the Gandharvas (celestial musicians). Dhṛtarāṣṭra means "watcher of lands".

There is a king Dhṛtarāṣṭra in the *Mahābhārata*. The war amongst his children and those of his younger brother Pāndhu for the throne of the Kuru - the Kauravas and the Pāndavas - forms the main action of the *Mahābhārata* war, around which the epic revolves (Basham: 408). It is thought that the story recounts a real war, although the dates are disputed.

Siddhaṃ

Tibetan – Uchen

ओं धृतराष्ट्रय स्वाहा

Devanāgarī

Lantsa

Transliteration

oṃ dhṛ ta rā ṣṭra ya svā hā

oṃ dhṛtarāṣṭraya svāhā

Note

There are some variations in the spelling of the name. I have also seen *dhṛtarāśtra* and *dhṛtarāṣṭṛa* in reputable sources.

Virūḍhaka

Japanese: *Zōjō-ten* (増長天); Tibetan: *Phakyepo* (འཕགས་སྐྱེས་པོ་)

King Virūḍhaka, king of the Southern quarter and lord of the Kumbhāṇḍas.

King of the South. Green in colour and holding a sword. King of the Kumbhāṇḍas, his name means "ever growing".

The Kumbhāṇḍas according to Sutherland are "a grotesque group of demons with testicles in the shape of a kumbha or pitcher". The Pāli commentaries describe them as having "huge stomachs, and their genital organs were as big as pots, hence their name".[181]

Siddhaṃ

ཨོཾ་བི་རཱུ་ཌྷ་ཀ་ཡ་སྭཱ་ཧཱ།

Tibetan – Uchen

ओं विरूढकय स्वाहा

Devanāgarī

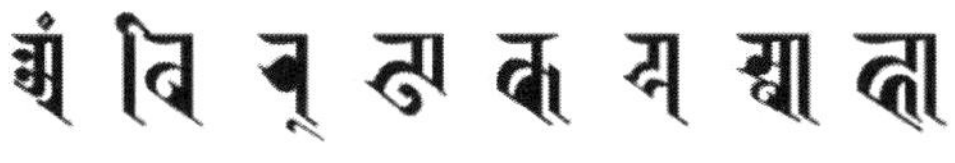

Lantsa

Transliteration

oṃ vi rū ḍha ka ya svā hā

oṃ virūḍhakaya svāhā

Notes

"*virūḍhaka kumbhāṇḍāye*" can be translated Virūḍhaka Lord of the Kumbhāṇḍas. *Bonji Taikan* has *yakṣādhipataye* but properly speaking Vaiśravaṇa is Lord of the Yakṣas, and Virūḍhaka is Lord of the Kumbhāṇḍas. I have taken a liberty here (the kind that tests the patience of traditionalists), but one that makes sense. Sometimes the tradition is wrong, or corrupt.

Virūpākṣa

Japanese: *Kōmoku-ten* (広目天); Tibetan: *Chenmizang* (སྤྱན་མི་བཟང་)

King Virūpākṣa, king of the Western quarter and lord of the Nāgas. Red in colour; holding a *stūpa*, and snake. King of the Nāgas. His name means something like "all seeing".

Virūpākṣa's association with serpents and water suggests a connection with the Vedic god Varuṇa. Initially

[181] (DA.iii.964)

a solar god, often paired with Mitra, Varuṇa was the guardian of *ṛta* - the cosmic order. Later, in the Hindu Epics, he was relegated to being a protector of water and was associated with animistic spirits, such as *nāgas*. Some scholars point to similarities with the Greek Titan Uranus (the names are phonetically similar).

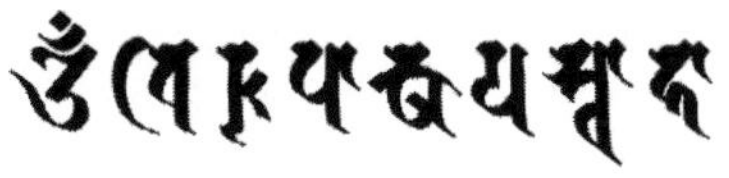

Siddhaṃ

Tibetan - Uchen

ओं विरुपाक्ष स्वाहा

Devānagarī

Lantsa

Transliteration

oṃ vi rū pā kṣa ya svā hā

oṃ virūpākṣaya svāhā

Notes

"*virūpākṣa nāgādhipataye*" can be translated as 'Virūpākṣa Lord of the Nāgas'. *Nāga* has several different meanings. Originally a reference to animistic water spirits, probably worshiped as deities; it also came to refer to serpents. In Pāli and modern Indian languages means elephant, and is also sometimes applied to any large animal such as a bull; the Buddha is sometimes refered to as a great *nāga*.

Vaiśravaṇa

Japanese: *Bishamon*-ten (毘沙門天); Tibetan: *Namthöse* (རྣམ་ཐོས་སྲས་)

King Vaiśravaṇa of the Northern quarter, Lord of the *Yakṣas*. Yellow in colour. Holding a (victory) banner and mongoose spitting jewels. The name means 'extensive hearing'. Vaiśravaṇa is also known as Kubera under which name he appears in the Śatapatha Brāhmaṇa. He goes by the name Vaiśravaṇa in the Mahābharata where he is the son of Pulastya, and half brother of Rāvaṇa. Kubera is a god of wealth and good fortune which is what the mongoose spitting out jewels symbolises. Vaiśravaṇa is the patron deity of the city of Khotan.

ཨོཾ་བཻ་ཤྲ་བ་ཎ་ཡེ་སྭཱ་ཧཱ།

Siddhaṃ

Tibetan - Uchen

ओं वैश्रवणये स्वाहा

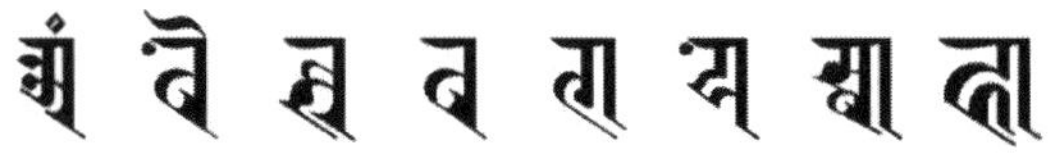

Devanāgarī

Lantsa

oṃ vai śra va ṇa ye svā hā

oṃ vaiśravaṇaye svāhā

This mantra is simply the name Vaiśravaṇa in the dative case (to or for Vaiśravaṇa) with *oṃ* and *svāhā*.

Notes on the Four Great Kings Collectively

A very early set of four directional gods appears in the *Yajurveda* with Agni (E), Yama (S), Savitṛ (W), and Varuṇa (N). The gods of the directions were shuffled around in Brāhmaṇa texts. Scholars, however, place there origins of the four Lokapālas in the pre-Āriyan indigenous population of India. I favour a hybrid approach. Since some of the figures clearly do relate to Vedic gods in some ways (e.g. Vaiśravaṇa and Kubera; Virūpākṣa and Varuṇa) I think that the Lokapālas, especially as we meet them in Buddhism, combine the chthonic local deities in the form of their followers (i.e. the *yakṣas*), but with Vedic inspired kings overlaid onto them. This is pure supposition however, and would need a lot more research to establish as fact.

The Lokapālas, or Mahārājas, feature widely in the Pāli texts (where they are known as the *Cātummahārājikā*), often visiting the Buddha at crucial times, or to hear the Dharma. In Pāli the names are: Dhataraṭṭha, Virūḷhaka, Virūpakkha, Vessavaṇa. A summary of the Great Kings in the Pāli texts is available in the Dictionary of Pāli Names.

One of the key texts featuring the Four Kings is the *Āṭānāṭiya Sutta* (DN 32). This is one of the traditional paritta texts which are chanted for protection from misfortune, and the *Āṭānāṭiya* is particularly concerned with protection from harmful 'spirits' ie *yakṣas* etc. *Yakṣas* etc. were minor gods with their own cults and shrines. Several *yakṣa* (P. *yakkha*) shrines are mentioned in the Pāli texts. Initially they were not much distinguished from *nāgas* and were nature spirits associated with water or trees. In one text there is a story of an anger-eating *yakkha* (SN 11.22).

One of the best known figures of the Vajrayāna, Vajrapāṇi, first appears in the *Ambaṭṭha Sutta* (DN 3) as the *yakkha* Vajirapani, the Pāli form of the name. He threatens to split the head of a Brahmin, who is lying to the Buddha about his ancestry, into seven pieces. Head splitting is, strangely, a regular topic in the canon - in the *Āṭānāṭiya* non-humans will split the head of any malicious spirit who attacks one of the Buddha's disciples, as long as the disciple will recite the sutta (this is very reminiscent of later Mahāyāna refrains!). Vajrapāṇi's progress to the pinnacle of the Vajrayāna pantheon is traced in David Snellgrove's Indo-Tibetan Buddhism.

The *Āṭānāṭiya* continues to be an important text into the Mahāyāna, and continues to develop as a text for several centuries at least. Peter Skilling has traced its development in his study of the so-called *rakṣā* [protection] texts. Later it is considered to be a *kriyā* (or action) class tantra.

The Four Great Kings make an appearance in the Golden Light Sutra where they promise to protect anyone who recites the sutra. They are the rulers of the chthonic forces of nature. In this context they are known as the Lokapālas: "They belong to the heavens, but they are in touch with the earth, and they are therefore able to keep the powerful energies of the earth under control, and prevent them from having a disruptive effect on the human world." [182]

In *maṇḍalas* the Kings guard the four gates in the four directions. Vessantara describes these protector figures as "beneficent forces at the summit of the mundane world who, whilst not themselves Enlightened, are receptive to the influence of the Buddhas and Bodhisattvas".

Maitiu O'Ceileachair has pointed out that these types of mantras: beginning with *oṃ*, followed by the name of the deity in the dative case (often with the case ending *–ye*), and ending in *svāhā*, are similar in form to some Vedic Mantras from the *Yajurveda*. What is suggested by this is that the mantra accompanied a libation (a liquid offering, probably ghee) is poured onto the sacrificial fire and dedicated to the named deity. The form was retained even when the sacrifices were internalised, that is, carried out imaginatively, and the mantras on their own came to suffice for the ritual. Later again they were adopted by Buddhists wishing to invoke Buddhas and Bodhisattvas and, as in this case, gods.

[182] Sangharakshita 1995: 134

Kṣitigarbha

Japanese: *Jizō Bosatsu* (地蔵 菩薩); Tibetan: *Sa Yi Nyingpo* (ས་ཡི་སྙིང་པོ)

KṢITIGARBHA IS ONE OF THE EIGHT Great Bodhisattvas. His name translates as earth (*kṣiti*) store or matrix (*garbha*). His special function is to descend into the hell realms to save the beings there. He responds to and helps all those in states of torment. In Japan his statue is often erected at crossroads and he is considered a protector of children.

He appears in the form of a *Sarvastivādin bhikṣu*, often standing on a golden lotus and carrying a mendicant's staff in his right hand. In his left hand he cradles a *cintāmaṇi* or wish-fulfilling jewel. The *cintāmaṇi* is sometimes also referred to as the 'pearl beyond price.'

An important source for Kṣitigarbha is *The Sūtra of the Past Vows of Kṣitigarbha Bodhisattva* (地藏菩薩本願經. T. No. 412) which recounts how he came to vow to rescue beings in hell.

Kṣitigarbha is one of the set of eight great bodhisattvas.

Seed Syllable

The seed syllable of Kṣitigarbha is *ha*.

Siddhaṃ

ཧ

Tibetan Uchen

Lantsa

ह

Devanāgarī

Mantra

Siddhaṃ

ཨོཾ་ཀྵི་ཏི་ག་རྦྷ་བོ་དྷི་ས་ཏྭ་ཡཿ།

Tibetan – Uchen

Lantsa

ओं क्षितिगर्भ बोधिसत्त्व यः

Devanāgarī

Transliteration

oṃ kṣi ti ga rbha bo dhi sa ttva yaḥ

oṃ kṣitigarbha bodhisattva yaḥ

Notes

As noted above *kṣiti* means 'earth', though it can also mean a dwelling or habitation. *Garbha* can mean womb, but more generally it means 'interior, middle, inside'. As such it is also used to refer to an inner sanctum or sanctuary in a temple.

I'm unsure what the *yaḥ* seed syllable relates to. In Shingon his *bīja* is *ha* which is far more widely known and used.

Shingon Mantra

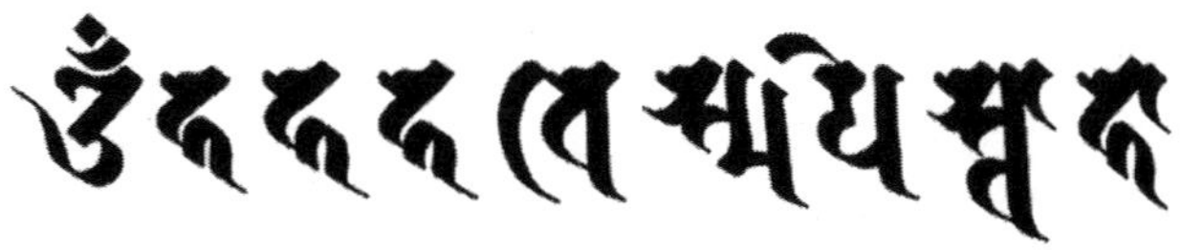

Siddhaṃ

ओं ह ह ह विस्मये स्वाहा

Devanāgarī

Transliteration

oṃ ha ha ha vi sma ye svā hā

oṃ ha ha ha vismaye svāhā

Notes

The word vismaya is a compound vi + smaya which means 'without (vi) pride or arrogance (*smaya*)', with the –*e* ending it is the dative – 'to the one without arrogance'.

Kurukullā

Tibetan: *Rikjéma*, (རིག་བྱེད་མ་).

KURUKULLĀ is possibly an Indian tribal deity who was assimilated by Buddhists. She became associated with Tārā and is sometimes called Red Tārā (T. *sgrol-ma dmar-po*). Incidently she was also adopted into the Hindu pantheon. In many ways she is similar to the *ḍakiṇī* figures such as Vajrayoginī.

Her name derives from her residence on Kurukulla Mountain in Lāṭadeśa (in present day Gujarat). In Tibetan her name is Rikjéma, which means "she who is the cause of knowledge".

Kurukullā is particularly associated with the Red Rite, the *Tantric Rite of Subjugation* or *Fascination* (*vaśikaraṇa*). The Sanskrit word *vaśi* means 'subjugation, fascination, bewitching', especially using magic to hold another to your will; and *karaṇa* 'making' is translated as 'rite'. She is red in colour, dancing on a red lotus and as Lokesh Chandra says "she beams with love in all the freshness of youth". The Red Rite on the mundane level associated with attracting lovers, and on the transcendental level relates to the 'sameness' Wisdom of Amitābha. Her seed syllable *hrīḥ* emphasises her relationship to Amitābha. There are some variations in her iconography but she is always shown with a pulled back bow and arrow, both covered in flowers. The flowery arrow will remind westerners of Cupid, the Roman equivalent of the Greek Eros, who is depicted as a cherub who goes about shooting people with arrows that make them fall in love. She also often holds an elephant goad and a noose, both of which are used to help to subjugate lovers.

Seed Syllable

Kurukullā's *bīja* mantra is *hrīḥ*

Siddhaṃ

Tibetan Uchen

Lantsa

Devanāgarī

Mantra

Siddhaṃ

ཨོཾ་ཀུ་རུ་ཀུ་ལླེ་ཧཱུཾ་ཧྲཱིཿསྭཱ་ཧཱ།

Tibetan

Lantsa

ओं कुरुकुल्ले हूं ह्रीः स्वाहा

Devanāgarī

Transliteration

oṃ ku ru ku lle hūṃ hrīḥ svā hā

oṃ kurukulle hūṃ hrīḥ svāhā

Notes

It is common to see the mantra without the *hūṃ*, that is: *oṃ kurukulla hrīḥ svāhā*, however the basic mantra is given with the *hūṃ* by Lokesh Candra's *Dictionary of Iconography*, and Stephen Beyer in *The Cult of Tārā*.

Kurukulle is the vocative singular of the name Kurukullā, meaning that she is being addressed by name.

Mahāsthāmaprāpta

Japanese: *Seishi Bosatsu* (勢至 菩薩); Tibetan: *Thuchentop* (མཐུ་ཆེན་ཐོབ་)

MAHĀSTHĀMAPRĀPTA is one of the set of thirteen Shingon deities (*Jūsanbutsu*). His name means he who has attained (*prāpta*) great (*mahā*) power (*sthāma*). In Japanese he is also called *Dai Seishi* which means 'proceeds with great power'.

He is shown here with the *añjali mudrā* but is also frequently seen with a lotus in his left hand and his right in the *viryā mudrā.* Along with Avalokiteśvara he attends on Amitābha.

He is a wisdom deity to complement Avalokiteśvara's compassion, and helps to awaken people to their Buddha-nature by illuminating the way to enlightenment. Sometimes he replaces Sarva-nīrvaṇaviṣkambhin in the group of eight great bodhisattvas. Apparently even amongst the Shingon deities he does not receive much attention

Seed Syllable

His seed syllable is *saḥ*.

Siddhaṃ

Tibetan Uchen

Lantsa

Devanāgarī

Mantra

Siddhaṃ

Tibetan – Uchen

Lantsa

ओं सं जं जं स्वाहा

Devanāgarī

Transliteration

oṃ saṃ jaṃ jaṃ saḥ svāhā

Maitreya

Japanese: *Miroku Bosatsu* (弥勒菩薩); Tibetan: *Jampa* (བྱམས་པ་)

MAITREYA WILL BE THE NEXT BUDDHA. His cult seems to have been known from very early and be common to early Buddhist schools as well as Mahāyāna. Buddhists can sometimes be heard to pray: "Come Maitreya, *come*!"

According to the *Cakkavatti Sīhanāda Sutta*, Metteyya, as he is called in Pāli, will be born, when human beings will live to an age of eighty thousand years, in the city of Ketumatī, present day Varanasi.[183] According to the *Anāgatavaṃsa Desanā*, Metteya is his family name, his personal name being Ajita (unconquered).[184] The *Mahāvaṃsa* relates that he is currently waiting in the Tuṣita heaven for his time on earth.[185] Shingon sources say this will be a period of 5,670,000,000 years after the death of Śākyamuni. After this period the Buddhadharma will have completely died out, and Maitreya will 'rediscover' it just as all previous Buddhas have done so.

Maitreya's emblem is the *stūpa*, sometimes sitting on a lotus, as in this image, and his *mudrā* is the *cakravartin* or wheel turning *mudrā* symbolising the teaching of the Dharma. He is sometimes shown as sitting in a chair western style, looking down with his hand raised and one finger resting on his cheek – contemplating the world. This is known as the Maitreya *mudrā*.

Seed Syllable

Maitreya's seed syllable is *maiṃ*. As in many cases this is the first syllable of Maitreya's name with an *anusvāra*. There are two forms for *maiṃ* in Siddhaṃ.

Siddhaṃ

Tibetan Uchen

Lantsa

Devanāgarī

Siddhaṃ alternate

[183] *Dīgha Nikāya* no.26. (PTS D.iii.75ff)

[184] *Anāgatavaṃsa Desanā* is a late Sri Lankan telling of the Metteya story – the version we have was compiled in the 14th century.

[185] Mhv.xxxii.73. The *Mahāvaṃsa* is a history of Buddhism written in Sri Lanka.

Mantra

Siddhaṃ

ཨོཾ་མཻ་ཏྲཱི་མ་ཧཱ་མཻ་ཏྲཱི་མ་ཏྲཱི་ཡེ་སྭཱ་ཧཱ།

Tibetan – Uchen

Lantsa

ओं मैत्री महामैत्री मैत्रीये स्वाहा

Devanāgarī

Transliteration

oṃ mai trī ma hā mai trī mai trī ye svā hā

oṃ maitrī mahāmaitrī maitrīye svāhā

Notes

The word *maitrī* means friendly, amicable, benevolent, affectionate. The Pāli equivalent is *mettā*. *Mahāmaitrī* is greatly friendly, and *maitrīye* is the dative form of the word and therefore means "to or for the friendly one". *Maitrī* is related to the word *mitra*. Mitra was a Vedic god (paired with Varuṇa) who oversaw the harmonious order of the universe (*ṛta*). He was concerned with order, and particular *moral* order and the word *mitra* was originally associated with a contract, or a formal bond. The IE root is *√*mei* 'to tie'. With an agentive suffix *-tṛ*; or with an instrumental suffix *–tra* (similar to *mantra,* Cf E. 'meter') mantra means 'one who ties' or 'that which ties' (i.e. a contract). This seems closer to the ancient function of the god *Mitra*, to which the sense of 'friend' came to be attributed later. The sense of 'friend' is restricted to Sanskrit and the word has few English cognates: some words related to threads, and *mitre* from a band which ties around the head (i.e. a turban).

In Shingon Maitreya has several seed-syllables, one of the most important is '*yu*' (right). Lokesh Candra suggests two possible connections: with the *yāna* of *mahāyāna* (which probably draws on the *arapacana* syllabary); and the '*yo*' of *yogacārā*. The traditional explanation relates to a mantra from the *Mahāvairocana-Abhisaṃbodhi Tantra* and says that *yu* come from √*yuj* (whence we get the word *yoga* which features in the mantra). Pilgrims on the Shikoku pilgrimage circuit known as '*Henro*' (遍路) often display '*yu*' on their robes.

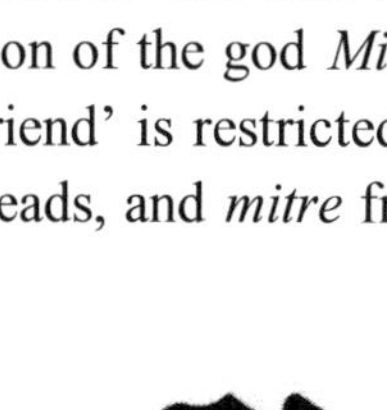

Mañjuśrī / Mañjughoṣa

Japanese: *Monju Bosatsu* (文殊菩薩); Tibetan: *Jampal* (འཇམ་དཔལ་) / *Jamyang* (འཇམ་དབྱངས་)

MAÑJUGHOṢA AND MAÑJUŚRĪ are names for the same figure, although there are sometimes slight iconographic differences between them in Buddhist art. In Sanskrit *mañju* means: 'beautiful, lovely, charming, pleasant, sweet'. *Ghoṣa* means 'voice' or 'sound'. *Śrī* has a range of meanings: 'light, lustre, radiance; prosperity, welfare, good fortune, success, auspiciousness; high rank, royalty'. So Mañjughoṣa can mean 'Beautiful Speech', and Mañjuśrī might be translated as 'Lovely Prince', or 'Beautiful Radiance', etc.

The emblems of both are the flaming sword in the right hand and the book in the left. Sometimes these are perched upon lotuses which are held in the relevant hand. Sometimes the book is held to the heart and sometimes out to the side. The book is the *Aṣṭasāhasrikā Prajñāpāramitā Sūtra* - the Perfection of Wisdom in 8000 lines.

He is sometimes known as Arapacana Mañjuśrī (in the *Mañjuśrīnāmasaṃgitī* for instance). This is a reference to his mantra which is also known as the Arapacana Mantra - see below. Another name he goes by is Vāgīśvara or Lord (*īśvara*) of Speech (*vāc*).

Seed Syllable

Mañjuśrī's seed syllable is *dhīḥ*, the seed syllable of perfect wisdom which he shares with Prajñāpāramitā.

Siddhaṃ

Tibetan Uchen

Lantsa

Devanāgarī

Mantra

Siddhaṃ

ཨོཾ་ཨ་ར་པ་ཙ་ན་དྷཱིཿ།

Tibetan – Uchen

Lantsa

ओं अ र प च न धीः

Devanāgarī

Transliteration

oṃ a ra pa ca na dhīḥ

Tibetan pronunciation is slightly different and so the Tibetan characters read:

oṃ a ra pa tsa na dhīḥ

Notes

The middle part of the mantra consists of the first five syllables of what is most likely the Gāndhārī alphabet - it is clearly not Sanskrit which has quite a different order. A short essay on the Arapacana alphabet is included in the book (see p. 34). *Dhīḥ* is strongly associated with the *prajñāpāramitā* tradition – see also the section on *dhīḥ*. One source of the alphabet is the *Pañcaviṃśatisāhasrikā Prajñāpāramitā Sūtra*:

akāro mukhaḥ sarvadharmāṇām ādyanutpannatvāt
repho mukhaḥ sarvadharmāṇāṃ rajo 'pagatatvāt
pakāro mukhaḥ sarvadharmāṇāṃ paramārthanirdeśāt
cakāro mukhaḥ sarvadharmāṇāṃ cyavanopapattyanupalabdhitvāt
nakāro mukhaḥ sarvadharmāṇāṃ nāmāpagatatvāt

a is an opening because of the primal quality of not arising of all mental phenomena.
ra is an opening because of absence of impurity of all mental phenomena
pa is an opening because it points to the highest truth about all mental phenomena

ca is an opening because of the non-perception of the causes of 'falling'[186] of any mental phenomena
na is an opening because of the absence of names of any mental phenomena

Each letter of this mystical alphabet then is associated with some point of the Dharma, and all together are referred to as the syllable-doors (*akṣāramukham*). Together they form a complex series of reflections on *śūnyatā* or the emptiness of dharmas (mental phenomena) of *svabhāva* (essence).

The first sentence in Sanskrit - *akāro mukhaḥ sarvadharmāṇāṃ ādyanutpannavāt* - went on to become a mantra in its own right in the *Hevajra Tantra* for instance (c.f. p. 35)

Vāgīśvara Mantra

Siddhaṃ

Tibetan – Uchen

Lantsa

ओं वागीश्वर मुः

Devanāgarī

Transliteration

oṃ vā gī śva ra muḥ

oṃ vāgīśvara muḥ

Notes

The epithet Vāgīśvara is also borne by Śiva, and by Indra before him in Vedic texts. *Vāc* is 'speech' in Sanskrit. In combination words *vāc* is treated as *vāk* and when followed by a vowel it becomes *vāg* (this is a *sandhi*; see glossary). In Vedic texts *Vāc* is treated as a Goddess in her

[186] 'falling' (*cyavana*) is a euphemism for dying.

own right. Vāgīśvara combines *vāc* and *īśvara* and means 'Lord of Speech'. Since it is *vāc* or speech that forms the basis of mantra, to be the Lord of Speech is to be Lord of Mantra. The fact that his mantra is the beginning of the alphabet also links Mañjuśrī to Vāc, since it was she who created the alphabet.

Sometimes instead of *muḥ* in this mantra what sees *muṃ* or even *maḥ*. Such variations are not untypical of mantras.

Prajñāpāramitā

Japanese: *hannya-haramitta* (般若波羅蜜多); Tibetan: *Sherchin* (ཤེར་ཕྱིན་མ་)

PRAJÑĀPĀRAMITĀ is a goddess of Wisdom. She is closely associated with the Perfection of Wisdom tradition, and indeed her name is usually translated as 'Perfection of Wisdom' or else as the wisdom (*prajñā*) which has crossed over (*pāramita*).[187] The Perfection of Wisdom tradition is one of the two great philosophical traditions of Mahāyana Buddhism. It is closely associated with Nāgārjuna who is said to have retrieved the texts from the *nāgas*. Prajñāpāramitā is the personification of the *prajñā*. Dharmacari Vessantara calls her "the book that became a goddess", and the tradition itself refers to her as the "Mother of all the Buddhas".

There are several forms of Prajñāpāramitā although she is always portrayed as a mature woman, with full breasts. In this four armed form her two main arms are held in the meditation mudra. The upper right arm is lightly holding a vajra, while the upper left arm holds the *Aṣṭasāhasrikā Prajñāpāramitā Sūtra* - the Perfection of Wisdom in 8000 lines.

Seed syllable

Prajñāpāramitā's seed syllable is *dhīḥ*, the seed syllable of perfect wisdom which she shares with Mañjuśrī.

Siddhaṃ

Tibetan Uchen

Lantsa

Devanāgarī

Mantra

Siddhaṃ

[187] For more on the word *pāramita* see below.

Tibetan – Uchen

Lantsa

ओं आः धीः हूं स्वाहा

Devanāgarī

Transliteration

oṃ āḥ dhīḥ hūṃ svāhā

Notes

Clearly this mantra is not translatable into English as it is composed entirely of seed syallables (taking *svāhā* as a *bīja*). To date I have not found any exegesis of this mantra, though see individual seed syllable pages later in the book.

Regarding the different translations of *pāramitā*, it derives from √*pṛ* which has two basic senses: 1. to bring over, to bring out (and therefore to deliver, rescue etc); and 2. to surpass, excel, the utmost. The underlying metaphor is reasonably clear. It is related on the one hand to crossing a river and on the other to crossing from this world to the next (in early Vedic rebirth one alternated between this world and the world of the fathers (*pitṛ*). Rivers in North India are often huge and represented natural barriers that could provide safety. *Pāramitā* is a past-participle indicating that the action of the verb has been completed i.e. crossed over, transcended etc and therefore perfected.

Salutation

The salutation *namo bhagavatyai āryaprajñāpāramitāyai* is used at the beginning of various Prajñāpāramitā sūtras, but can equally apply to the deity Prajñāpāramitā. Edward Conze sprinkles it liberally around in his published work on the texts. When used as a mantra, *oṃ* is placed at the beginning.

Siddhaṃ

ཨོཾ་ན་མོ་བྷ་ག་ཝ་ཏྱཻ་ཨཱ་རྱ་པྲ་ཛྙཱ་པཱ་ར་མི་ཏཱ་ཡཻ།

Tibetan

ओं नमो भगवत्यै आर्यप्रज्ञापारमितायै

Devanāgarī

Lantsa

Transliteration

oṃ na mo bha ga va tyai ā rya pra jñā pā ra mi tā yai

oṃ namo bhagavatyai āryaprajñāpāramitāyai

Notes

Conze translates this as "homage to the perfection of wisdom, the lovely, the holy." *Namo* (q.v. p. 203) is salutation or homage, a respectful greeting. *Bhagava* (here in the feminine and dative case) means 'fortunate, prosperous, happy; glorious, illustrious, devine, adorable, venerable'. The Buddha is most frequently addressed as *bhagavat*, and this form of address is still popular for saints in India, hence: "Bhagawan Śrī Rajneesh". *Ārya* is most often translated as 'noble', and Conze renders it as 'holy'. The dictionary also gives 'respectable, honourable'. In a Buddhist context it applies to someone who is at least a stream-entrant, i.e. someone who has achieved some measure of insight into the nature of experience.

Samantabhadra

Japanese: *Fugen bosatsu* (普賢菩薩); Tibetan: *Kuntuzangpo* (ཀུན་ཏུ་བཟང་པོ་)

SAMANTABHADRA is one of the thirteen main deities in Shingon Buddhism, though less well known in the west. In Tibet there is also a Buddha called Samantabhadra who is the *ādibuddha* for the Nyingma School. *Samanta* mean 'universal, whole, entire, all'; while *bhadra* means 'blessed, auspicious, fortunate, good, gracious, excellent, beautiful.' His name is translated as Universal Good and elaborations on this.

He is portrayed here holding a lotus in his left hand, on which is balanced a sword, and his right hand is in the *varada* or giving *mudrā*. There are many variations in his iconography, often involving a *cintāmani*. Samantabhadra is frequently depicted riding a white elephant.

He is, along with Mañjuśrī, an attendant of Śākyamuni and is thought to represent compassion. He features prominently in the *Avataṃsaka Sūtra*, especially in Chp. 56 (which circulates separately as the *Gaṇḍavyūha Sūtra*), where he makes ten vows or resolutions (*praṇidhāna*) which are frequently cited in Mahāyāna Buddhism.

Seed Syllable

The seed syllable of Samantabhadra is *aṃ*.

Siddhaṃ

Tibetan Uchen

Lantsa

Devanāgarī

Mantra

Siddhaṃ

ཨོཾ་ས་མ་ཡ་སྟྭཾ།

Tibetan Uchen

Lantsa

ओं समयस्त्वं

Devanāgarī

Transliteration

oṃ sa ma ya stvaṃ

oṃ samayas tvaṃ

Japanese pronunciation: *on sanmaya satoban*

Notes

Samaya is an agreement or contract, the nominative singular is *samayaḥ* which changes to *samayas* when followed by the *t* of *tvaṃ* meaning 'you' also nom. sg. So that part means "you are bound", or "there is an agreement or contract with you". It probably refers to the tantric vows one takes before *abhiṣeka*. The final *–s* of *samayas* coalesces with *tvaṃ* to form a single syllable: *stvaṃ*.

Tārā

Japanese: *Tara Bosatsu* (多羅菩薩); Tibetan: *drölma* (སྒྲོལ་མ་)

THE BODHISATTVA TĀRĀ was born from the tears of Avalokiteśvara as he looked down on the sorrows of the world. Her name comes from the Sanskrit word *tāra* and means: “carrying across, a saviour, protector; a star, shining”. For other names see the notes below. Tārā is usually depicted with the Tathāgata Amitābha in her head-dress.

Her right hand is in the mudra of giving, and her left hand in the mudra of fearlessness through going for refuge to the three jewels. Her left leg is tucked up in the meditation posture and her right leg is stepping down into the world. The left leg symbolises her meditation, while the right symbolises her compassionate activity in the world.

Despite the connection with the Padma family via Amitābha and Avalokiteśvara, she is also considered member of Amoghasiddhi’s *karma* or action family, as she appears as his consort or *prajñā* in yab-yum (father-mother) depictions.

Seed Syllable

The seed Syllable of the Tārā’s is *tāṃ*

Siddhaṃ

Tibetan Uchen

Lantsa

Devanāgarī

mantra

Siddhaṃ

Tibetan

Lantsa

ओं तारे तुत्तारे तुरे स्वाहा

Devanāgarī

Transliteration

oṃ tā re tu ttā re tu re svā hā

oṃ tāre tuttāre ture svāhā

Notes

Tārā is known by many names. Some of the more common and important are:

English	Sanskrit	Tibetan	
Green Tārā	*śyāma-tārā*	*drölmajangu*	སྒྲོལ་མ་ལྗང་གུ
		dröljan	སྒྲོལ་ལྗང
Noble Tārā	*ārya–tārā*	*pakma drölma*	འཕགས་མ་སྒྲོལ་མ
Exalted-Tārā		*jetsün drölma*	རྗེ་བཙུན་སྒྲོལ་མ
Tārā of the bond	*samaya-tārā*	*damtsik drölma*	དམ་ཚིག་སྒྲོལ་མ

In Tārā's mantra *tāre* is probably the feminine vocative of Tārā's name[188] and is therefore a call to her by name: "O Tārā". *Tu* can mean "to be strong, or to have authority; to make strong or efficient; to be able;" or it can mean "pray, I beg, do, now, then"; and is also sometimes used as an expletive. So *Tuttāre* could be "O Tārā be strong", or "O Strong Tārā" though it's not clear why the '*ta*' doubles. There is a Sanskrit word *tura* which means "quick, willing, prompt", and *ture* would be that word in the feminine vocative: O (she who is) quick, willing etc., which would fit the mythology of Tārā.

A traditional explanation of the mantra is that *tāre* represents deliverance from mundane suffering; while *tuttāre* represents deliverance into the spiritual path conceived in terms of individual salvation; and finally *ture* represents the culmination of the spiritual path in terms of deliverance into the altruistic path of universal salvation.

Wayman quotes an explanation from the *Kusumāñjali-guhyasamāja-nibandha-nāma* by Ratnākaraśānti (a commentary on the *Guhyasamāja Tantra*) which suggests that *tāre* is related to *tāra* 'carrying across'; *tuttāra* is related to the root √*tud* 'suffering' because she protects devotees from pain; while tura is as above 'fast' because she responds rapidly when called

[188] This assumes Classical Sanskrit case endings. For more on this see my essay *Words in mantras that end in –e* (p.64).

upon.[189] I'm doubtful about √*tud* though because it means: "to push, to strike, goad, bruise, sting", and refers to pain only in the sense that "this wound pains me" (i.e. hurts me).

[189] Wayman, A. 'The Significance of Mantras…'. p. 427-8.

Tārā - White

Tibetan: *drölma karpo* (སྒྲོལ་མ་དཀར་པོ་); or *drölkar* (སྒྲོལ་དཀར་).

WHITE TĀRĀ is also known as Sita Tārā - the Sanskrit *sita* simply means white or pure, and is also a name for the planet Venus. See also Green Tārā.

White Tārā is distinguished from Green Tārā (other than by their colours) by having both legs tucked up in the meditation posture, and by having seven eyes: the two usual ones, and then one in her forehead (the Wisdom Eye) and one in each palm and the soles of her feet.

White Tārā is associated with the Padma family of Amitābha, who in graphical representations appears in the form of Amitāyus (Infinite Life) and sits in her head-dress, or above her head.

White Tārā's devotees pray to her to extend their life span – see notes on her mantra below.

Seed Syllable

White Tārā's seed Syllable is the same as Green Tārā - *tāṃ* (see previous pages for Tārā). See also the notes on *tāṃ* on p. 195.

Siddhaṃ

Tibetan Uchen

Lantsa

Devanāgarī

mantra

Siddhaṃ

ཨོཾ་ཏཱ་རེ་ཏུ་ཏྟཱ་རེ་ཏུ་རེ་མ་མ་

ཨཱ་ཡུཿ་པུ་ཎྱ་ཛྙཱ་ན་པུ་ཥྚིཾ་ཀུ་རུ་སྭཱ་ཧཱ།

Tibetan – Uchen

Lantsa

ओं तारे तुत्तारे तुरे मम

आयुःपुण्यज्ञान पुष्टिं कुरु स्वाहा

Devanāgarī

Transliteration

oṃ tā re tu ttā re tu re ma ma ā yuḥ pu ṇya jñā na pu ṣṭiṃ ku ru svā hā

oṃ tāre tuttāre ture mama āyuḥ puṇya jñāna puṣṭiṃ kuru svāhā

Notes on the mantra

White Tārā's mantra is the basic Tārā mantra with an extra phrase inserted. The extra phrase is *mama āyuḥ-puṇya-jñāna puṣṭiṃ kuru*. *Mama*, being the genitive singular of the first person pronoun, means 'my' or 'mine'. *Pushtiṃ* means 'increase' and *kuru* is the second person imperative of the verb √*kṛ* 'to do, to make'. *Āyuḥ*, *puṇya* and *jñāna* mean life, merit and wisdom so the overall meaning is 'make my life, merit and wisdom increase'.

This mantra uses the word *āyus* 'life'. Different versions of the mantra use slightly different versions. The form ā*yuḥ* is demanded by Sanskrit sandhi rules as it is followed by the p of *puṇya*. This form is used in the Siddhaṃ above. However the *sādhana* of White Tārā as passed down from Dhardo Rinpoche, via Sangharakshita, to the Triratna Order, uses ā*yur* which is a corruption. Some schools of thought suggest that the mantra should be pronounced exactly as transmitted, and others say that if along the way the Sanskrit has been corrupted then it should be corrected and pronounced correctly. And thus lineages diverge.

The mantra is also known as 'the long life mantra' because it is used in rituals which are said to extend one's life. White Tārā is one of a trinity of long life deities with Amitāyus (see p. 106.) and Uṣṇīṣavijaya.

The mantra can be modified by replacing the 'mine' (*mama*) with the name of a person whom you wish to benefit - like transference of merit. (see below for an example of this with the honorific *bhante*).

Strictly speaking, using Wylie, the *jñāna* in the White Tārā mantra should be written *dznyāna* as *nya* is a regular Tibetan letter. I have seen the mantra written in Tibetan with *jñāna* spelt *dzñāna*.

Other forms of the mantra

The 'White Tārā' mantra is the Tārā mantra with some extra words which request long life, merit and wisdom for the practitioner. A variety of other forms of the mantra are given to request other qualities or perform particular actions. [190] I've indicated the most likely grammatical forms because they are clear in my sources, but don't worry if you don't know Sanskrit grammar just insert the word as you know it - mantras seldom stick to Classical grammar in any case.

For mantras of increase simply insert the Sanskrit word for the quality you want to increase into the mantra *oṃ tāre tuttāre ture mama* ______ *puṣṭiṃ kuru svāhā*. For example to increase life use: *oṃ tāre tuttāre ture mama āyuḥ puṣṭiṃ kuru svāhā*. Words used in this type of mantra seem to be either stem forms or nominative singular. Some examples are:

puṇya - merit
jñāna - wisdom
karuṇā - compassion
vīrya - energy, vitality, or courage.
kṣānti - forbearance, forgiveness

The mantra can also be used to pacify. In this case the template is *oṃ tāre tuttāre ture sarva* ______ *śānti kuru svāhā*. Which means make all X be pacified. To pacify bad dreams use: *oṃ tāre tuttāre ture sarva duḥsvapnān śānti kuru svāhā*. For this function use words in the accusative plural case, for example:

grahān - evil spirits
jvarān - fevers
upadravān - injuries
duḥsvapān - bad dreams
cittākulāni - confusions

Protection is also a function of the mantra, in which case the template is: *oṃ tāre tuttāre ture sarva* ______ *raksaṃ kuru svāhā*. For example for protection from diseases use: *oṃ tāre tuttāre ture sarva vyādibhyo raksaṃ kuru svāhā*. Examples are:

---

[190] see for instanc Beyer *Magic and Ritual in Tibet* p.277-8; and Mullin *Meditations on the Lower Tantras*, p.101-3

grahebhyo - evil spirits
śatrubhyo - enemies
yuddhebhyo - battles
akālamṛtyubhyo - untimely death

The *-ebhyo* is the ablative plural form of masculine nouns ending in *–a*, meaning 'from', the base form is *-ebhyaḥ* but it changes to *-ebhyo* when followed by *r*.

There are many possibilities here for asking Tārā for help and assistance. The type of request need not be limited to just these examples, and need not be limited by your knowledge of Sanskrit.

White Tārā for Bhante Sangharakshita

In the Triratna Buddhist Community we often chant the White Tārā mantra for the benefit of our founder Sangharakshita, using the familiar honorific *Bhante*.

Siddhaṃ

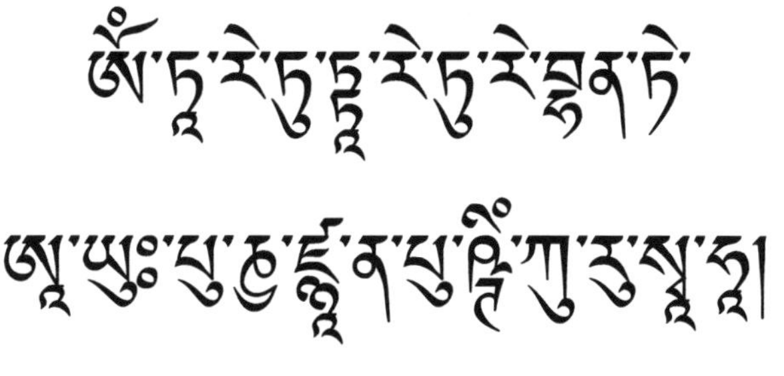

Tibetan – Uchen

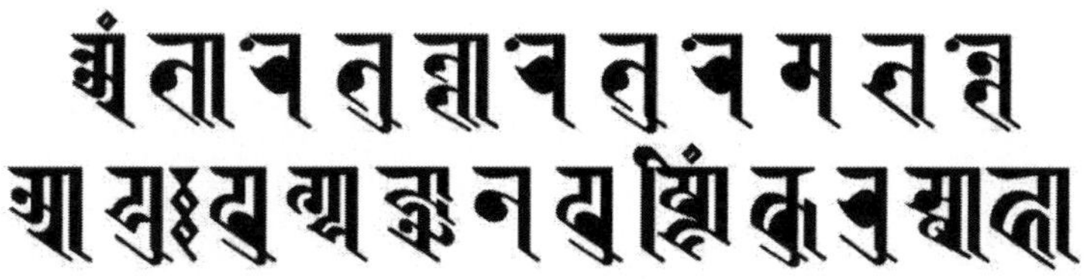

Lantsa

ओं तारे तुत्तारे तुरे भन्ते
आयुःपुण्यज्ञान पुष्टिं कुरु स्वाहा

Devanāgarī

Transliteration

oṃ tā re tu ttā re tu re bha nte ā yuḥ pu ṇya jñā na pu ṣṭiṃ ku ru svā hā

oṃ tāre tuttāre ture bhante āyuḥ puṇya jñāna puṣṭiṃ kuru svāhā

Notes

The honorific '*bhante*' is used when addressing monks, and dates from the days when Sangharakshita was a Theravādin bhikkhu. *Bhante* is a contraction probably from *bhadanta* which is a respectful form of address to a senior – junior monks call senior monks *bhante*. An English equivalent might be 'sir'. The –e ending is likely to be a Magadhism, a left over from the Magadha dialect which has a nominative in *–e* where Pāli has *–o* and Sanskrit *–aḥ*.

Vajrapāṇi

Japanese: *Kongōshu* (金剛手); Tibetan: *Chakna Dorje* (ཕྱག་ན་རྡོ་རྗེ་)

VAJRAPĀṆI IS A BODHISATTVA who appears in a primative form in the Pāli *Ambaṭṭha Sutta* (DN 3) as the *yakkha* (Sanskrit *yakṣa*) Vajirapāni, a kind of daemonic or chthonic spirit. His name means "Thunderbolt in Hand". In the Vajrayāna he becomes a central figure, where he frequently also goes by the name Guhyapati (Lord of Secrets). In the Tantric texts he is often seen in dialogue with the *Dharmakāya* Buddha Mahāvairocana.

The form depicted here is his peaceful manifestation, sitting in the 'royal ease' posture and balancing the vajra in the palm of his hand. Vajrapāṇi is deep blue in colour. He also has a wrathful form - his body swollen with the energy of liberation is surrounded by a wreath of flames; he roars (*rava*) his *bīja* mantra *hūṃ* and draws his hand back to hurl the vajra at you in order to break through your obscurations. He is frequently depicted trampling on the Hindu god Śiva whom he defeats in a contest of magic in the *Sarvatathāgata-tattvasaṃgraha Tantra*, first killing him and then reviving him with mantras, thus converting him to Buddhism.

Vajrapāṇi belongs to the *Vajra* Family which is headed by Akṣobhya. In Japan he is also known as Vajrarakṣa.

Seed Syllable

The seed syllable *hūṃ* is shared by a number of Buddhas and Bodhisattvas, especially those associated with the *Vajra* family of which Vajrasattva is the epitome.

Siddhaṃ

Tibetan Uchen

Lantsa

Devanāgarī

Mantra

Siddhaṃ

ཨོཾ་བཛྲ་པཱ་ཎི་ཧཱུྃ།

Tibetan – Uchen

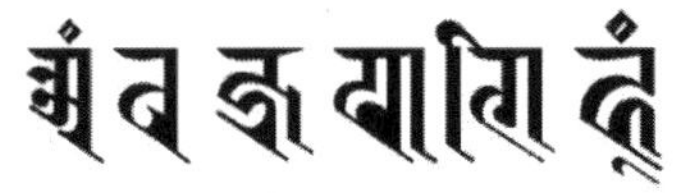

Lantsa

ओं वज्रपाणि हूं

Devanāgarī

Transliteration

oṃ va jra pā ṇi hūṃ

oṃ vajrapāṇi hūṃ

Notes

The Tibetan pronunciation of Vajrapāṇi's name is *ba dzra pā ṇi*, and the Tibetan version of the mantra reflects this.

Vajrayoginī Ḍākiṇī

Tibetan: *Dorje Naljorma* (རྡོ་རྗེ་རྣལ་འབྱོར་མ་)

VAJRAYOGINĪ is a tantric deity with no counterpart in Mahāyana Buddhism. She is a *ḍākiṇī*. The Tibetan translation *khandroma* (*mkha' 'gro ma*) means 'sky dancer'. The Sanskrit may derive via Prakrit from √*śak* 'able, powerful' (with ś > ḍ). Figuratively the *ḍākiṇī* is a wild spirit who dances ecstatically in the clear blue sky of *śūnyatā*. She is usually depicted as blood red in colour, naked except for elaborate ornaments of human bone, and a necklace of skulls, corresponding to the sixteen vowels and thirty-four consonants of the Sanskrit alphabet, and symbolising the purification of speech. In her right hand she holds a flaying knife with a vajra handle - a vajra-chopper - which she uses to cut off attachments. In her left hand is a skull cup filled with *mahāsukha* (the great bliss) which she pours out like wine to her devotees. In the crook of her left arm she cradles a *khaṭvāṅga* or magic staff. Her iconography is rich and multifaceted, and draws on Śaiva Tantra imagery.[191]

Practices and mantras associated with Vajrayoginī are often considered secret - although the mantras are now widely published. Many traditional practitioners are uncomfortable with this breaking of the traditional secrecy around these practices.

Short Mantra

Siddhaṃ

Tibetan - Uchen

Lantsa

[191] The history of Vajrayoginī and her iconography is explored in English (2000).

ओं वज्रयोगिनी हूं फट् स्वाहा

Devanāgarī

Transliteration

oṃ va jra yo gi nī hūṃ pha ṭ svā hā

oṃ vajrayoginī hūṃ phaṭ svāhā

Tibetan Transliteration

oṃ ba zra yo gi nī hūṃ pha ṭa svā hā

Long Mantra

This mantra is one that I have received several inquiries about, questioning the wisdom of making it available. I am sympathetic to these concerns. This mantra is from the *Anuttara Yoga Tantra* - the most esoteric and generally speaking most secret level of Tibetan Buddhism. While the lower (or outer) Tantras are often treated as open and accessible to the public, many people consider this mantra to be "secret". It is something of an open secret however as there are several books which reveal it, and many internet sites. Andy Weber, a very well known Western practitioner of Tibetan artistic traditions, has made the mantra into a postcard![192]

In the Triratna Buddhist Order we do not necessarily approach mantra on the terms of Tibetan Tantric Buddhism. From the traditional point of view this mantra should be used under the guidance of a qualified teacher. Especially if you are involved in a Tibetan Tradition you should consult your Buddhist teacher if you want to use this mantra in your practice. Vajrayoginī practices require specific initiations and carry samaya vows.

Siddhaṃ

[192] http://www.andyweberstudios.com [viewed 3.11.10]

ཨོཾ་ཨོཾ་ཨོཾ་ས་རྦ་བུ་དྡྷ་ཌཱ་ཀི་ཎཱི་ཡེ་བཛྲ་བརྞ་ནཱི་ཡེ་

བཛྲ་བཻ་རོ་ཙ་ནཱི་ཡེ་ཧཱུྃ་ཧཱུྃ་ཧཱུྃ་ཕཊ་ཕཊ་ཕཊ་སྭཱ་ཧཱ།

Tibetan

Lantsa

ओं ओं ओं सर्वबुद्धडकिणीये वज्रवर्णनीये

वज्रवैरोचनीये हुं हुं हुं फट् फट् फट् स्वाहा

Devanāgarī

Transliteration

oṃ oṃ oṃ sa rva bu ddha ḍa ki ṇī ye va jra va rṇa nī ye

va jra vai ro ca nī ye hūṃ hūṃ hūṃ pha ṭ pha ṭ pha ṭ svā hā

oṃ oṃ oṃ sarvabuddhaḍākiṇīye vajra varṇanīye

vajra vairocanīye hūṃ hūṃ hūṃ phaṭ phaṭ phaṭ svāhā

Mantras of Historical Figures and Teachers of the Past

The follow mantras and chants are associated with people who actually lived. We know varying amounts about these people. Ānanda features prominently in Buddhist texts, but there is no physical evidence for him. Padmasambhava and Kūkai were near contemporaries but we have only legend and hagiography for the former, whereas for the latter we have actual letters he wrote and other samples of his handwriting. Kūkai is a more substantially historical figure though there are things about his story that remain unclear. Dr Ambedkar is the only recent figure and I include him because he is so very important to new Buddhists in India, especially to my colleagues in the Triratna Order. Indeed Dr Ambedkar's story is one that can inspire anyone.

Dr. B.R. Ambedkar
Ānanda
Kūkai / Kōbōdaishi
Milarepa
Padmasambhava

Dr. Bhimrao Ramji Ambedkar
डॉक्टर् भीम्रव राम्जी आंबेढकर

डॉक्टर् 'बबसहेब'
भीम्रव राम्जी आंबेढकर

Dr. B. R. Ambedkar (1891 - 1956) was the revered leader of Dalits[193] in India, and also inspires many Western Buddhists. Against heavy odds he became educated and worked for the benefit of his people. Dr. Ambedkar was India's first Law Minister, and fought hard to outlaw caste prejudice in India. In this he was opposed by Gandhi who saw caste as important to Indian culture.

Ambedkar had grown up in an untouchable caste and decided that in order to escape the oppression of caste he would need to leave Hinduism behind. After considering his options he converted to Buddhism. Millions of his followers also converted in mass conversion ceremonies.

Though untouchability was outlawed, in practice it is still a great social problem in parts of India and Dr Ambedkar's people face daily prejudice and hardship as a result – despite concessions such as quotas for government jobs.

Dr. Ambedkar is also known affectionately as Babasaheb.

Jai Bhim

Indian Buddhists greet each other with Jai Bhim! This means "victory to Bhim", ie victory to Dr. Ambedkar. Here are three ways of writing Jai Bhim.

Hindi

जै भीम

jai bhīm

Sanskrit

जय भीम

Devanāgarī

Siddhaṃ

In Hindi the word for 'victory' can be written *jai* (pronounced to rhyme with the English 'may'), whereas in Sanskrit the word is *jaya*. Hindi obviously comes from the root of Sanskrit

[193] Dalit means 'oppressed' and refers to various down-trodden groups in India, including people from castes (*jati*) whose mere touch was considered to be ritually polluting necessitating purification rituals involving cow excrement.

but the pronunciation has changed, especially at the ends of words. In Hindi the *virāma* on the *m* is not always added since it is routinely pronounced. I have added it in the Siddhaṃ.

Chants

Below are some chants which you will hear in India from followers of Dr. Ambedkar. They are in the Hindi style of Devanāgarī which differs in some minor respects from Sanskrit.

ढॉक्टर् भीम्रव् राम्जी आंबेढकरांचा विजय असो

ḍaoktar bhīmrav rāmjī āṃbeḍkarāṃcā vijaya aso

Dr. B. R. Ambedkar... may he succeed!

ढॉक्टर् भीम्रॉ राम्जी आंबेढ्करं ज़िंडाबाड्

ḍaoktar bhīmrao rāmjī āṃbeḍkaraṃ ziṃdābād

Long live Dr. B. R. Ambedkar

Notes

The standard Romanisation of Dr. Ambedkar's name hides a lot from the uninitiated, and it took quite a bit of consultation with an Indian friend to find the correct spelling in Devanāgarī. A more accurate transliteration of the Devanāgarī would be: *ḍaokṭar bhīmrao rāmjī āṃbeḍkar.* Hindi (and Marathi) speakers tend to pronounce (and transliterate) *rava* (as in *bhīmrava*) as *rao* – they drop the final vowel and the /v/ sound more like English /w/. The Hindi use of Devanāgarī also has the possibility of the *ao* vowel so can write is rao रॉ.

The word *ziṃdābād* apparently comes from a Hindi/Urdu adaptation of the Russian slogan "long live the revolution", ie *inquilab zindabad*, so might be translated as *viva*! The *za* sound is indicated by a dot under the letter *ja.*

Kūkai (空 海) aka Kōbōdaishi (弘法大師)

KŪKAI, ALSO KNOWN AS KŌBŌDAISHI, was a tantric master who established the *Vajrayāna* teachings in Japan in the early 9th century. He travelled to China in 804 and returned with many new texts, including early tantras, in 806.

Because of the necessity to preserve the correct pronunciation of the mantras they were often not translated or transliterated, but preserved in the Siddhaṃ script, and so along with the tantra itself, Kūkai introduced the study of Sanskrit and Siddhaṃ into the Shingon syllabus. This in turn had a direct influence on the development of the Japanese Kana scripts.

Kūkai combines two elements. Firstly *Kū*, which in Sanskrit is *ākāśa* and means space, or emptiness (in the sense of *Śūnyatā*). Kūkai had a strong association with the Bodhisattva Ākāśagarbha, known in Japanese as Kokūzo. The second element is *Kai* which means 'sea' and perhaps relates to the story recounted by Oliver Statler that Kūkai attained enlightenment on the southern coast of Shikoku Island.[194]

Kōbōdaishi is a title posthumously awarded in the year 921, after the preist Kangen (観覧) lobbied Emperor Daigo (醍醐天皇). *Kōbō* means 'to spread the Dharma' while *daishi* means 'great teacher'. Kūkai is also known simply as The Daishi or affectionately in Shingon circles as Odaishisama. O- and –sama are the most respectful general honorifics.

Mantra or Hōgō 保譽

Kūkai also has a mantra of his own (see below) which is chanted by Shingon practioners. In Japanese this is known as a hōgō (保 譽)

Transliteration

na mu dai shi hen jō kon gō

namu daishi henjō kongō

南 無 大 師 遍 照 金 剛

[194] Statler *Japanese Pilgrimage* p.68.

Notes

This mantra is Japanese rather than Sanskrit, but Siddham can be used to write Japanese with some modifications (I discuss some of these below). In the Shingon school of modern times the 'Daishi mantra' is very important as he is treated as a Bodhisattva figure to whom one can appeal, as Tibetans do to Avalokiteśvara, with the hope of rebirth in Amitābha's pure land.

Hōgō means "treasure name". It is also applied to the Nembutsu (see Kūkai calligraphy below), which is a mantra associated with Amitābha. The modern Hōgō was in common use during the Muromachi era (ca 1336 - 1573), but seems to have been created in the mid Kamakura Era by Dōhan (道範, 1178-1252) of the monastery Shōchi-in. It appears in Dōhan's work Himtsu nenbutsu shō (秘密念仏抄).[195]

Namu is the Japanese pronunciation of the Sanskrit *namo* and means 'homage'. *Daishi* means "great teacher". And *henjō kongō* is Kūkai's tantric name: "Vairocana Vajra" in Sanskrit, and means something like "Illuminating Reality", or "Illuminating Diamond/Thunderbolt" in English.

Siddhaṃ lacks a character for the Japanese long *ō* sound.[196] So what I have done is invent a way of indicating it. There are two ways of writing ā, one using the right-hand vertical curve at the top right of the character, and one which uses the horizontal curve at the bottom of the character. So I indicate *ō* by adding the latter to the diacritics for *o*. This is similar also to how Tibetan adds a marker for long vowles at the bottom of letters (see right).

I've written the mantra *he n jō* rather than conjuncts *he njō* here for aesthetic reasons – the *njō* character would be a bit unwieldy. In any case in Japanese the syllables are hen jō.

[195] See SHINJO Hinonishi; LONDO William (trans.) 'The Hōgō (treasure name) of Kōbō Daishi and the development of beliefs associated with it,' *Japanese religions*. 2002, vol. 27, no1, pp. 5-18

[196] Actually Sanskrit *o* is a long monophthong *ō* and the short *ŏ* which existed in Proto-Indo-European has been assimilated to the vowel *a*. It is not marked as long because there is no confusion with the diphthong *au*. Japanese does distinguish between o and ō so two signs are needed.

Kūkai's Calligraphy

Kūkai was honoured as one of the three great calligraphers of his age. On the right is a fine example of Chinese brush style calligraphy by Kūkai. The mantra is *namo amitabaḥ* which is the mantra Amitābha. It includes on the left Kūkai's signature and below it his seal.

Syllabary

On the facing page is calligraphy of the alphabet is by Kūkai. It begins with the words '*siddhaṃ rastu*' which are Sanskrit for: 'may there be perfection!'[197] In Gupta era India (ca. 3rd to 6th centuries CE) this was traditionally written at the head of every text, and the script associated with the Gupta's became known as Siddhaṃ as a result.

The syllables as written are:

si	ddhāṃ	ra	stu	
a	ā	i	ī	
u	ū	e	ai	
o	au	aṃ	aḥ	
ṛ	ṝ	ḷ	ḹ	
ka	kha	ga	gha	ṅa
ca	cha	ja	jha	ña
ṭa	ṭha	ḍa	ḍha	ṇa
ta	tha	da	dha	na
pa	pha	ba	bha	ma
ya	ra	la	va	śa
ṣa	sa	ha	llaṃ	kṣa

Notes

The brush style *u* and *ū* are a bit different to the modern pen style, as is the character for *la*. Kūkai has used an alternative form of the *tha* syllable. Kūkai has made a good distinction between *ba* and *va*. These two characters are frequently mixed up as they are so similar, especially in brush style calligraphy, but they need not be as this shows! Kūkai has included all of the vowels (*ṝ ḷ ḹ*) which are often left out because they so seldom occur in mantras; and an extra conjunct consonant (*llaṃ*).

[197] The Sanskrit should be *siddhir astu*, but this clearly became corrupted early on. See also *Beginning and End Markers*, p.245ff.

The images of Kūkai's calligraphy are originally from a collection reproduced in five large concertina fascicles by the Japanese monk Sō-gen in 1837 under the title of *Ashara-jō*.[198] Sō-gen traced fine examples of Siddhaṃ calligraphy and then inked in the middle, thereby creating reasonably accurate facsimiles. The original of the mantra calligraphy was 74cm high (and therefore done with quite a large brush), while the syllabary was 90cm. The *Ashara-jō* was republished as *Sanskrit bījas and mantras in Japan* edited by Raghu Vira and Lokesh Chandra (New Delhi: International Academy of Indian Culture, 1965). These images were also reproduced in R.H. Van Gulik. *Siddham: An Essay on the History of Sanskrit Studies in China and Japan* (New Delhi, Jayyed Press, 1981).

[198] *Ashara-jō* is out of copyright restrictions.

Milarepa

Tibetan: milaraspa (མི་ལ་རས་པ་)

MILAREPA LIVED IN TIBET in the 11th century. As a young man he used black magic to take revenge on his wicked uncle. Appalled by the results of the magic he seeks advice, and he is told to seek out Marpa who will teach him the Dharma. Marpa puts Milarepa through a series of trials, and then gives him the abhiṣeka. Milarepa's two main disciples were Rechungpa and Gampopa. One of Gampopa's disciples became the first Karmapa, and founded the Kargyu lineage which is one of the four major lineages of Tibetan Buddhism.

One of the classic poses in which Milarepa is depicted shows him cupping his right hand to his ear. Vessantara suggests that he appears to be listening to an inner voice of the Dharma, but that some authorities say that it is a yogic posture designed to affect the body's subtle energies. Milarepa is often coloured light green, due it is said, to his diet of nettle soup during his long period of solitary meditation.

Mantra

Tibetan (Uchen)

Siddhaṃ

Lantsa

ओं आः गुरु हसवज्र सर्वसिद्धि हूं

Devanāgarī

Transliteration

oṃ āḥ gu ru ha sa va jra sa rva si ddhi hūṃ

oṃ āḥ guru hasavajra sarvasiddhi hūṃ

Notes

Guru is of course 'teacher'. The word *hasa* means 'laughing' – Milarepa being sometimes known as the Laughing Vajra (T. *bzhad pa rdo rje* pronounced '*zhepa dorje*'). *Sarvasiddhi* means 'all accomplished', or 'all accomplishing'. There are some variations on this mantra.

oṃ āḥ guru hasavajra hūṃ

Used for instance in the Shambala Milarepa Day celebrations.

oṃ āḥ guru hasavajra sarvasiddhi phala hūṃ -

Phala means 'fruit' or 'result' and in this context is a synonym for *siddhi.* It is recommended by Lama Yeshe for benefiting animals.

My sketch of Milarepa draws on traditional iconography, but also a drawing in Eva Van Dam, *The Magic Life of Milarepa*, published by Shambhala.

Padmasambhava

Tibetan: *Pema-jungné* (པདྨ་འབྱུང་གནས་)

Padmasambhava was probably an historical character, but has been elevated to the Bodhisattva pantheon.

Padmasambhava has many different forms. In this image he is portrayed as a *siddha*, but wears a *bhikṣu's* robe, a *pandit's* hat, and the implements of a *siddha*. In his right hand he brandishes a vajra held in the warding-off evil mudra; while in his left hand he cradles a skull cup filled with *amṛta* - the ambrosia of the gods which gives immortality. In the crook of his left elbow is his *khaṭvāṅga* or magical staff which is a flaming trident decorated with severed heads in various stages of decay.[199]

Padmasambhava played a crucial role in establishing Buddhism in Tibet where he is revered as a second Buddha particularly by the Nyingma School. He used his magical powers to subdue the demons of Tibet in order to allow Buddhism to take root there. In Tibet he is referred to as Guru Rinpoche (Precious Teacher), or the Vajra Guru. His mantra is also known as the *Vajra Guru* mantra.

guru rinpoche in Tibetan Uchen

Mantra

Siddhaṃ

Tibetan – Uchen

[199] The trident staff is part of the distinctive equipment of the Śaiva ascetic in present day India.

Lantsa

ओं आः हूं वज्रगुरु पद्म सिद्धि हूं

Devanāgarī

Transliteration

oṃ āḥ hūṃ va jra gu ru pa dma si ddhi hūṃ

oṃ āḥ hūṃ vajraguru padma siddhi hūṃ

Notes

A traditional commentary on the Vajra Guru Mantra shows that each syllable or word has many esoteric associations. For instance *oṃ, āḥ* and *hūṃ* represent the "supreme essence" of Body, Speech, and Mind (what would be called the Three Mysteries in Shingon, I think). While *vajra, guru, padma, siddhi* and *hūṃ* represent the supreme essence of the five Buddha families, diamond, jewel, lotus, action, and Buddha respectively. A different explanation is given for each of the eight main manifestations of Padmasambhava.[200]

The Skull Garland Mantra

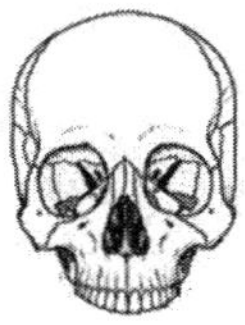

༄ ཨོཾ་ཨཱཿཧཱུྃ་བཛྲ་གུ་རུ་པདྨ་ཐོད་ཕྲེང་རྩལ་

བཛྲ་ས་མ་ཡ་ཛཿསིདྡྷི་ཕཱ་ལ་ཧཱུྃ་ཨཱཿ།

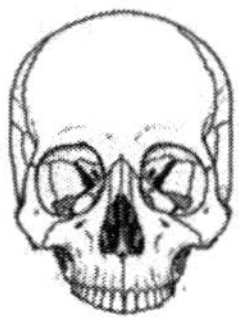

oṃ āḥ hūṃ badzra gu ru padma thod phreng rtsal

badzra sa ma ya jāḥ siddhi phā la hūṃ āḥ.

Notes

The Tibetan words *thod phreng rtsal*, pronounced *thöthrengtsal*, translate the Sanskrit *kapālamālā* meaning 'garland of skulls'. *Vajrasamaya* means adamantine (*vajra*) bond or pledge (*samaya*), or possibly 'whose bond is unbreakable', while *siddhiphāla* means 'the fruit of perfection' or 'whose fruit is perfection'. Tibetans often substitute *pema* for *padma*

[200] *Crystal Mirror* Vol.2, p.17-38.

when chanting the mantra, and this is the way it is usually pronounced by Triratna Buddhists.

The Seven Line Invocation

This popular prayer is chanted by Padmasabhava devotees. Slight variations of spelling and writing occur but this one seems to be fairly common and has been checked by a Tibetan speaker.

༄༅། ཧཱུྃ༔

ཨོ་རྒྱན་ཡུལ་གྱི་ནུབ་བྱང་མཚམས༔

པདྨ་གེ་སར་སྡོང་པོ་ལ༔

ཡ་མཚན་མཆོག་གི་དངོས་གྲུབ་བརྙེས༔

པདྨ་འབྱུང་གནས་ཞེས་སུ་གྲགས༔

འཁོར་དུ་མཁའ་འགྲོ་མང་པོས་བསྐོར༔

ཁྱེད་ཀྱི་རྗེས་སུ་བདག་བསྒྲུབ་ཀྱི༔

བྱིན་གྱིས་བརླབ་ཕྱིར་གཤེགས་སུ་གསོལ༔

གུ་རུ་པདྨ་སིདྡྷི་ཧཱུྃ༔

Transliteration	*Pronunciation*
hūṃ |	hūṃ
o rgyan yul gyi nub byang mtshams |	orgyen yul gyi nub chang tsam
padma ge sar sdong po la |	padma kesar dongpö la
ya mtshan mchog gi dngos grub brnyes |	yathsen chok gi ngö drup nye
padma 'byung gnas zhes su grags |	padma jungne shesu drak
'khor du mkha' 'gro mang pos bskor |	khor do khandro mangpö kor
khyed kyi rjes su bdag bsgrub kyi |	khye kyi je su dak drup kyi
byin gyis brlab phyir gshegs su gsol |	chin gyi lap chir shek su sol
gu ru padma siddhi hūṃ |	guru padma siddhi hūṃ

Translation

hūṃ
To the North-west of the land of Urgyen,
On the calyx of a lotus flower,
O wondrous, the highest siddhi has been attained!
Thus Padmasambhava declares
O thou who art encircled with an entourage of *ḍākinīs*
Following thy example will I work
Thou must come here to give me thy blessing
guru padma siddhi hūṃ.[201]

[201] Translation by Urgyen Sanghrakshita according to the oral explanation of Dhardo Rinpoche.

Bīja mantras – Seed Syllables

THE RELATIONSHIP between a mantra or deity and their seed-syllable (*bījākṣāra*) is often a mystery. For some it is simply the first syllable of their name with an added *anusvāra* (nasalisation) or *visarga* (aspiration), with the latter is more common in early Tantra and the Far East; the former in later Tantra and Tibet. Others are an identifiable word which has a clear association, like the syllable *dhīḥ* which means 'wisdom'. Others don't seem to have any logical connection – *hūṃ* is not a word and is the *bīja* for many different deities. Sometimes the *bīja* will occur in the mantra, but sometimes not: e.g. Avalokiteśvara whose mantra is *oṃ maṇipadme hūṃ*, but whose *bīja* is *hrīḥ*.

All we can say is that at some point in time, for whatever reason, that syllable seemed to sum up something about the deity for someone. In all likelihood the source was a vision or mystical experience rather than a cool logical process, though I must say that working out the associations can be a stimulating and far from cool activity for me.

The following pages not only show more variations on the form of the *bīja* than is presented with on the deity pages, but also contain my notes on each *bīja*. Some of these notes are purely conjectural – I prefer to put forward some theory then remain completely silent. I endeavour to mark my own thoughts as distinct from the traditional explanations.

The Seed Syllable *a*

THE LETTER 'A' is the first letter of the Indic alphabets. It is the short 'a' sound that we find in the English word 'but', written 'ə' in the phonetic alphabet. The syllable *a* is said to represent the perfection of wisdom (see p.180f.). The esoteric meaning of 'a' is *anutpāda* or "unarisen". This is a reminder that because all things arise in dependence on causes that nothing is permanent, and that nothing has any essential characteristic outside of those causes.

As a *bīja*, 'a' is seed syllable of Vairocana in the *Garbhadhatu Maṇḍala*, and more generally of Mahāvairocana as the *Dharmakāya* Buddha. Meditation on the syllable 'a' is a central practice in Shingon Buddhism.

Siddhaṃ Tibetan (Uchen) Devanāgarī Lantsa

Comparing the Tibetan Uchen 'a' with the Siddhaṃ one can see that they contain the same graphic elements with minor differences. This is because they both derive from the same earlier script, which was related to the Brāhmī script which was one of the scripts used by King Aśoka to write his famous pillars. The diagram below shows how the Siddhaṃ and Uchen scripts are related by using hypothetical intermediates to demonstrate that they contain the same graphic elements.

Uchen and the other Tibetan scripts are also related to the Lantsa or Ranjana script which Tibetans still use to write Sanskrit sometimes. Robert Beer, the well known artist, has created a decorative 'a' which is for sale as a postcard on this website.

You can read about the meditation on the syllable 'a' on James Deacon's *Reiki Website*,[202] and also in the book *Shingon: Japanese Esoteric Buddhism*, by Taiko Yamasaki, which is available from the Shingon Buddhist International Institute.

In the *Mahāvairocana Abhisaṃbodhi Tantra* the four basic variations on the letter *a* (i.e. *a ā aṃ aḥ*) occur in the 'Four Syllable Mantra': *namaḥ sarvatathāgatebhyo viśvamukhebhyaḥ sarvathā a ā aṃ aḥ.*[203] In another section of the text the four seed-syllables are linked to the four stages of practice: *bodhi* (i.e. *bodhicitta*), *carya*, *saṃbodhi*, *nirvāṇa.*[204] Adrian Snodgrass notes that a Shingon commentary also links these four to the four Buddhas of the *Garbhadhātu Maṇḍala.*[205]

---

[202] http://www.geocities.com/fascin8or/jsp_ajikan.htm [viewed 7.10.2008]
[203] Stephen Hodge. *The Mahāvairocana Abhisaṃbodhi Tantra* (VI.19, p.173)
[204] Stephen Hodge. *The Mahāvairocana Abhisaṃbodhi Tantra* (IV.15, p.162)
[205] Snodgrass, vol.2, p.748-9.

Letter	Direction	Buddha Name		Stage
		Sanskrit	*Japanese*	
a	E	Ratnaketu	Hōdō	*bodhi*
ā	S	Saṃkusumita Rāja	Kaifuke-ō	*carya*
aṃ	W	Amitāyus	Amida	*saṃbodhi*
aḥ	N	Divyadundubhi-mehganirghoṣa	tenkuraion	*nirvāṇa*
āṃḥ	Centre	Mahāvairocana	Dainichi	

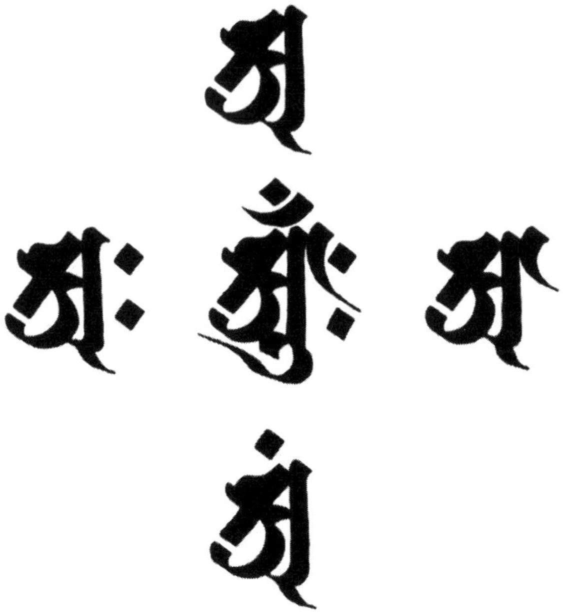

Note that East is oriented up in maṇḍalas. This arrangement takes into account the esoteric symbolism of *anusvāra and visarga* (see p. 31f.). So we could see the four syllables are representing

a the initial insight (*bodhi*), *bodhicitta* as aspiration to *bodhi*,

ā that insight drawn out by practice (*carya*),

aṃ *carya* resulting in a direct experience of *śūnyatā* (represented by the *anusvāra* or 'void point'),

aḥ Direct experience of śūnyatā resulting in liberation *nirvāṇa* (represented by the visarga or '*nirvāṇa* points).

The four syllables can all be combined into one syllable, *āṃḥ*, which represents the culmination of the Spiritual path, and Mahāvairocana at the centre of the maṇḍala. The Shingon perspective is that the *maṇḍala*, and indeed all forms, sounds, and thoughts, emanate from Mahāvairocana, and that, by the same token, forms etc. are the body, speech and mind of Mahāvairocana. As Kūkai says the created is the creator, and the creator is the created. Note that the actual form of *āṃḥ* incorporates both of the alternate ways of representing *ā* (see *āḥ*, p. 184). In linguistic terms no syllable can have both *anusvāra* and *visarga* (see p. 31f.), but that fact helps to make this a distinctive symbol.

The Essence of All Mantras

The syllable 'a' is the *sine qua non* of Tantric Buddhist. Not only is it the quintessence of the perfection of wisdom, but it is also called the Essence or the Mother of all Mantras.[206] There is a *sūtra*, which only survives in Tibetan translation called the *Perfection of Wisdom in a Single Letter*, and that letter is 'a'.

One explanation is that the letter *a*, when added to the beginning of most Sanskrit nouns and adjectives, it turns them into their opposite: *vidyā* is knowledge, while *avidyā*, is ignorance. This allows us to use the letter 'a' to stand for the Truth which cannot be fully comprehended by language: it is possible to negate any definite statement about the transcendental (including this one!). However I don't think this alone accounts for the notion that the letter a is the source of all mantras, if only because the *a-* prefix for verbs usually indicates the imperfect past-tense rather than any sense of negation.

Another idea relates to the way that Indic alphabets attach an inherent short letter *a* to each consonant. Thus the Sanskrit consonants are written as syllables or phonemes - called *akṣāra* - (e.g. *ka kha ga gha ṅa*); not, as in the English alphabet, simply letters (e.g. k kh g gh ṅ). Once again there is a flaw in this suggestion. The vowels, except for *ā*, *aṃ* and *aḥ*, can't really be considered to derive from the letter *a*. All vowels are similar in that they are voiced similarly - differences in sound are due to shifts in the tongue and lips changing the resonant frequency of the vocal track, but it doesn't seem to be enough to consider, say, the letter *ī* to derive from the letter *a*. Graphically the vowels are mostly not related to the shape of the letter a either. This is all true of the Brāhmī derived scripts. In Devanāgarī the sixteen vowels are:

अ आ इ ई उ ऊ ऋ ॠ ऌ ॡ ए ऐ ओ औ अं अः.

The Brāhmī or Siddhaṃ vowels are no more similar to each other than these. However there is one ancient Indian script which does not derive from Brāhmī and which has some interesting features. The Kharoṣṭhī is associated with the area known as Gandhāra which covered present day north-east Afghanistan and north-west Pakistan (roughly the area presently controlled by the Taliban!). We now know, thanks to research by Professor Richard Salomon, that the Arapacana alphabet (see also p.34f.) is simply the alphabet of Gāndhārī, the language of Gandhāra. We can also be reasonably sure that Kharoṣṭhī is based on the Aramaic script used by the Persian administrators of the region during the Buddha's lifetime (known as the Achaemanids).[207]

As well as retaining some of the letters (with the same phonetic value) of Aramaic, Kharoṣṭhī retains several features from Aramaic: it is written right to left for instance. One important feature is the lack of signs for initial vowels. Aramaic being based on Semitic languages which do not begin words with vowels, did not need separate signs for vowels and indicated them using modifications of consonant signs. When designing a script to write Indic languages one needs to be able to write initial vowels, for instance: *evam mayā śrutaṃ* (Thus have I heard which begins all Buddhist sūtras). Brāhmī scripts use a different sign for each vowel (although long vowels are indicated with diacritics marks in most cases).

[206] See for instance: Stephen Hodge. *The Mahāvairocana Abhisaṃbodhi Tantra* (XVIII.3, p.326-7)

[207] The Achaemanids ruled Gandhāra ca. 558-380 BCE. There is other evidence of Persian influences on India and on Buddhism, for which see http://jayarava.blogspot.com/2008/06/persian-influences-on-indian-buddhism.html

Kharoṣṭhī created a single vowel sign on the model of the consonant signs - it is simply 'a' if unadorned, but can become any vowel with diacritic marks (See right).

Kharoṣṭhī vowels
a e i o u

My suggestion is that the special function of the letter *a* in Buddhism is a relic of the Gandhāra area. It is only in Kharoṣṭhī that all signs for letters derive from, or contain, the short *a*.

One piece of supporting evidence comes from the Sūtra of Perfect Wisdom in 25,000 Lines. This sutra was probably composed in the 2nd or 3rd century, and is preserved in a variety of Sanskrit originals, as well as in Tibetan and Chinese translations. In the sūtra the alphabet is used as a mnemonic for a series of reflections on the nature of phenomena. Each letter is indicated by a keyword starting with that letter; and each word is the basis for a line of verse. Being a Sanskrit text one might expect the Sanskrit alphabet to be used, but it is not. The alphabet is a partially Sanskritised version of the Arapacana alphabet. Even in the fully Sanskritised version of this practice - present for example in the *Mahāvairocana Abhisaṃbodhi Tantra* - the vowels are sometimes left off so we have the Sanskrit consonants, but the syllable *a* as the only vowel.[208] In the next layer of tantra – represented by the *Sarvatathāgata-Tattvasaṃgraha Tantra* the whole thing is boiled down to just the letter a. The tradition is preserved and the trail seems to lead back to Gandhāra, at least on Indian soil.

I say "on Indian soil" because the use of alphabetical verses, that is to say verses in which the first letter of the first word of each line are in alphabetical order (a kind of acrostic) is unknown in pre-Buddhist India. Verses were organised by length, and by numerical schemes, but not alphabetically. Verses were arranged alphabetically in Semitic cultures, so there are Old Testament psalms and Manichean hymns with verses in alphabetical order. This brings us around in a circle to the Semitic origins of Kharoṣṭhī.

The letter *a*, then, is the source of all the other letters in the alphabet; and the alphabet is the source of all the mantras - hence the composer(s) of the *Mahāvairocana Abhisaṃbodhi Tantra* could say that "from [a] arise mantras without number".

[208] See for instance MAT ii.84 (Hodges p.132-3).

The Seed Syllable āḥ

THE SEED SYLLABLE *ĀḤ* is associated with Amoghasiddhi and the action (*karma*) family.

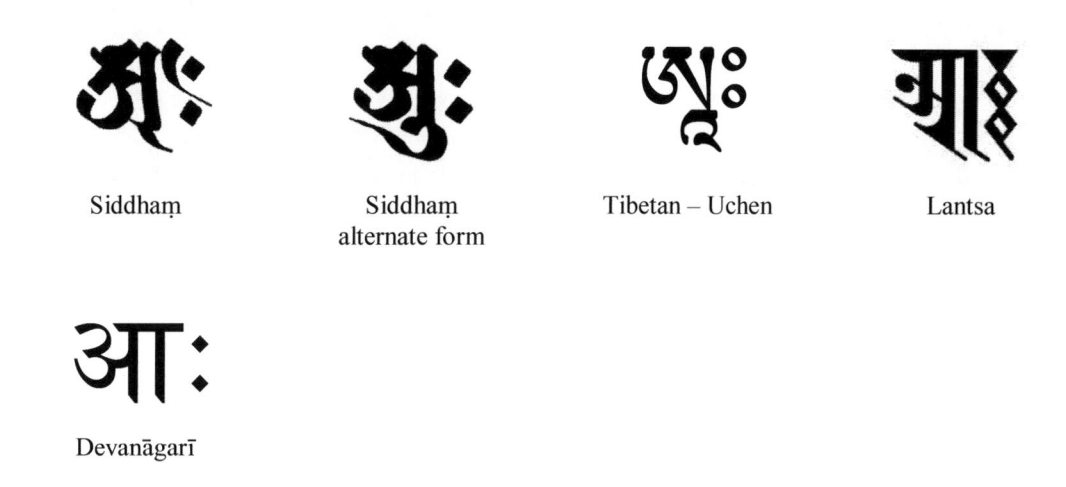

Siddhaṃ

Siddhaṃ
alternate form

ཨཱཿ

Tibetan – Uchen

Lantsa

आः

Devanāgarī

Notes

In Sanskrit *āḥ* is an exclamation of either joy or indignation[209] – similar to the way we might use the same sound in English. The pronunciation of the visarga is usually described as a soft echo of the vowel something. As well as appearing on its own *āḥ* occurs in the set of syllables: *oṃ āḥ hūṃ*. (see p. 210)

Notice the similarities between the *alternate* form of the Siddhaṃ and the Tibetan *āḥ*. Tibetan uses a marker to indicate long vowels which is the same for all vowels:

ཨ

a

ཨཱ

ā

It seems that there is a memory of this, perhaps older, form in the alternate Siddhaṃ form. It is only used in this syllable and in Vairocana's other seed syllable *vāṃḥ*. (see p. 94, 198.)

[209] Macdonell *A Sanskrit Grammar* p.158.

The Seed Syllable dhīḥ

DHĪḤ IS THE SEED SYLLABLE of perfect wisdom or *prajñāpāramitā*, and by association of Mañjuśrī.

Siddhaṃ

Tibetan – Uchen

Lantsa

Devanāgarī

Note that in John Stevens' book he writes *dhiḥ* with a short *i*, as is common practice in Japan. However I am sure that the long *ī* is correct. This example is for comparison.

The syllable *dhīḥ* is sometimes combined with *mma* which stands for Mañjuśrī (although we would expect *maṃ* here) resulting the complex syllable is *dhīṃmma* which is the seed-syllable of the Heart Sūtra. As above the Japanese also use *dhiḥ*.

Notes

The Monier-Williams *Sanskrit-English Dictionary* definition of *dhī* is:

> "1. to perceive , think , reflect"
> "2. (feminine noun) thought , (esp.) religious thought , reflection , meditation , devotion, prayer (pl. Holy Thoughts personified); understanding , intelligence , wisdom (personified as the wife of Rudra-manyu), knowledge , science , art; mind , disposition , intention , design; notion , opinion , the taking for (comp.) "

Dhīḥ, with the *visarga* (*ḥ*), is either the nominative or the vocative singular form of the noun – i.e. it is either a name or attribute; or form of address 'O wisdom'. The word occurs rarely in the *Ṛgveda* where it's usually translated as 'intelligence' or 'prayer', though clearly the connotations are much broader. Antonio T. De Nicolas translates it as vision in his essay *Religious Experience and Religious Languages*.[210] According to William Mahoney, the Vedic

[210] http://www.infinityfoundation.com/mandala/i_es/i_es_denic_religious.htm

concept of *dhī* draws on the *ṛṣi*'s ability to see the divine realm and its inhabitants, and his ability to communicate with them through the *sūktas* or hymns.[211]

Monier-Williams definition 2. is clearly interesting territory for Buddhists and not surprisingly *dhīḥ* became the seed syllable – the sonic quintessence – of the goddess of wisdom in Buddhism, Prajñāpāramitā, who names means 'that wisdom that has gone to the other shore' or the 'perfection of wisdom'. It occurs in the middle of her mantra: *oṃ āḥ dhīḥ hūṃ svāhā* (see p. 147).

Gelugpa monks invoke Mañjuśrī when making logical points in their ritualised debates. Holding their left hand out palm up, they strike it with the palm of the right, drawing the right hand back in the same motion. At the point of contact they shout *dhīḥ!* The opponent is left to answer as best they can, if they can.

In some Mañjuśrī *sādhanas* one is instructed to recite *dhīḥ* as many times as possible in one breath.

211 see for instance: Mahony, W.K. 1998. *The Artful Universe*, p.7.

The Seed Syllable hrīḥ

HRĪḤ IS THE SEED SYLLABLE of Amitābha and so represents the qualities of the Buddha of the western quarter: chiefly meditation and compassion. It is also associated with the bodhisattva Avalokiteśvara or *Chenrezik.*

Siddhaṃ

Tibetan – Uchen

Lantsa

Devanāgarī

In China and other places in East Asia there are variants of Lantsa script which have been altered to look like Chinese Characters, especially to look like the Seal Script.

Notes

It is possible that the *bīja hrīḥ* is related to the Sanskrit word *hrī* 'modesty' or 'moral shame'. In the dictionary *hrī* is defined as:

> *Verb*: to feel shame, blush, be bashful or modest, be ashamed of anyone or anything.
> *Noun*: shame, modesty, shyness, timidity.

It's not clear however what the connection is to Amitābha or the quality of compassion. The quality *hrī* is directly praised in the *Mahāvairocana Abhisaṃbodhi Tantra* (MAT), as someone who possesses modesty will act ethically and be praised by the Buddhas for doing so, and they will gain insight and "companionship" with the Buddhas and Bodhisattvas. They will also be reborn in either the human world or the god realms.[212]

We can see *Hrīḥ* as made up of four sounds – *ha* + *ra* + *ī* + *ḥ* – each with its own esoteric significance. Lama Govinda provides one analysis in his book *Foundations of Tibetan Mysticism*. However, he says that as the Tibetans seldom pronounce the *visarga* (*ḥ*) they analyse *hrīḥ* as only three sounds. According to this scheme the *ha* symbolises: "the breath, the symbol of all life"; while *ra* is "the sound of fire", and *ī* is "the vowel of high intensity and stands for the highest spiritual activity and differentiation"[213]

According to the MAT '*ha*' stands for *hetu* or 'cause' in the sense of 'original cause', and 'ra' is *raja* or defilement - the point being that *dharmas*, phenomena, lack either an original cause or defilements. The MAT doesn't say anything about the vowels or the *visarga*. Kūkai treats the alphabet more comprehensively. In his scheme: *ha* is 'cause' [*hetu*], *ra* is taint [*raja*], *ī* is senses [*indriya*], and *visarga* is release.[214] This kind of analysis has roots in the Perfection of

---

212 Hodge, Stephen. 2003. *The Mahā-Vairocana-Abhisaṃbodhi* p.168. (MAT vi.9)
213 Govinda, Lama. 1959. *Foundations of Tibetan Mysticism*. (London : Rider). p.183, note 1.
214 Abe, Ryuchi. 1999. *The Weaving of Mantra.* (New York : Columbia University Press). p.291-2.

Wisdom tradition and is found in the larger texts like the *Perfection of Wisdom in 25,000 lines*. Before that there are links back to the Abhidharma tradition. Similar kinds of analyses are found in the *Chāndogya Upaniṣad* which is thought to predate Buddhism.

The Seed Syllable hūṃ

HŪṂ IS A VERY COMMON *bīja* which occurs at the end of many mantras. Its associations are many and varied, and it is probably the most common *bīja* at the end of Buddhist mantras.

Siddhaṃ

Siddhaṃ alternate

Tibetan – Uchen

Devanāgarī

Lantsa

Lantsa alternative

Imitation Chinese Seal Script[215]

The Architecture of hūṃ

The diagram below shows how *hūṃ* is put together from various elements which are more or less the same in both Siddhaṃ and Tibetan, because they both come from the Gupta script.

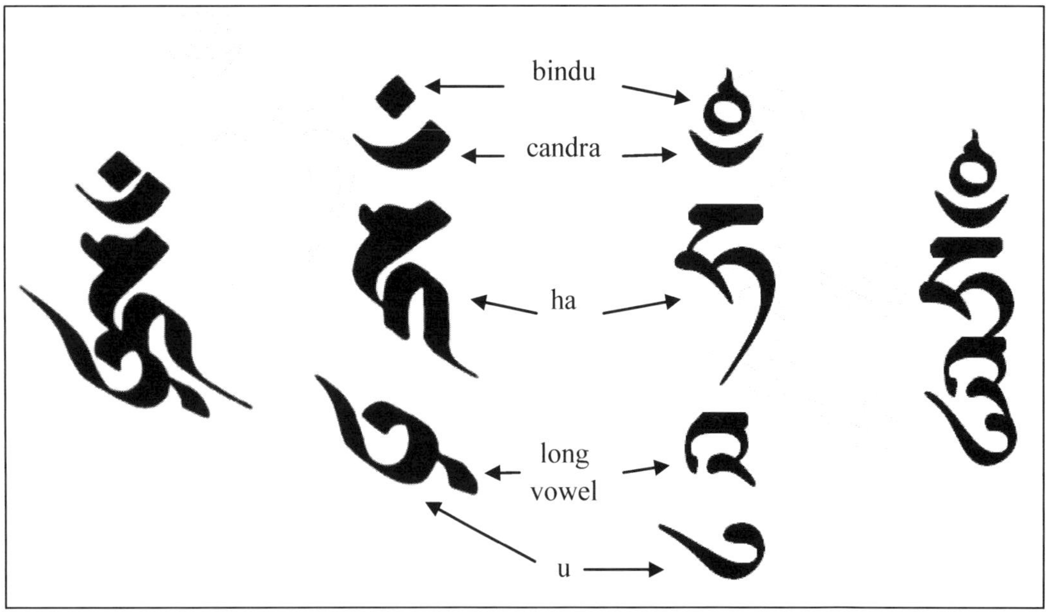

[215] based on an image in a British Museum book called *Buddhism: Art and Faith* by W. Zalf, which is no longer in print, but is often available in second hand bookshops.

For more on the *candra-bindu* see the section on *anusvāra* (p. 34f.).

Kūkai's Commentary on hūṃ

In his *Ungi gi 'The Meanings of the Word Hūṃ'* Kūkai makes *hūṃ* a cipher for understanding the nature of reality. He breaks it into its constituent sounds: *ha* + *a* + *ū* + *ṃ*. The various aspects of the syllable take in all truths, all teachings, all practices, and all attainments. It summarises the two basic false views of nihilism and eternalism, and shows them to be false. The Truth of things is that they are neither real nor unreal, these categories do not apply – this is a restatement of the Buddha's fundamental insight into the nature of phenomena, couched in the language of the Madhyamaka.

Kūkai discusses *hūṃ* on three levels: invariant, ultimate, and synthetic. Each aspect of *hūṃ* is capable of infinite associations. The invariant meanings are the esoteric associations via the alphabet of wisdom, thus: *ha* = *hetu* (cause); *a* = *anutpāda* (unarisen); *ū* = *ūna* (wanting); and *ṃ* = *ātman* (self). In practice we would take each element as a meditation practice by inserting it into a general formula. For example the seed syllable *ha* 'is a door to all dharmas because they are *without a cause*', the idea being that each phrase, one for each of the letter of the alphabet, points to the *śūnya* nature of dharmas, i.e. that they lack *svabhāva* or self-being.

The ultimate meanings are difficult to sum up simply because the possible associations are so extensive and the *Ungi gi* is a very dense and terse text - summaries which do justice to the text end up being the same size as the text itself. All I can do here is offer some indications to give a taste and suggest the reader gets hold of *Ungi gi.*

The ultimate meaning of *a* is that it is the first sound and therefore represents relative being; it is non-arising (*anutpāda*) and therefore empty (*śūnya*); *a* is also uncreated and therefore is the source of all things. *A* is the first sound because it begins the alphabet; it is the first sound that comes when you breath out; and it is said to be present in all letters – consonants have an implicit accompanying *a* vowel. Because *ha* the first cause is unobtainable we should know that predications of all things are only our mind, and that the real feature of our mind is all-inclusive wisdom. *Ū* means that because all things are *ūna*, or wanting, the ultimate meaning is that no existence is found wanting of Buddhahood; the 'One Mind' is perpetual and doesn't increase or decrease; it is eternity, bliss, the self, purity; in short the nature of suchness (*tathatā*) pervades all beings. Finally the ultimate meaning of *ṃ* is the all-embracing equality, the transformation of Mahāvairocana into all things; it is the sole great self of selfless existence.

Note that although Kūkai adopts the language of permanence and even 'self' (*ātman*), he is not negating the principle of *pratītyasamutpāda*: the contradiction is more apparent than real. Kūkai accepts a radical form of the idea that all things interpenetrate. This is not explicit in *pratītyasamutpāda* but which can be deduced from it, and came to prominence with the *Avataṃsaka Sūtra* around the 2nd century CE. In this view all dharmas are fully and perfectly interpenetrated by all other dharmas. This includes the Buddha and the principle of Buddhahood (*Dharmakāya*). The phenomenal world is not solid and real, but neither is it illusion and unreal. Neither real nor unreal can fully describe reality. We must keep in mind that Kūkai's rhetoric is shaped partly by the early Vajrayāna texts, but also as a reaction to the scholastic formalism in 9th century Japan.

Kūkai's synthetic meanings can be glossed as: *ha* summarises all religious teachings; *a* is absolute reality; *ū* includes all religious practices; while *ṃ* encompasses all religious attainments. The '*a*' *bīja* symbolizes the Dharmakāya; it is neither being nor non-being, nor both, nor neither, being beyond such dualities; '*a*' is the negative prefix in Sanskrit which forms a negative to any noun when added to the beginning; this is the truth that all Buddhists teachings are pointing to, so '*a*' summarises them all.

In Kūkai's analysis then *hūṃ* is a hermeneutical device, a way of interpreting, which can unlock the true nature of reality. It is massively polyvalent and polysemic, which is to say that it has almost infinite power and meaning, because it exists at the centre of a network of interconnected associations.

The Seed Syllable ma

Ma is used in a variety of seed-syllables: *maṃ* associated with Mañjuśrī, *māṃ* with Māmaki, *maiṃ* (rhymes with 'mine') is the seed syllable of Maitreya, and *muḥ* is also associated with Mañjuśrī. It also appears in the complex seed-syllables *dhīmmaḥ* and *hāmmāṃ* (see Complex Seed-syllables below).

Siddhaṃ

maṃ māṃ maiṃ muḥ

Tibetan

མཾ མཱཾ མཻཾ མུཿ

maṃ māṃ maiṃ muḥ

Lantsa

maṃ māṃ maiṃ muḥ

Devanāgarī

मँ माँ मैं मुः

maṃ māṃ maiṃ muḥ

The Seed Syllable oṃ

THE FIRST APPEARANCE OF *OṂ* in a sacred text is in the *Yajurveda*, composed sometime after 1000 BC but before the Buddha. In the Vedic rtituals it was to be uttered loudly by the *hotṛ* Brahmin at the end of the invocation to the god being sacrificed to (*anuvākya*), as an invitation to partake of the sacrifice.[216] By the time of the Upaniṣads *oṃ* had taken on a greater significance as a sonic symbol of *brahman* - the universal absolute. See also notes below

Oṃ seems not to have been used by Buddhists until the middle Tantric period as it does not appear in early Mahāyāna *dhāraṇī*, nor in the *Mahāvairocana Abhisaṃbodhi Tantra* (ca mid 7th century). In the latter, mantras typically begin "*namaḥ samanta buddhānaṃ*". However it becomes the standard way to begin a mantra at some point after this. Buddhist mantras always seem to use *oṃ* rather than *auṃ*. Although Tibetan exegesis gives *oṃ* a variety of different associations and significances, the main function of *oṃ* in Buddhist mantras seems to be to mark what follows as a mantra. According to Lama Govinda, *oṃ* represents Buddhahood in potential, and is contrasted with *hūṃ* which represents Buddhahood made manifest.

Siddhaṃ

Tibetan – Uchen

Tibetan – Ume

Lantsa

Devanāgarī

Imitation Chinese Seal Script[218]

Korean[217]

Oṃ and Auṃ

The prominence of *auṃ* ॐ in Hindu traditions is explained by reference to two of the *Upaniṣads* which are amongst the later of the 'early' Upaniṣads. The *Maitrī Upaniṣad* divides *oṃ* into *a* + *u* + *m*. The three aspects are said to represent, amongst other things, the Hindu trinity or *trimurti* in their aspects as creator (Brahmā), sustainer (Viṣṇu), and destroyer (Śiva). The *Māṇḍūkya Upaniṣad* takes this one step further and makes *oṃ* itself the fourth aspect which allows it to be related to all manner of four fold lists and symmetries: particularly the four-fold Vedas, the four faces of Brahmā, the four Great Elements (earth, water, fire, air), etc. This

[216] The Vedic sacrifice involved a number of priests in different roles. The *hotṛ* accompanied each ritual action with a mantra.

[217] This *oṃ* inspired by an image from a Korean temple on Parhessiastes' Flickr site. Online: http://www.flickr.com/photos/parrhesiastes/487612545/

[218] based an image in a British Museum book called Buddhism: Art and Faith, which is no longer in-print but is often available second hand.

theory of associations was an aspect of Vedic thinking millennia before it was incorporated into Tantric systems.

One interesting point here is that the character ॐ is clearly based on a script much closer to Siddhaṃ than it is to Devanāgarī which would write *oṃ* or *auṃ* as ओं or औं. Buddhist mantras use *oṃ* exclusively as far as I am aware.

oṃ and *auṃ*
in Siddhaṃ

Oṃ was supplanted by *a* in Buddhism as the seed syllable which encapsulated the religion. There is a parallel with early Vedic exegesis (in the *Āraṇyaka* texts) which treat the phoneme '*a*' as the first phoneme in the syllable and therefore give it precedence, however I think it is unlikely, given Buddhist thinking on the syllable *a*, that Buddhists were drawing on these sources.

For the early history of *oṃ* see especially: André Padoux. 1990. *Vāc: the concept of the word in selected Hindu Tantras*. (Trans. 1992 by Jacques Gontier) Delhi: Sri Satguru Publications.

Auṃ

ॐ औं

Devanāgarī

The Seed Syllable tāṃ

TĀṂ IS THE SEED SYLLABLE of Tārā in all her forms, being the first syllable of her name (*tā*) plus the *anusvāra* (*ṃ*).

Siddhaṃ — Tibetan – Uchen — Lantsa — Devanāgarī

White Tara and Tāṃ

White Tārā appears to have a special relationship to the Mandala of the Five Buddhas. I originally noticed this while contemplating the yellow Buddha Ratnasambhava whose *mudrā* is *varada* or giving. This is also the mudrā of White Tārā's right hand. It occurred to me that White Tārā's left hand was in the *abhaya mudrā* which is the mudrā of Amoghasiddhi. These two Buddhas sit opposite each other in the mandala. White Tārā has Amitābha sitting in her head-dress - which places him in the appropriate place for the mandala. And she sits in the Vajrāsana and the vajra is the symbol of Akṣobhya. In the centre of the mandala usually sits Vairocana. However when a figure is white we can consider that they have moved to the centre, so White Tārā replaces Vairocana to complete the mandala.

The same relationship can be seen in the *tāṃ*. Following the same order... the right-hand of the *tāṃ* stretches out and down just like Ratnasambhava; the left-hand is represented by the *ā* mark and looks like the *mudrā* of Amoghasiddhi; the *anusvāra* represents Amitābha sitting in Tārā's head-dress; and the stem of the *tāṃ* is the *vajra* of Akṣobhya.

This could all be a coincidence of course, and I have not come across it in any of texts on Tārā. However the world view of Tantra is that knowledge is based on resemblance and relationship, whereas the modern scientific worldview seeks knowledge through identity and separation (this difference is explored in Michel Foucault's *The Order of Things*). For example in Tantra we see associations between the five Buddhas, the five wisdoms, the five elements, the five directions (compass points plus centre), and the five poisons. In the Vedic tradition this correspondence is known as *bandhu* 'a bond'. It is this kind of bond which allows a mantra or seed-syllable to represent a Buddha, for instance.

One of the mysteries about White Tārā is that she has seven eyes. These are explained in various ways - for instance they represent the four noble truths and the three liberations. This has always struck me as somewhat arbitrary, and does seem to have much connection with the myth of Tārā. If we accept the correspondence with the mandala then perhaps five of the eyes might represent Buddhas. Four of the eyes are at the extremities, and that the extremities stretched out are at the corners of a square - which suggests a mandala. A fifth eye is in the centre of White Tārā's forehead. This is traditionally the wisdom eye - the 'eye' which opens in Buddhas when they awaken. The fifth eye is, then, at the centre of the mandala. This leaves two eyes in the usual places - White Tārā's own eyes. So far I've found no traditional confirmation of this scheme, but I find it quite a pleasing explanation.

Even though they are commonly depicted in human form the Buddhas and bodhisattvas are not really people in the sense of flesh and blood human beings. The pictures are symbols. The true nature of Buddhas and Bodhisattvas is formless. In the west we can lose sight of this and when this happens there is an unfortunate resonance with Christian imagery. The Buddha can come to be seen as a man sitting on a lotus floating up in the sky, and bodhisattvas start to look a bit like angels. I think this is worth reflecting on. Sounds are equally good representations of Buddhas and bodhisattvas, as are written mantras and seed-syllables. We should not become fixated on the anthropomorphic representations, and chosing a written seed-syllable as a symbol can help us keep this in mind.

The Seed Syllable traṃ/trāḥ

THE SYLLABLE *TRA* MEANS PROTECTING, while *trā* is a protector or defender. *Traṃ* is the seed syllable of the Ratnasambhava, the Buddha of the southern quarter. In early mandalas Ratnaketu is in the south and his *bīja* is *traḥ*.

Siddhaṃ | Tibetan – Uchen | Lantsa | Devanāgarī

Trāḥ occurs in the mantra of Ākāśagarbha.

Siddhaṃ | Tibetan Uchen | Lantsa | Devanāgarī

Notes

The syllable *tra* occurs for instance in words like *gotra* 'cow-shed'; *tvaktra* 'armour', literally 'skin-protection'. Some traditional explanations of what the word *mantra* suggest that it means that which protects (*tra*) the mind (*manas*).

The Seed Syllable vaṃ

Vaṃ is the *bīja* of Mahāvairocana in the *Vajradhātu Maṇḍala,* associated with the *Vajraśekhara Sūtra,* and is seen in many contexts, particularly on the Japanese grave markers known as *sotoba*[219] (卒塔婆). The Tibetans substitute *ba* for *va* when writing Sanskrit, so we write *baṃ* and *bāṃḥ* when using the Tibetan script.[220]

Siddhaṃ | Tibetan Uchen | Lantsa | Devanāgarī

The *vaṃ* syllable is also elaborated as *vāṃḥ* suggesting *va vā vaṃ* and *vaḥ* combined similar to what happened with the seed syllable *a*.

Siddhaṃ | Tibetan Uchen | Lantsa | Devanāgarī

Va presumable comes from the first syllable of Vairocana's name. Its esoteric meaning is *vāc* 'voice' (also speech, word). *Vāc* is both speech and the old Vedic goddess of speech. Mantra is the quintessence of *vāc*, the speech of Reality.

---

[219] *sotoba* is the Japanese pronunciation of *stūpa*, and the wooden *sotaba* has the outline of a *stūpa*.

[220] One theory to account for this is that the Tibetans mainly drew their Sanskrit teachings from a part of India which pronounced *va* as *ba*.

Complex Seed-Syllables

A number of these complex syllables are used which combine more than one syllable. All these examples are in the Siddhaṃ script. Notes on the following page.

dhīḥmma

hāmmāṃ

kālacakra

bhrūṃ

stryi

jñā

Dhīḥmma

Dhīḥmma combines the seed syllable *dhīḥ* from Prajñāpāramitā with *ma* representing Mañjuśrī (whose seed-syllable is actually *maṃ*). It is associated by John Stevens with the Heart Sūtra.[221]

Hāmmāṃ

Associated with the figure of Acala-vidyārāja, *hāmmāṃ* is a combination of the two final seed-syllables *hāṃ* and *māṃ* from his mantra.

Kālacakra

This is a complex seed-syllable associated with the *Kālacakra Tantra*, written in the Siddhaṃ script. The seed-syllable combines a number of syllables from the Kālacakra mantra: *haṃ kṣaḥ ma la va ra ya*. Also included are the *anusvāra* (*ṃ*) and *visarga* (*ḥ*) and the vowel *a* which is included in all consonants by default. The mantra itself is: *oṃ haṃ kṣaḥ ma la va ra ya svāhā*.

Bhrūṃ

This syllable is pronounced *boron* in Japan and is associated with the figure called *Ekākṣara-uṣṇīṣa-cakra* (*Ichijikinrin*) which means 'single-letter-crown-wheel'. *Ekākṣara* means single (*eka*) letter (*akṣara*) and *uṣṇīsa* is literally 'a turban' or any head gear, but here refers to one of the 'thirty-two marks' of the Buddha - the bump on the top of his head.

Stryi

This syllable associated with the *Karaṇḍamudrā dhāraṇī*. This text begins:

> नमस्त्र्यध्विकानां सर्व तथागतानां
> namastryadhvikānāṁ sarva tathāgatānāṁ
> homage to all the Tathāgatas of the three times.

namastryadhvikānāṁ breaks down into *namas tryadhvikānāṁ*. *Namaḥ* meaning homage, and swapping *ḥ* for *s* due to Sanskrit sandhi (qv) rules. *Tradhvikānāṁ* = *tri* (three) + *adhvan* (times) + *-ika* (belonging to) + *-nāṃ* (genitive plural case ending). When followed by a vowel, i becomes y, so *tri* > *try*.

Adhvan + *ika* > *adhvika* is a *taddhita* compound, although we would usually expect the initial vowel of the base to lengthen (*ādhvika*) in cases like this. The grammar in *dhāraṇī* is often not what you might expect from Classical Sanskrit, most likely because they were not composed in Classical Sanskrit but one of the vernaculars. Broken into syllables for writing in an Indic script (such as Siddhaṃ or Devanāgarī) they read:

> न म स्त्र्य ध्वि का नां
> na ma strya dhvi kā nāṁ

---

[221] Stevens Sacred Calligraphy, p.62. Stevens has *dhi* and *dhiḥmma* both with a short *i*, this is probably traditional but incorrect: both should have the long *ī*: *dhīḥ* and *dhīḥmma*.

It's not clear why *strya* becomes *stryi*. However, as the first syllable following the *namaḥ* (homage) it comes, by metonymy, to stand for the whole *dhāraṇī*.

Jñā

Jñā is an important Sanskrit root found in the word *jñāna* which is more or less cognate with English *know*. Other related words are *samjñā*, *vijñāna*, and *prajñā* the definitions of which are complex because they are used differently at different times (and sometimes they are synonymous).

Mantric Words

A few words are included as mantras that in some ways function like *bījas*. These are

namaḥ
phaṭ
svāhā

Namas

This word is ubiquitous in Indian religion, and *namaste* is perhaps the most common greeting in India today. Because of Sanskrit *sandhi* rules (qv) there are three forms of this word which are essentially the same. Here are all the forms in Devanāgarī:

नमः	नमो	नमस्
namaḥ	namo	namas

Namaḥ in other scripts:

Siddhaṃ

ན་མཿ
Uchen

Lantsa

Notes

Namas occurs in a number of contexts in Buddhism. For instance when we salute a shrine we say

> *namo buddhāya, namo dharmāya, namo saṅghāya, namo namaḥ.*

We can translate this as "homage to the Buddha, homage to the Dharma, homage to the Saṅgha, homage homage". The different spellings of *namo* and *namaḥ* are simply sandhi variations (see below) and don't mean different things.

In the tantric context most mantras in the *Mahāvairocana Abhisaṃbodhi Tantra* (MAT) begin with:

> *namaḥ samantabuddhānāṃ or namaṃ-samantavajrānāṃ.*

These mean 'homage to all the Buddhas', or to all the vajras. The *-ānāṃ* ending is a genitive plural, usually used to indicate possession. A literal reading might be 'the homage of all the Buddhas' but I think the idea is homage *to* the Buddha. Stephen Hodge renders it as "salutations to all the Buddhas" in his translation of the MAT.

Modern grammarians consider *namaḥ* to be the basic form with changes depending on what follows.[222] Classical Sanskrit sandhi rules tell us that:

namaḥ followed by a voiced consonant (e.g. ba, dha, na) > *namo*
namaḥ followed by a dental consonant (ta, tha, da, dha, na, and sa) > *namas*
when *namaḥ* is followed by 'a' > *namo* and drop the 'a'
    (e.g. *namaḥ amitābha > namo 'mitābha*)

[222] Others consider *namas* to be the most basic form.

namaḥ remains the same otherwise.

From this you can see that *namo sanghāya* is not quite correct. It should be *namas saṅghāya* but conventional usage often over-rides grammatical rules.

Namaste, actually two words – *namas te* – means 'homage to you'. *Te* is a form of the second person singular dative pronoun 'to you'.

Phaṭ

Phaṭ is pronounced as a single syllable, but in Indic scripts must be written as two characters. In Buddhist Tantra it functions in the same way as a seed-syllable, and is often associated with the mantras of wrathful deities. The word *phaṭ* means something like ‘crack!’ or ‘bang!’, and is imported from the Vedic tradition. In the Vajrasattva mantra it is added when the mantra is used to subdue demons.

The *ṭ* is written with a *virāma* diacritic to indicate that it has no following vowel, though the *virāma* is routinely left out in Tibetan.

Siddhaṃ   Tibetan – Uchen   Lantsa   Devanāgarī

Notes

The word p*haṭ* occurs in mantras for Vajrasattva, Vajrayoginī, and the Dharma doors mantra which occurs in the Hevajra Tantra and in the offering section of tantric rituals for Tārā and Vajrayoginī. We can see it is therefore more often associated with wrathful figures and figures from the more esoteric Tantras (called by the Tibetans the *yoga* and *atiyoga* tantras).

The syllable *pha* is always pronounced ‘p-ha’ (p^h in the phonetic alphabet) and never like /f/. It is like a breathy /p/. The vowel is the short *a* so that *phaṭ* sounds like the English word ‘putt’.

In Tibetan retroflex consonants such as *ṭa* are written by using the mirror image of the matching dental: e.g. ta = ཏ and ṭa = ཊ.

Svāhā

Svāhā is not really a seed-syllable, since it is two syllables, but in Buddhist mantras it does function in the same way as a seed-syllable.

Siddham

སྭཱ་ཧཱ

Tibetan – Uchen

Lantsa

स्वाहा

Devanāgarī

Notes

Monier-Williams says the etymology is probably *su* (good, well, whole, etc) + √*ah* (to call, to say, to speak, etc); though *āha* is a past perfect form, so that it would literally mean something like: "well spoken". Conze translates it as "all hail" and most other translators seem to follow him. However he admits that it is not a very satisfactory translation. He refers to *svāhā* as a term of blessing: "an ecstatic shout of joy, expressive of a feeling of complete release".[223]

Svāhā is imported from Vedic ritual, where it was used when making oblations to the sacred fire. After each ladle of offering the priest exclaims *svāhā*! In the *Yajurveda* there are long lists of phrases which have the name of a god in the dative form (meaning 'to' or 'for' the deity) followed by svāhā, e.g *agnaye svāhā*, *somāya svāhā* (*Taittirīra Saṃhitā* 7.1.14.1). These may be the precursors of Buddhist mantras.[224] *Svāhā* first shows up in Buddhist texts in the *dhāraṇīs* which were interpolated into *Mahāyāna* texts such as the *White Lotus Sūtra* and the *Golden Light Sūtra.*

It becomes a standard ending for Buddhist mantras, and although Conze suggests that *svāhā* is reserved for feminine deities[225], this is clearly not the case. *Svāhā* occurs at the end of the mantras for Śakyamuni, Maitreya, Bhaiṣajyarāja (The Medicine Buddha), Locanā, Māmakī, Pāṇḍaravāsinī, Tārā, Ākāśadhātvīśvarī, and in the Heart Sutra Mantra.

Svā is a conjunct consonant which combines *sa* and *va* with the long *ā* diacritic.

[223] Conze *Buddhist Wisdom Books*, p.128
[224] The connection between Yajurveda and Buddhist mantras was suggested to me by Maitiu O'Ceileachair.
[225] Conze *Buddhist Wisdom Books*, p.106.

Miscellaneous Mantras

The Heart Sūtra mantra is somewhat unique in the West in being the only one associated with a text. There are in fact a number of these in other Mahāyāna *dhāraṇī* texts but, perhaps because they have not been translated into English, they are not yet popular in the west. The *dhāraṇī sūtras* were, and are, very popular in China and the Far East.

Tantric rituals use mantras to mark each activity in the *sādhana* and so there are many mantras which are associated with activities rather than deities. One of the key activities of any *sādhana* is preliminary purification – both the *śūnyatā mantra* and *śuddha mantra* (which is also, paradoxically, known as the *śūnyatā mantra*) are associated with this initial purification, though the *śuddha* mantra is often chanted when dismantling a shrine on Triratna Buddhist Community retreats. The *śānti* mantra is chanted at the conclusion of Triratna Buddhist Community sevenfold pujas.

The Alphabet as Mantra

IN MANY SĀDHANAS the meditator is instructed to recite the entire Sanskrit alphabet.[226] Sometimes this is part of the preliminary practices, and at other times comes in the main part of the sādhana. In the *Mahāvairocana Abhisaṃbodhi Tantra* (MAT) the meditator imagines the letters of the alphabet positioned around their body. Frequently the letters are placed on the rim of an eight-spoked wheel – in some cases the vowels form one circle and the consonants another, each moving in different directions around the wheel. This wheel is then known as *cintacakra* – often translated as 'wish-fulfilling wheel – though it literally means thought-wheel.

Siddhaṃ

अ आ इ ई उ ऊ ऋ ॠ ऌ ॡ ए ऐ ओ औ अं अः
क ख ग घ ङ च छ ज झ ञ ट ठ ड ढ ण त थ द ध न
प फ ब भ म य र ल व श ष स ह क्ष

Devanāgarī

ཨ་ཨཱ་ཨི་ཨཱི་ཨུ་ཨཱུ་ཨྲྀ་ཨྲཱྀ་ཨླྀ་ཨླཱྀ་ཨེ་ཨཻ་ཨོ་ཨཽ་ཨཾ་ཨཿ

ཀ།ཁ་ག།གྷ་ང་ཙ་ཚ་ཛ་ཛྷ་ཉ་ཊ་ཋ་ཌ་ཌྷ་ཎ་ཏ་ཐ་ད་དྷ་ན

པ་ཕ་བ་བྷ་མ་ཡ་ར་ལ་ཝ་ཤ་ཥ་ས་ཧ་ཀྵ།

Tibetan

[226] Recall that the 'alphabet' is made up of *syllables* rather than *letters*.

Lantsa

Transliteration

a ā i ī u ū ṛ ṝ ḷ ḹ e ai o au aṃ aḥ

ka kha ga gha ṅa ca cha ja jha ña ṭa ṭha ḍa ḍha ṇa ta tha da dha na

pa pha ba bha ma ya ra la va śa ṣa sa ha kṣa

Notes

As far as I am aware the alphabet used in this context is usually the Sanskrit alphabet, rather than the Arapacana or Wisdom Alphabet. In the MAT the alphabet is the Sanskrit but only includes the vowel 'a', and therefore seems to be an echo of the Arapacana (c.f. p. 34ff.).

The transliteration of the letters is subject to quite a lot of variation, often because diacritics are not used. Each of the syllables has a distinct sound. See also the section on Sanskrit pronunciation (p.14.).

The vowel ḹ is usually included though it is only a theoretical possibility and is not used in Sanskrit in practice. *Anusvāra* and *visarga* are included in the vowels though they can apply to any vowel. *Kṣa* is routinely included in the syllabary though it is strictly speaking a conjunct made up of *k* + *ṣa*, it makes the number of syllables up to fifty made up of sixteen vowels and thirty-four consonants. Sometimes in tantric syllabaries another conjunct is included *llaṃ*.

Often the syllabary is written in rows according to the place of articulation in the mouth – with the vowels first, then velar, palatal, retroflex, dental, labial, semivowels, and sibilants.

a ā i ī u ū ṛ ṝ

ḷ ḹ e ai o au aṃ aḥ

ka kha ga gha ṅa

ca cha ja jha ña

ṭa ṭha ḍa ḍha ṇa

ta tha da dha na

pa pha ba bha ma

ya ra la va

śa ṣa sa ha kṣa

See p. 171 for a facsimile of a syllabary brushed by Kūkai.

Oṃ āḥ hūṃ

THIS IS THE MANTRA OF BODY, SPEECH AND MIND. The division of a person into 'body, speech and mind' is one of the classic analyses of Buddhist thought. Morality is often conceived of as relating to actions of the body, of speech and thoughts. The *dasakusala-karma* or ten skilful actions have three precepts each for the body and the mind, and four for speech.

Siddhaṃ

ཨོཾ་ཨཱཿ་ཧཱུྃ།

Tibetan – Uchen

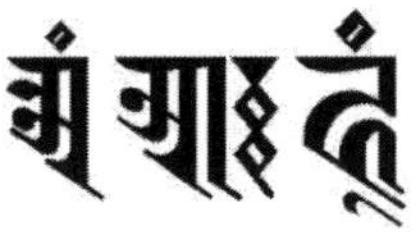

Lantsa

ओं आः हूं

Devanāgarī

Transliteration

oṃ āḥ hūṃ

Notes

Some Tibetan teachers recommend visualising the syllables at the higher three *cakras* – between the eyes, at the throat, and at the heart – and spending some time chanting each syllable as a purification practice. The three *cakras* stand for the body, speech, and mind respectively – note that the body *cakra* is in the head, and the mind cakra is over the heart. Or you can recite the mantra itself: *oṃ āḥ hūṃ*.

If you look on the back of a genuine Tibetan Thangka you will find there three syllables painted over the *cakras* of the figure(s) represented.

These syllables also occur at the beginning of the Padmasambhava mantra, where they have a number of different associations (see p. 176).

Heart Sutra Mantra

This is the mantra from the *Prajñāpāramitahṛdaya Sūtra* or *The Sūtra of the Heart of the Perfection of Wisdom*, or *Heart Sūtra* for short. Prajñāpāramita, the bodhisattva, has another mantra.

Traditionally thought to be a Sanskrit text, it now seems almost certain that the Heart Sūtra was composed in China around the 7th century, although it incorporates verses from the Chinese version of the Large *Prajñāpāramita* texts. It is entirely possible that Xuanzang back-translated it into Sanskrit during his trip to India. The evidence for this conclusion are presented in an article by Jan Nattier: 'The Heart Sūtra: a Chinese apocryphal text?' *Journal of the International Association of Buddhist Studies*. 1992 Vol. 15 (2), p.153-223. I have a précis of this article on my blog.[227]

The script on the left is *hṛdaya* in Siddhaṃ.

Seed Syllable

The seed syllable dhīḥ is associated with the Heart Sūtra.

Siddhaṃ

Tibetan – Uchen

Lantsa

Devanāgarī

Another Seed syllable is found in the Shingon tradition which combines *dhīḥ* with *ma* representing Mañjuśrī

Mantra

Siddhaṃ

[227] http://jayarava.blogspot.com/2007/09/heart-stra-indian-or-chinese.html

ག་ཏེ་ག་ཏེ་པཱ་ར་ག་ཏེ་པཱ་ར་སཾ་ག་ཏེ་བོ་དྷི་སྭཱ་ཧཱ།

Tibetan – Uchen

Lantsa

गते गते पारगते पारसंगते बोधि स्वाहा

Devanāgarī

Transliteration

ga te ga te pā ra ga te pā ra saṃ ga te bo dhi svā hā

gate gate pāragate pārasaṃgate bodhi svāhā

Notes on the Heart Sutra Mantra

Conze's translation reads: "gone, gone, gone beyond, gone altogether beyond, oh what an awakening, All hail!"

There has been much speculation on the meaning of this particular mantra. *Gate* has been analysed as Classical Sanskrit. Conze was of the opinion that gate is in the feminine vocative case. The vocative case indicates that someone is being addressed. so that *gate* means not simply 'gone', as it is usually translated, but "O she who is/has gone!".

I am not entirely convinced by Conze's suggestion. There are six ways to derive *gate* from the verbal root √*gam*. We may either take it to be a past passive participle or a past active participle. In either case it may be a masculine or neuter locative, or a feminine vocative. A passive participle of the word gata would mean in English 'he/she/it who is gone to'; while the active would translate as 'he/she/it who went'. I summarise the possibilities in the table below.

past passive participle	masc. loc	in/on he who is gone to.
	neut. loc	in/on it that is gone to.
	feminine voc	in/on she who is gone to.
past active participle	masc. loc	in/on he who went
	neut loc	in/on it that went
	feminine voc	in/on She who went

You will see that none of these six options matches Conze's translations. This is because Conze is giving the participle a perfect aspect. Participles are imperfect unless they are part of a relative clause, when there is a finite verb. "O she who is gone" would need to be something like '*gate abhavat*' with the verb to be (√*bhū*). So Conze is seemingly in error in this case.

All this presumes that *gate* is Classical Sanskrit. In my online essay I have explored the possibility that the *–e* ending is simply a nominative in either Buddhist Hybrid Sanskrit or Magadhi. In which case it would simply mean: "he who is gone".[228] The fact is that we don't know and that all of the explanations we have are *ad hoc*.

It is common-place for Buddhist *dhāraṇī* to use this device. Later tradition interprets it as addressing Prajñāpāramita (ie Wisdom, considered feminine in India), and most scholars seem to accept that the feminine vocative is intended. Kern, in his 1884 translation of the *Sadharmapuṇḍarika Sūtra*, related the use of the feminine vocative in *dhāraṇī* to the worship of Durga.

The Heart Sutra itself describes the mantra as:

mahāmantro mahā-vidyā mantro 'nuttara mantro samasama-mantraḥ

The translates as "The great mantra, the great knowledge mantra, the unexcelled mantra, the whole, complete mantra". Conze relates these epithets to traditional epithets for the Buddha, so the mantra is being likened to, or equated with, the Buddha.[229]

There are many commentaries to the Heart Sutra which attempt explanations of the mantra. Seven are recorded in the Tibetan canon. However as Alex Wayman notes that in the commentaries on the Tibetan versions that each exposition reflects the learning and tradition of the author rather than an inherited tradition associated with the text.[230] Similarly having surveyed the Indian commentaries preserved in the Tibetan Canon, as well as some of the later Tibetan commentaries, Donald Lopez concludes that they provide no explanation of the function of the mantra within the sūtra and that even sādhanas make only a 'perfunctory reference' to the mantra.[231]

A tradition which seems to originate with Atiśa (982-1054) relates the parts of the mantra to the stages of the path as set out in the Abhisamayalamkara (attributed to Maitreya):

gate	Path of merit / accumulation
gate	Path of preparation
paragate	Path of insight (1st Bodhisattva bhumi)
parasamgate	Path of meditation (2nd to 10th Bodhisattva bhumis)
bodhi	Buddhahood

[228] 'Words in Mantras that end in –e.' *Jayarava's Raves* 6.6.2009. http://jayarava.blogspot.com/2009/03/words-in-mantras-that-end-in-e.html
[229] Conze *Buddhist Wisdom Books*, p.104
[230] Wayman. *Secret of the Heart Sutra* p.136
[231] Lopez. *The Heart Sutra Explained*. p.120.

Jaḥ hūṃ vaṃ hoḥ

This mantra is used in Tantric rituals, along with the appropriate *mudrā*, to summon deities into a *maṇḍala* and bind them there, or to do the same in a *sādhana*.

Siddhaṃ

ཛཿ ཧཱུྃ་བྃ་ཧོཿ།

Tibetan Uchen

Lantsa

जः हूं वं होः

Devanāgarī

Transliteration

jaḥ hūṃ vaṃ hoḥ

The Tibetan transliteration substitutes *baṃ* for *vaṃ* as usual.

Notes

This text is found in the *Sarvatathāgata-tattvasaṃgraha*[232] where it is accompanied by the phrase:

> *jaḥ hūṃ vaṃ hoḥ* ||
> *mahāsatvākarṣaṇapraveśanabandhanavaśīkaraṇahṛdayama* ||
>
> *jaḥ hūṃ vaṃ hoḥ* - The innermost heart of summoning, entrance of, binding with, and subjugation of the great hero

The long compound breaks down to: *mahāsatvā-karṣaṇa-praveśana-bandhana-vaśīkaraṇa-hṛdayama*, i.e. great-heros - summoning - entering - binding - subjugating - heartmost.
Here it is referring to the functions of the four door guardians of the *maṇḍala*. When constructing a maṇḍala the deities must be invited in and made to stay.

---

[232] Online. http://www.sub.uni-goettingen.de/ebene_1/fiindolo/gretil/1_sanskr/4_rellit/buddh/sarvttsu.htm

In a generic tantric *sādhana* the idea is to imagine oneself as a deity (the *samayasattva*), then to invoke the actual deity externally (the *jñānasattva*), which is then merges with the *jñānasattva* transforming the *sādhaka* into the Buddha that one is imagining. The mantra *jaḥ hūṃ vaṃ hoḥ* effects this invitation, entry, binding and 'subjugation' of the deity.

mantra	**function**		**guardian**	
jaḥ	*karṣaṇa*	summoning	*vajrāṅkuśa*	vajra-hook
hūṃ	*praveśana*	entering	*vajrapāśa*	vajra-noose
vaṃ	*bandhana*	binding	*vajrasphoṭa*	vajra-expansion[233]
hoḥ	*vaśīkaraṇa*	subjugating	*vajrāveśa*	vajra-penetration

The word *vaśīkaraṇa* is undoubtedly 'subjugation' but this needs to be qualified. The terminology developed from Vedic sacrificial rituals where the object was to compel the gods to follow the natural order of the universe – to bring the rains on time etc. This developed into a magical system for obtaining personal goals, and then underwent a transformation when adopted by Buddhists. Subjugating Buddhas and Bodhisattvas is hardly likely to be beneficial, and since they very much want to do what they can to help un necessary. So generally speaking the interpretation of *vaśīkaraṇa* is less wilful. For instance we find some authors translating this in terms of 'pervading' the *maṇḍala* or 'becoming inseparable' from the *sādhaka*, which is reflected in the name of the corresponding door guardian.

Note also here that though Buddhists often misspell *bodhisattva* with one 't', that *mahāsattva* 'great hero' here is intended. Compare with notes on the word bodhisattva on p. 119.

[233] Snellgrove translates this name 'vajra-fetter'. Indo-Tibetan Buddhism, p.223.

Karaṇḍamudrā Dhāraṇī

Japanese: *Hōkyōin darani* (宝篋印陀羅尼)

Seed-syllable stryi

THE KARAṆḌAMUDRĀ DHĀRAṆĪ is an important litugical text in Japan. The dhāraṇī comes at the end of: 一切如來心祕密全身舍利寶篋印陀羅尼經 (Taisho T19 no.1022a). In Sanskrit the title would be:

Sarvatathāgata-adhiṣṭhāna-hṛdaya-guhya-dhātu-
karaṇḍamudrā-dhāraṇī Sūtra
सर्वतथागताधिष्ठानहृदयगुह्यधातुकरण्डमुद्रा धारणी सूत्र

i.e. The sutra of the spell (*dhāraṇī*) which is the symbol (*mudrā*) of the casket (*karaṇḍa*) of the secret heart element (*hṛdaya-guhya-dhātu*) which is the basis (*adhiṣṭhāna*) of all the awakened (*tathāgata*). A better English translation would be '*The sūtra of the spell symbolising the casket containing the mysterious essence of the basis for all the Awakened.*'

The *Karaṇḍamudrā dhāraṇī* is associated with the complex seed-syllable (*bījākṣara*) *stryi* (see above), which is seen on some Japanese stupas. This appears to derive from the first few syllables of the *dhāraṇī*:

नमस्त्र्यध्विकानां सर्वतथागतानां
namastryadhvikānāṃ sarvatathāgatānāṃ

homage to all the Tathāgatas of the three times.

'*Namastryadhvikānāṃ*' breaks down into *namas tryadhvikānāṃ*. *Namaḥ* means homage, and Sanskrit sandhi rules require swapping ḥ for s when followed by t.

Tradhvikānāṃ = *tri* + *adhvan* + *–ika* + *–nāṃ*; *tri* (three) *adhvan* (times) *–ika* (belonging to) *–nāṃ* (genitive plural case ending). When followed by a vowel, *i* becomes *y*, so *tri* > *try*. *Adhvan* + *ika* > *adhvika* is a *taddhita* compound, although we would usually expect the initial vowel of the base to lengthen (*ādhvika*) in cases like this. The grammar in *dhāraṇī* is often not what you might expect from Classical Sanskrit - most likely because they were not composed in Classical Sanskrit but one of the vernaculars.

Now broken into syllables for writing in Siddhaṃ:

na ma *strya* dhvi kā nāṃ

As the first syllable following the *namaḥ* (homage) *strya* comes, by metonymy, to stand for the whole *dhāraṇī*.

In the Chinese Tripiṭaka in the Taisho edition the Siddhaṃ script version of the *dhāraṇī* reads: *na maḥ stryi dhvi ka nāṃ sa rva ta thā ga ta nāṃ*... Someone has made a pdf of 1022a from the CBETA reader software.[234] It's not clear why the syllable became *styri* with an *i*, but I

[234] http://www.suttaworld.org/Collection_of_Buddhist/Taisho_Tripitaka/pdf/t19/T19n1022A.pdf

suspect that it was how the mantra was heard, by the translator - running the syllables together in normal speech it does sound rather like *namas stryi adhvikanāṃ*.

Karaṇḍamudrā means 'seal (*mudrā*) of the casket (*karaṇḍa*)' - a *karaṇḍa* was used for keeping relics.[235] In Japan the *dhāraṇī* is associated with the *hōkyōintō* (宝篋印塔) style of *stūpa* on which one sees the syllable *stryi* carved.

Karaṇḍamudrā Dhāraṇī

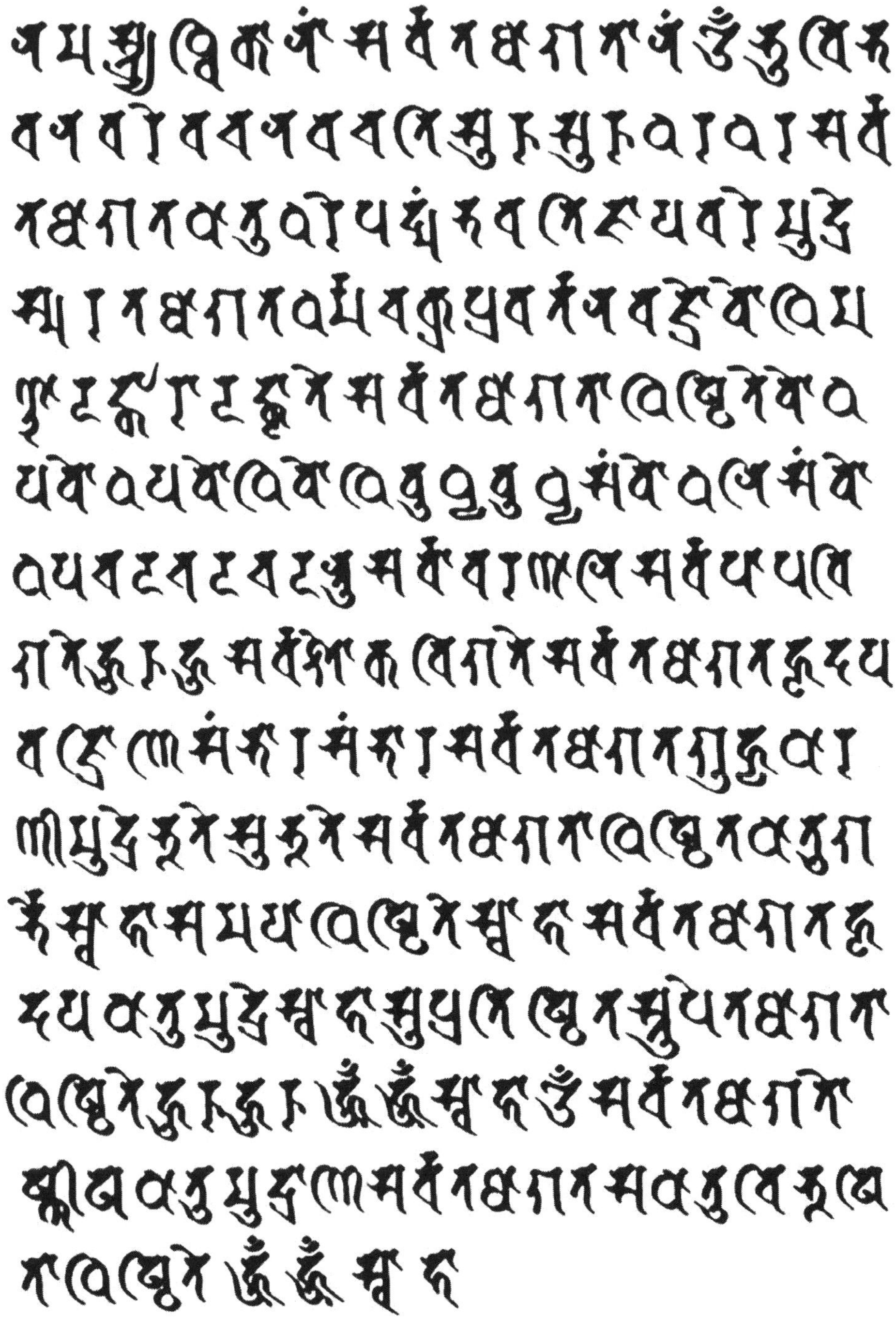

[235] (see Studholme, A. The Origins of Oṃ Maṇipadme Hūṃ : a Study of the Kāraṇḍavyūha Sūtra. SUNY Press. p.10).

Transliteration

namastryadhvikānāṃ sarvatathāgatānāṃ | oṃ bhuvibhavanavare vacanavacati | suru suru dhara dhara | sarvatathāgatadhātu dhare padmaṃ bhavati | jayavare mudre | smaratathāgata-dharmacakrapravartana vajre bodhimaṇḍālaṅkārālaṅkṛte | sarvatathāgatādhiṣṭhite | bodhaya bodhaya bodhi bodhi budhya budhya | saṃbodhani saṃbodhaya | cala cala calantu sarvāvaraṇāni | sarvapāpavigate | huru huru sarvaśokavigate | sarvatathāgatahṛdayavajriṇi | saṃbhāra saṃbhāra | sarvatathāgataguhyadhāraṇī mudre | bhūte subhūte | sarvatathāgatādhiṣṭhitadhātu garbhe svāhā | samayādhiṣṭhite svāhā | sarvatathāgatahṛdayadhātu mudre svāhā | supratiṣṭhitastūpe tathāgatādhiṣṭhite huru huru hūṃ hūṃ svāhā | oṃ sarvatathāgatoṣṇīṣadhātu mudrāṇi sarvatathāgatasadhātu vibhūṣitādhiṣṭhite hūṃ hūṃ svāhā ||

Devanāgarī

नमस्त्र्यध्विकानां सर्वतथागतानां । ओं भुविभवनवरे वचनवचति । सुरु सुरु धर धर । सर्वतथागतधातु धरे पद्मं भवति । जयवरे मुद्रे । स्मरतथागतधर्मचक्रप्रवर्तन वज्रे बोधिमण्डालङ्कारालङ्कृते । सर्वतथागताधिष्ठिते । बोधय बोधय बोधि बोधि बुध्य बुध्य । संबोधनि संबोधय । चल चल चलन्तु सर्वावरणानि । सर्वपापविगते । हुरु हुरु सर्वशोकविगते । सर्वतथागतहृदयवज्रिणि । संभार संभार । सर्वतथागतगुह्यधारणी मुद्रे । भूते सुभूते । सर्वतथागताधिष्ठितधातु गर्भे स्वाहा । समयाधिष्ठिते स्वाहा । सर्वतथागतहृदयधातु मुद्रे स्वाहा । सुप्रतिष्ठितस्तूपे तथागताधिष्ठिते हुरु हुरु हूं हूं स्वाहा । ओं सर्वतथागतोष्णीषधातु मुद्राणि सर्वतथागतसधातु विभूषिताधिष्ठिते हूं हूं स्वाहा ॥

Note

I've consulted several sources for this and found that most versions break sandhi to facilitate reading and/or chanting. I've reconstructed the Sanskrit with sandhi as best I can. There are a number of problems with the Sanskrit in the Taisho version of the text.

Nīlakaṇṭha Dhāraṇī

THE *NĪLAKAṆṬHA DHĀRAṆĪ* IS also known as the *Mahākaruṇika Dhāraṇī*. Nīlakaṇṭha means blue-throated, while Mahākaruṇīka means Greatly Compassionate. It is preserved in several versions in the Chinese canon, but in each case the Sanskrit is badly corrupted. I use the reconstucted Sanskrit version by Lokesh Chandra working from the various versions in his article *Origin of the Avalokitesvara of Potala*. The text contains many obvious features assimilated from both Śaiva and Vaiṣṇava milieus - the very name Nīlakaṇṭha is strongly associated with Śiva.

Mantra over the page.

Notes

The Nīlakaṇṭha Dhāraṇī was translated into Chinese four times: first by Vajrabodhi (fl. 719-741) Taisho 1112, then twice by his pupil Amoghavajra (ca 723-774) T. 1111, 1113b[236], and lastly in the fourteenth century by Dhyānabhadra T. 1113a. In addition some Chinese and Central Asian texts have been discovered at Dunhuang. Amoghavajra's version (T. 1113A) which is preserved along with a (badly corrupted) Siddhaṃ script Sanskrit version is the most popular form of the dhāraṇī and is popularly chanted in East Asia.

More information on this dhāraṇī and it's variations can be found in Lokesh Chandra. *The Thousand-Armed Avalokitesvara*. The blue throat is related to an ancient Indian myth of churning the ocean of milk (*samudra manthan*) - a contest between the *devas* and *asuras* - with the goal of producing amṛta, the nectar of immortality. There are several versions of this story but in some the amṛta becomes poisoned (by the asuras) and in order to prevent all life being destroyed someone drinks it. In some versions is it Śiva who drinks it, in Buddhist legends Vajrapāṇi or Avalokiteśvara. Whoever drinks it, it turns their throat (or in Vajrapāṇi's case his whole body) blue. Hence the name blue (*nīla*) throated (*kaṇṭha*) (this is an example of a *bahuvrīhi* compound). Note that the peacock has a blue throat and because it occasionally eats snakes is thooought to be immune to poison.

Many of the epithets in this *dhāraṇī* are adopted from Śaiva or Vaiṣṇa sources. Names associated with Viṣnu include: *padmahasta*, *vajrahasta*, *cakrahasta*, *varāhamuka*. As I have pointed out Nīlakaṇṭha is a name for Śiva; we also find siddhayogīśvara. We find many examples of Buddhists purposefully absorbing material, iconography and ritual elements from other religious milieus.

[236] link to CBETA romanised version in Google Books: http://is.gd/fdKHa

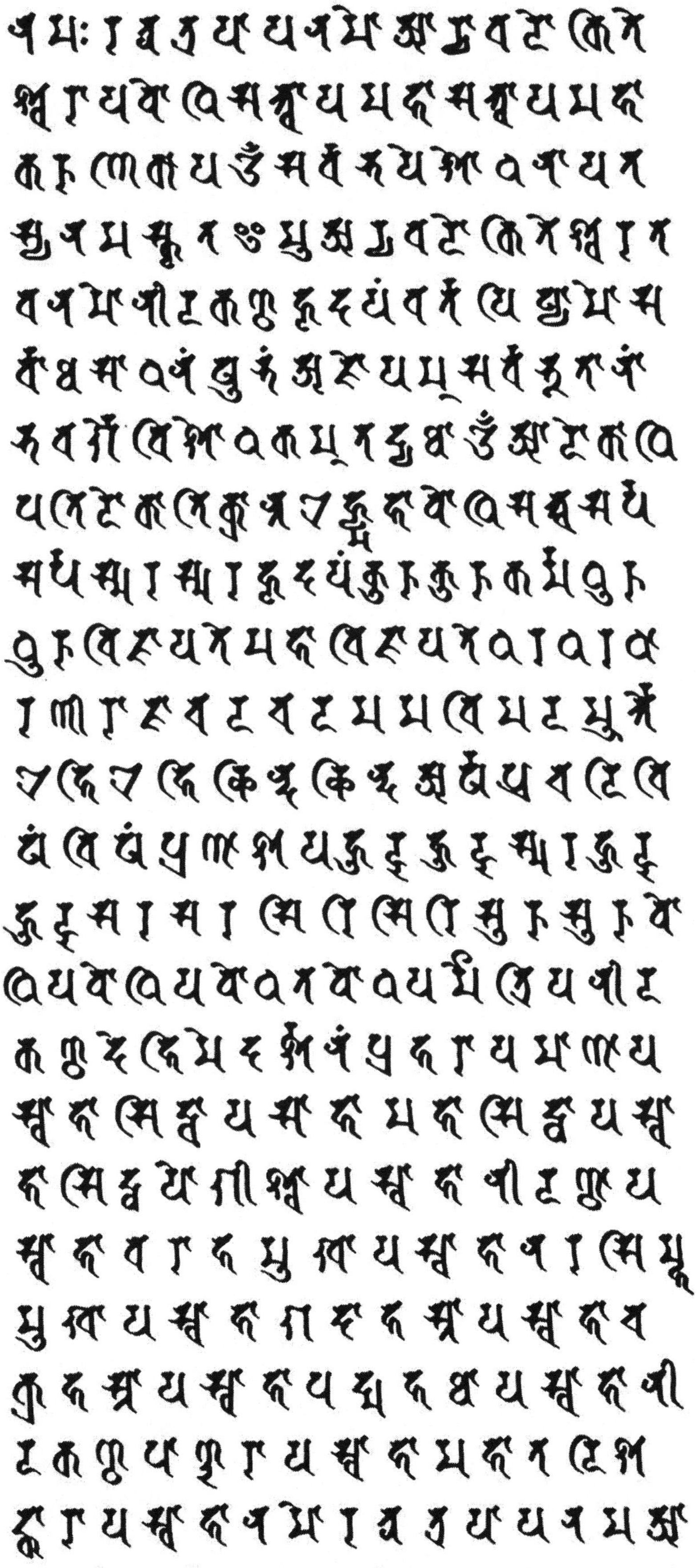

Transliteration

na maḥ ra tna tra yā ya na mo ā ryā va lo ki te
śva rā ya bo dhi sa ttvā ya ma hā sa ttvā ya ma hā
ka ru ṇi kā ya oṃ sa rva bha ye śo dha nā ya ta
sya na ma skṛ ta i mu ā ryā va lo ki te śva ra ta
va na mo nī la ka ṇṭha. hṛ da yaṃ va rta yi ṣyā mo sa
rvā tha sā dha naṃ ṣu bhaṃ a je ya m sa rva bhū tā nāṃ
bha va ma rge vi śo dha kam ta dya thā oṃ ā lo kā dhi
pa ti lo kā ti krā nta e hyma hā bo dhi sa ttva sa rpa
sa rpa sma ra sma ra hṛ da yaṃ ku ru ku ru ka rma dhu ru
dhu ru vi ja ya te ma hā vi ja ya te dha ra dha ra dhā
ra ṇī rā ja ca la ca la ma ma vi ma la mū rtte
e hi e hi chi nda chi nda a rṣa pra c ali vi
ṣaṃ vi ṣaṃ pra ṇā śa ya hu lu hu lu sma ra hu lu
hu lu sa ra sa ra si ri si ri su ru su ru bo
dhi ya bo dhi ya bo dha ta bo dha ya mai tri ya nī la
ka ṇṭha de hi me da rśa naṃ pra ha rā ya mā ṇā ya
svā hā si ddhā ya svā hā ma hā si ddhā ya svā
hā si ddha yo gī śva rā ya svā hā nī la ka ṇṭhā ya
svā hā va rā ha mu khā ya svā hā na ra si mha
mu khā ya svā hā ga dā ha stā ya svā hā ca
kra ha stā ya svā hā pa dma ha thā ya svā hā nī
la ka ṇṭha pā ṇḍa rā ya svā hā ma hā ta li śa
ṅka rā ya svā hā na mo ra tna tra yā ya na ma ā ryā
va lo ki te śva rā ya bo dhi sa ttvā ya svā hā

Namaḥ ratnatrayāya. Namo āryāvalokiteśvarāya bodhisattvāya mahāsattvāya mahākaruṇikāya.

Oṃ sarvabhaye śodhanāya tasya namaskṛta imu āryāvalokiteśvara tava namo nīlakaṇṭha. hṛdayaṃ vartayiṣyāmo sarvātha-sādhanaṃ ṣubhaṃ. ajeyam sarvabhūtānāṃ bhava-marge-viśodhakam tadyathā:

oṃ ālokādhipati lokātikrānta ehymahābodhisattva sarpa-sarpa smara smara hṛdayam kuru kuru karma dhuru dhuru vijayate mahāvijayate dhara dhara dhāraṇīrāja, cala cala mama vimala-mūrtte, ehi ehi chinda chinda arṣapracali viṣam viṣam praṇāśaya hulu hulu smara hulu hulu sara sara siri siri suru suru bodhiya bodhiya bodhata bodhaya maitriya nīlakaṇṭha dehi me darśanaṃ. Praharāyamāṇāya svāhā siddhāya svāhā mahāsiddhāya svāhā siddhayogīśvarāya svāhā nīlakaṇṭhāya svāhā varāhamukhāya svāhā narasimhamukhāya svāhā gadāhastāya svāhā cakrahastāya svāhā padmahathāya svāhā nīlakaṇṭhapāṇḍarāya svāhā mahātali-śaṅkarāya svāhā

namo ratnatrayāya nama āryāvalokiteśvarāya bodhisattvāya svāhā

The Śānti Mantra

THE ŚĀNTI MANTRA is used to invoke the peace of liberation or *nirvāṇa*. The word *śānti* simply means 'peace'. This mantra is used at the end of pujas in the Triratna Buddhist Community.

Siddhaṃ

ཨོཾ་ཤཱནྟི་ཤཱནྟི་ཤཱནྟི།

Tibetan – Uchen

Lantsa

ओं शान्ति शान्ति शान्ति

Devanāgarī

Transliteration

oṃ śā nti śā nti śā nti

oṃ śānti śānti śānti

The Śūnyatā Mantra

Śūnyatā or emptiness is a Buddhist technical term which refers to the fact that phenomena lack permanence and substantiality (or essence). This mantra is used in tantric rituals to remind the *yogin* of this basic Buddhist teaching, and to try to evoke the experience of it - normally we experience a series of jolts when we discover that things don't last, or provide satisfaction because we fail to see the true nature of things. The *Śūnyatā* mantra helps us tune into impermanence and insubstantiality. The mantra appears in visualisation practices as a prelude to visualising the *yidam*.

There is another mantra which is commonly called the *Śūnyatā Mantra* which I have labelled the *Śuddha Mantra* to distinguish it from this mantra (since it actually features the word *śuddha*).

Siddhaṃ

Tibetan Uchen

Lantsa

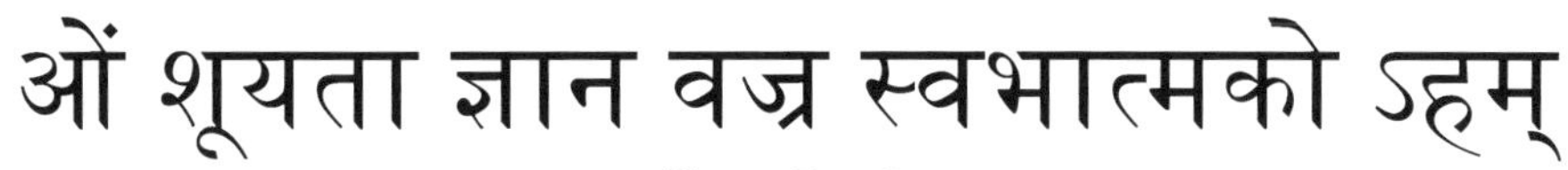

ओं शूयता ज्ञान वज्र स्वभात्मको ऽहम्
Devanāgarī

Transliteration

oṃ śū nya tā jñā na va jra sva bhā vā tma ko 'ham

oṃ śūnyatā-jñāna-vajra-svabhāvātmako 'ham

Comments

Translates literally as: "oṃ emptiness knowing diamond self-nature-essence I". In *The Cult of Tārā* Stephan Beyer renders it: "*oṃ*. I am the very self whose essence is the diamond knowledge of emptiness." Or it could go: "oṃ I am the *vajra* essential-own-being which is the knowledge of *śūnyatā*."

The word *jñānavajrasvabhāvātmakaḥ* is a compound of *jñāna* + *vajra* + *svabhāva* + *ātma* + (suffix) *ka*. Long compounds are often difficult to unravel: *ātmaka* means 'belonging to' or 'having the nature'; *svabhāva* means intrinsic nature'; *vajra* is, of course, 'diamond'; and *jñāna* means knowledge'. The compound means something like 'having a nature whose essence is the diamond knowledge'.

The '*ham* on the end is not a seed-syllable, it is an artefact of *sandhi* or euphony rules. Without *sandhi* the words are: *jñānavajrasvabhāvātmakaḥ aham*; with *sandhi -aḥ* followed by *a* becomes *o* '. The apostrophe in '*ham* is a representation of the Devanāgarī symbol ऽ known as *avagraha*, and marks the missing '*a*'. In Tibetan the avagraha is indicated by ྅ and this is used in the Derge and Lhasa editions of the Tibetan Tripiṭaka, though it is not universal in Tibetan manuscripts. The form ending *jñānavajrasvabhāvātmako 'ham* tells us that this is a case where Sanskrit *sandhi* rules have been applied, hence we must treat the stem forms of the other words as forming a compound.

Maitiu O'Ceileachair says that Tibetan *sādhanas* tend to avoid the vowel sandhi between *bhāva* and *ātma* in this mantra. In Sanskrit the two become *bhāvātma*, but in Tibetan texts the two are kept separate.

The Śuddha - Purity Mantra

This mantra is frequently referred to as Śūnyatā Mantra, although the words themselves focus on *śuddha* or purity, so I have called it the Purity Mantra to distinguish it from the mantra which focuses on the word *śūnyatā*,

Siddhaṃ

Tibetan – Uchen

Lantsa

ओं स्वभाव शुद्धाः सर्वधर्माः स्वभाव शुद्धो ऽहं

Devanāgarī

Transliteration

oṃ sva bhā va śu ddhāḥ sa rva dha rmāḥ sva bhā va śu ddho ‘haṃ

oṃ svabhāva śuddhāḥ sarvadharmāḥ svabhāva śuddho ‘haṃ

Comments

Translates literally as: “*oṃ* (by) self-nature pure (are) all dharmas; by self-nature pure (am) I.” Which I would render: *oṃ*. all dharmas in their own-being are pure; in my own-being I too am pure!

Notes

Apart from *oṃ* the sentence is well formed Sanskrit, with correctly declined words and sandhi applied.

Sūtras

This section consists of extracts of Buddhist texts from both Pāli and Sanskrit. Sūtras are the fundamental texts of Buddhism. The word literally means 'thread' though it is usually translated as 'discourse' or something along those lines. In Buddhist traditions the sūtras were records of the teachings given by the Buddha and remembered by Ānanda.

Some comments on the word sūtra.

The Buddhist use of the Sanskrit word *sūtra* is based on the notion that the Prakrit (especially Pāli) word *sutta* derives from the Sanskrit word *sūtra*. This is understandable since Pāli resolves almost all conjunct consonants to double consonants. But if you ever look at a Brahmanical *sūtra* you can easily see that they are an entirely different genre of texts. Brahmanical *sūtras* have more in common with *abhidhamma* style texts. They are terse, almost like bullet points. There is none of the narrative style of the Buddhist *sūtra*. It is far more likely that *sutta* derives from another Sanskrit word: *sūkta*. Both *sūkta* and *sūtra* resolve to *sutta* in Pāli. *Sūkta* means 'well spoken' from *su* + *ukta*, where *su-* means "good or well"; *ukta* is a past-participle formed (irregularly) on the verbal root √*vac* 'speech or words'. *Sūkta* is also a name for the verses of the Vedas, and it seems likely that this is case of conscious imitation of Brahmins by Buddhists – other examples include '*tevijja*' the Buddha's three kinds of special knowledge which references the three Vedas; and the 'three fires' of greed, hatred and delusion which references the three sacred fires of the Vedic sacrificial enclosure.

The useage of *sūtra* is now so well established that even though it is probably wrong, it is unlikely ever to be corrected to *sūkta*.

Thus have I heard

THESE WORDS ARE considered to begin every genuine Buddhist *sūtra*. The voice is that of Ānanda, the Buddha's cousin and attendant for his last twenty-five years. According to the Buddhist tradition Ānanda was present at many teachings and after the Buddha's death was called on to recite all of them. What he recalled became the *sūtrapiṭaka* (Pāli: *suttapiṭaka*) or collection of discourses.

There is a little discussion about whether to translate these words as: "Thus I heard. At one time..." or "Thus I heard at one time". The next part always says where the Buddha was living (*viharati*) at the time the discourse was delivered.

It is sometimes said that the language spoken by the Buddha was Pāli. However scholars agree that this is extremely unlikely. The Buddha is likely to have spoken a Prakrit related to the dialect known as Magadhi. Pāli is founded on Magadhi but with admixtures of other Middle-Indic dialects and some Sanskritisation. The Pāli texts have been translated at least once.

Sanskrit

𑖊𑖪𑖽 𑖦𑖧𑖯 𑖫𑖿𑖨𑖲𑖝𑖽 𑖊𑖎𑖭𑖿𑖦𑖰𑖡𑖿𑖭𑖦𑖧𑖸

Siddhaṃ

एवं मया श्रुतं एकस्मिन्समये

Devanāgarī

Transliteration

e vaṃ ma yā śru taṃ e ka smi nsa ma ye

evaṃ mayā śrutaṃ ekasmin samaye...

Pāli

𑖊𑖪𑖽𑖦𑖸𑖭𑖲𑖝𑖽𑖊𑖎𑖽𑖭𑖦𑖧𑖽

Siddhaṃ

ඒවං මේ සුතං ඒකං සමයං

Sinhala

एवं मे सुतं एकं समयं

Devanāgarī

Transliteration

e vaṃ me su taṃ e kaṃ sa ma yaṃ

evaṃ me sutaṃ ekaṃ samayaṃ

Notes

This phrase is a good case study of the similarities differences between Pāli and Sanskrit. The conjunct *śru* devolves to the simple *su*. Also note the case endings, which show the grammatical relationship of the words, is different. Otherwise the words are very similar.

Karaṇīya Mettā Sutta

THIS IMPORTANT SUTTA from the Pāli canon describes the Buddhist path in terms of loving kindness or *mettā* (Sanskrit: *maitrī*). It is found in the Sutta Nipāta which is considered to be amongst the earliest layers of the composition of the canon. Also known as simply the *Mettā Sutta*, although there is another text with that name, the *Karaṇīya Mettā Sutta* is one of the best known *paritta* texts which were and still are chanted for protection against harm. The Pāli commentary records that it was taught to a group of bhikkhus who were having problems with tree devas.[237] The Pāli text comes from the Pāli text society edited version.

Pāli text in roman script

Karanīyam atthakusalena
yan taṃ santaṃ padaṃ abhisamecca:
Sakko ujū ca sūjū ca
suvaco c'assa mudu anatimānī,

Santussako ca subharo ca
appakicco ca sallahukavutti
Santindriyo ca nipako ca
appagabbho kulesu ananugiddho,

Na ca khuddaṃ samācare kiñci
yena viññū pare upavadeyyuṃ
Sukhino vā khemino hontu
sabbe sattā bhavantu sukhitattā:

Ye keci pāṇabhūt' atthi
tasā vā thāvarā vā anavasesā
Dīgha vā ye mahantā vā
majjhimā rassakā aṇukathūlā

Diṭṭhā vā ye vā addiṭṭhā
ye ca dūre vasanti avidūre
Bhūtā vā sambhavesī vā
sabbe sattā bhavantu sukhitattā

Na paro paraṃ nikubbetha
nâtimaññetha katthacinaṃ kañci
Vyārosanā paṭighasaññā
nâññamaññassa dukkham iccheyya

Mātā yathā niyaṃ puttaṃ
āyusā ekaputtam anurakkhe
Evam pi sabbabhūtesu
mānasam bhāvaye aparimāṇaṃ

Mettañ ca sabbalokasmiṃ
mānasam bhāvaye aparimāṇaṃ
Uddhaṃ adho ca tiriyañ ca
asambādhaṃ averaṃ asapattaṃ

Tiṭṭhaṃ caraṃ nisinno vā
sayāno vā yāvat' assa vigatamiddho
Etaṃ satiṃ adhiṭṭheyya
brahmam etaṃ vihāraṃ idha-m-ahu

Diṭṭhiñ ca anupagamma
sīlavā dassanena sampanno
Kāmesu vineyya gedhaṃ
na hi jātu gabbhaseyyaṃ punar etī ti

Siddham text following page

[237] I have translated the story. 'How the Mettā Sutta Came About' : http://jayarava.blogspot.com/2010/06/how-karaniya-metta-sutta-came-about.html

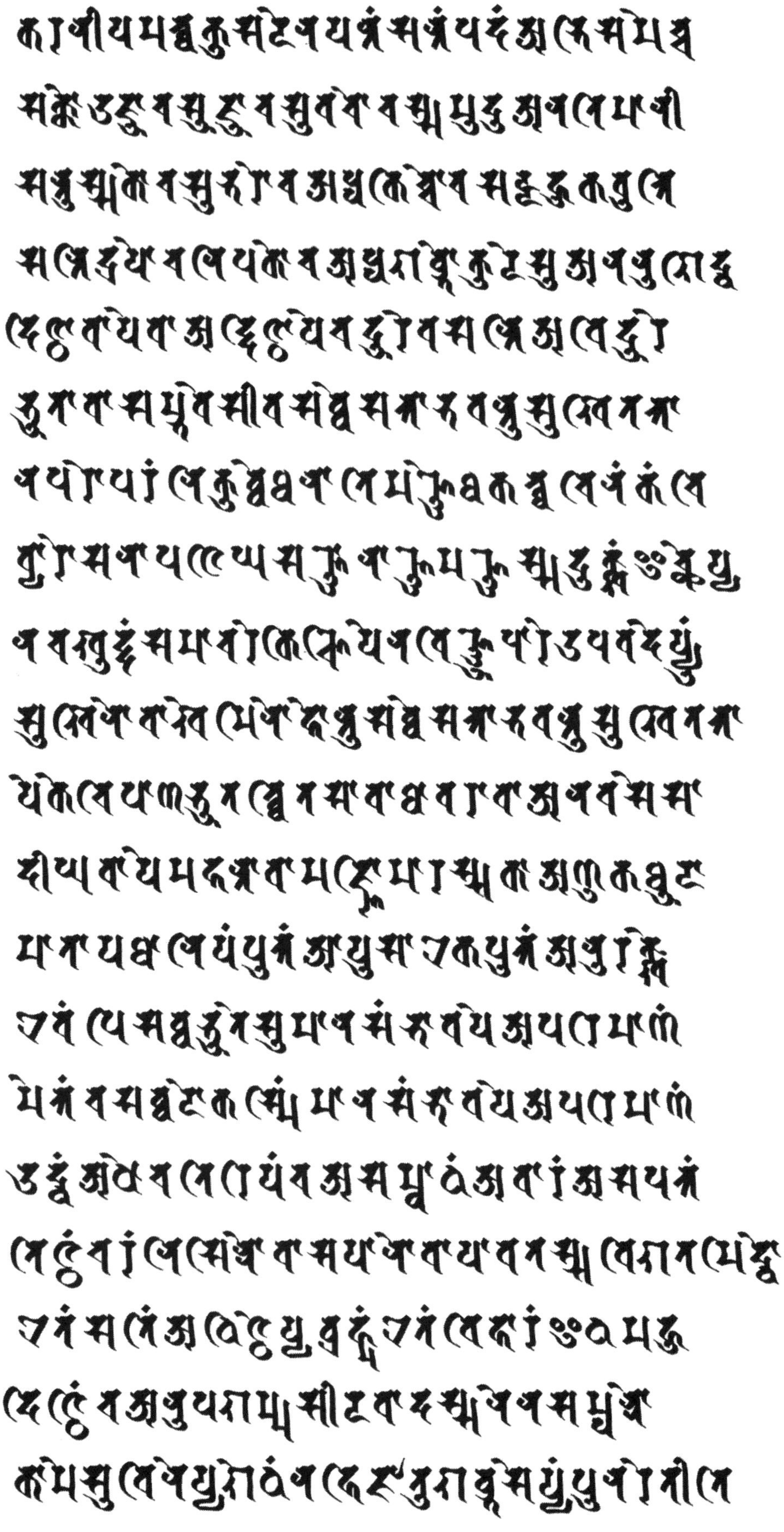

English Translation

This is what ought to be done by one skilled in the good
Having understood the path to peace
Able, straight forward and 'straight up',
polite, they should be mild and not arrogant

Contented and frugal,
with few responsibilities and easy going,
grounded, and not impulsive;
not chasing status

And not doing the slightest thing
which is denounced by the Wise in others
May they have happiness and peace;
May all beings be happy in themselves

Whatever living beings there are
fearful or fearless – without remainder
Huge, large,
medium, small. Fine or coarse.

Seen or unseen,
Remote or living nearby,
Born or seeking birth:
May all beings be happy in themselves

Not humiliating, or despising
anyone anywhere
Though anger or experiencing repugnance:
[they] should not wish suffering for another.

Like a mother's own child,
[she will] protect that only child with her life
Thus for all beings should
the heart become infinite

And friendliness for all the world,
[should] the heart become infinite
In all the directions of space,
unobstructed, peaceable, without enmity

Standing, walking, sitting
or lying down, As far as possible without sluggishness
This mindfulness should be undertaken;
[It is like] dwelling with god here and now

Not falling into views,
ethical and with perfect vision
Having given up greed for sensory pleasures,
freed without doubt from birth.

Mettā Sutta in Sinhala Script

මෙත්තසුත්තං

කරණීයමත්ථකුසලෙන, යන්ත සන්තං පදං අභිසමෙච්ච;
සක්කො උජූ ච සුහුජූ ච, සුවචො චස්ස මුදු අනතිමානී.
සන්තුස්සකො ච සුභරො ච, අප්පකිච්චො ච සල්ලහුකවුත්ති;
සන්තින්ද්‍රියො ච නිපකො ච, අප්පගබ්භො කුලෙස්වනනුගිද්ධො.
න ච ඛුද්දමාචරෙ කිඤ්චි, යෙන විඤ්ඤූ පරෙ උපවදෙය්‍යුං;
සුඛිනො ව ඛෙමිනො හොන්තු, සබ්බසත්තා භවන්තු සුඛිතත්තා.
යෙ කෙචි පාණභූතත්ථි, තසා වා ථාවරා වනවසෙසා;
දීඝා වා යෙ ව මහන්තා, මජ්ඣිමා රස්සකා අණුකථූලා.
දිට්ඨා වා යෙ ව අදිට්ඨා, යෙ ව දූරෙ වසන්ති අවිදූරෙ;
භූතා ව සම්භවෙසී ව, සබ්බසත්තා භවන්තු සුඛිතත්තා.
න පරො පරං නිකුබ්බෙථ, නාතිමඤ්ඤෙථ කත්ථචි න කඤ්චි;
බ්‍යාරොසනා පටිඝසඤ්ඤා, නාඤ්ඤමඤ්ඤස්ස දුක්ඛමිච්ඡෙය්‍ය.
මාතා යථා නියං පුත්තමායුසා එකපුත්තමනුරක්ඛෙ;
එවම්පි සබ්බභූතෙසු, මානසං භාවයෙ අපරිමාණං.
මෙත්තඤ්ච සබ්බලොකස්මිං, මානසං භාවයෙ අපරිමාණං;
උද්ධං අධො ච තිරියඤ්ච, අසම්බාධං අවෙරමසපත්තං.
තිට්ඨං චරං නිසින්නො ව, සයානො යාවතාස්ස විතමිද්ධො;
එතං සතිං අධිට්ඨෙය්‍ය, බ්‍රහ්මමෙතං විහාරමිධමාහු.
දිට්ඨිඤ්ච අනුපග්ගම්ම, සීලවා දස්සනෙන සම්පන්නො;
කාමෙසු විනය ගෙධං, න හි ජාතුග්ගබ්භසෙය්‍ය පුනරෙතීති.

Notes

The translation is by Jayarava and is an original, fairly literal rendering.

Siddhaṃ is a fine script for writing Pāli although it would not have been traditional to do so. Siddhaṃ was developed for writing Sanskrit, but the two languages are so similar that it presents no difficulties. Pāli was in fact recorded mainly in the Sinhala script in Sri Lanka and the Burmese Script in Burma - both of which also derive ultimately from Brāhmī Script (see p. 19f.).

It's not often commented on but this '*sutta*' is not actually a *sutta* at all because it does not begin *evaṃ me sutaṃ* - thus have I heard - and does not finish with a response from the audience which are the two main criteria for a sutta. I suppose it is really an example of a *gatha* or verse.

The Last Words of the Buddha

THESE WORDS ARE TRADITIONALLY said to be the last that the Buddha uttered to an audience of Arahants, just before he passed into *parinibbāna*. The source text is chapter six of the *Mahāparinibbāna Sutta* (*Dīgha Nikāya* 16.6.8).

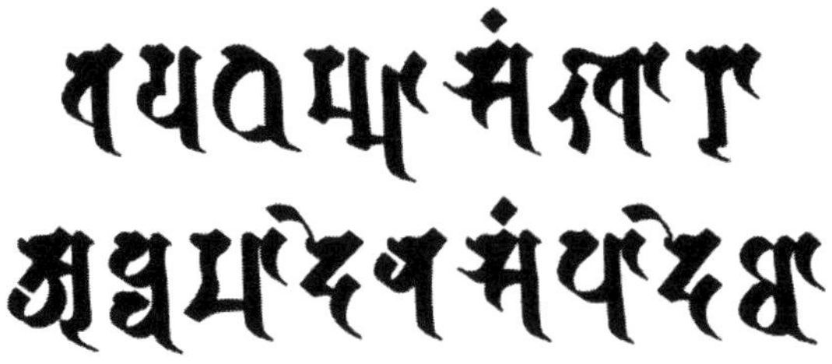

Siddhaṃ

වයධම්මා සඞ්ඛාරා

අප්පමාදේන සංපදේථා

Sinhala

Transliteration

vayadhammā saṅkhārā

appamādena saṃpadethā

Translation

Conditioned things are perishable;
with vigilance strive to succeed.

or alternatively

All experiences are disappointing
it is through vigilance that you succeed[238]

[238] See my commentary on the Buddha's last words: http://jayarava.org/buddhas-last-words.html

Prajñāpāramitā Ratnaguṇasaṁcayagāthā

Prajñāpāramitā Ratnaguṇasaṁcayagāthā

The *Prajñāpāramitā Ratnaguṇasaṁcayagāthā* - The Verses on the Perfection of Wisdom Which is the Storehouse of Precious Virtues - is the verse summary of the *Aṣṭasāhasrikā Prajñāpāramitā Sūtra* - the Perfection of Wisdom in 8000 lines - the two together being the earliest Prajñāpāramitā Sūtras. This first *gāthā* captures something beautiful about the approach of Mahāyāna Buddhism.

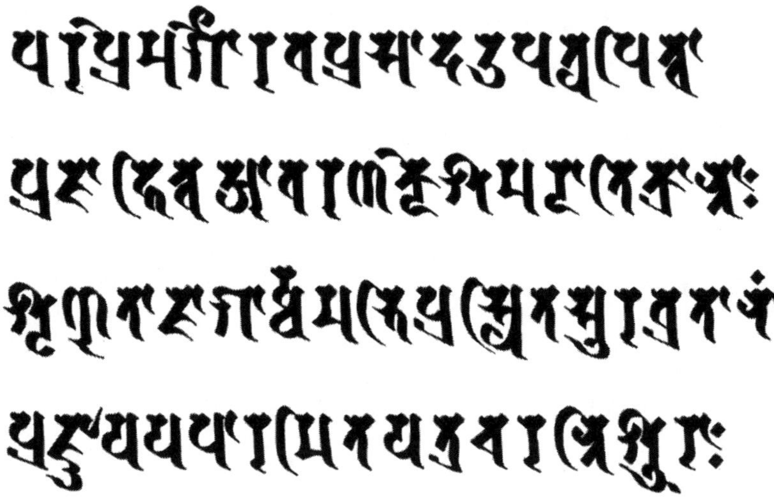

Transliteration

para prema gaurava prasāda upasthapitvā
prajahitva āvaraṇa kleśamalātikrāntāḥ
śṛṇutā jagārthamabhiprasthita suravratānāṁ
prajñāya pāramita yatra caranti śūrāḥ

Translation

Call forth as much as you can of love, of respect and of faith!
Remove the obstructing defilements, and clear away all your taints!
Listen to the Perfect Wisdom of the gentle Buddhas
Taught for the weal of the world, for heroic spirits intended!

Notes

Sanskrit text from Digital Sanskrit Buddhist Canon.[239] Translation by Edward Conze. 1983. *Perfection of Wisdom in Eight Thousand Lines and its Verse Summary*. San Francisco, Four Seasons Foundation, p.9.

[239] http://www.uwest.edu/sanskritcanon/Sutra/roman/Sutra%2028/Sutra28-1.html

The Doors to the Deathless are Open

Deathless is a very evocative synonym for *nirvāṇa* and features in these words, which were spoken to *Brahmasahampati* by the Buddha just after his Awakening. The Buddha paused for dramatic effect to consider whether he should teach, or whether it might be too difficult. After a request from Brahmā the Buddha 'realised' that he must teach.

The locus classicus is the Pāli *Ariyapariyesanā Sutta*, but as shown below there are parallels in later biographical texts as well. I've chosen to illustrate the version in the *Lalitavistara Sūtra* (LV 25.34) because it is in Sanskrit:

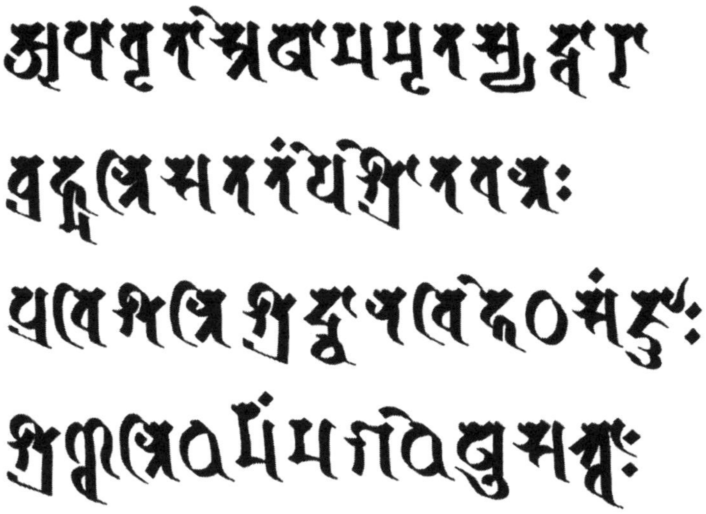

Transliteration

apāvṛtāsteṣāmamṛtasya dvārā
brahman ti satataṁ ye śrotavantaḥ |

praviśanti śraddhā naviheṭhasaṁjñāḥ
śṛṇvanti dharmaṁ magadheṣu sattvāḥ ||

Translation

The door to the undying is laid open
O Brahma, constantly to those with ears.

They enter non-harmful thoughts faithfully
The beings of Magadha listen to the doctrine.

Notes

There are parallel verses in the Pāli Canon in the *Ariyapariyesanā Sutta* (MN 26, PTS M i.170), and in the *Mahāvastu* (Mv 3.319). They are quite different in places. It is likely that the Pāli represents a truer memory of the text.

The *Aryapariyesanā Sutta* reads:

> *apārutā tesaṃ amatassa dvārā*
> *ye sotavanto pamuñcantu saddhaṃ*
> *vihiṃsasaññī pagunaṃ na bhāsiṃ*
> *dhammaṃ paṇītaṃ manujesu brahme ti*
>
> The doors of the deathless are open for them -
> let those who have ears give up the funeral rites
> Forseeing bother, Brahmā, I did not speak
> the rarified, subtle Dhamma among human beings

The *Mahāvastu* reads:

> *apāvṛtaṃ me amṛtasya dvāraṃ brahma ti bhagavantaṃ ye śrotukāmā śraddhāṃ pramuṃcantu viheṭhasaṃjñāṃ*
>
> *viheṭhasamjño praguṇo abhūṣidharmo aśuddho magadeṣu pūvaṃ*
>
> I have opened the doors to the Deathless, Brahma. Let those who desire to hear the Blessed One give up the funeral rites based on a harmful idea.
>
> For already there has arisen among the Magadhans a Dharma that is impure, based on a harmful idea, and wrong.

Buddhist Chants & Phrases

These chants and phrases usually have canonical precedents but have become independent of their textual context – unlike the previous section. Phrases such as *sabbe sattā sukhi hontu* are not easily distinguishable from mantras.

Ye dharmā hetuprabhava – Causation

THIS VERSE FROM THE VINAYA beginning "*ye dharmā hetuprabhava*" are the words spoken by the Arahant Assaji (S. Aśvajit) to Upatissa, later to become known as Sariputta (S. Śāriputra). Sāriputta along with his boyhood companion Kolita, later called Moggallāna (S. Maudgalyayana), was one of the two chief disciples of the Buddha. Upon meeting Assaji, Sariputta was impressed and asked after his teacher and the dhamma that he taught. Assaji demurred, being "only a beginner", but eventually responded with the now famous verse, and before he had finished Sariputta had a decisive break through.

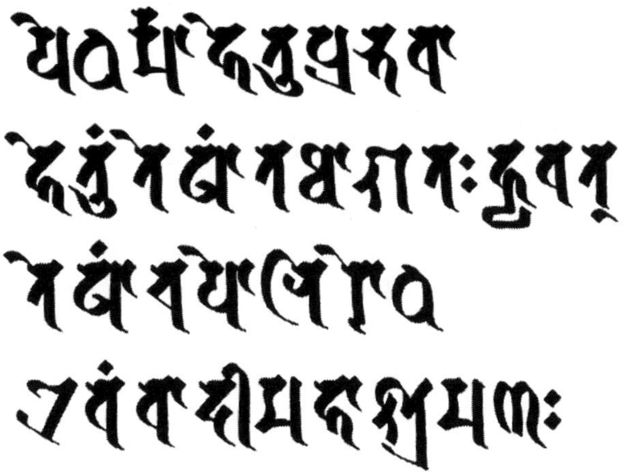

Transliteration

Ye dha rmā he tu pra bha vā
he tuṃ te ṣāṃ ta thā ga taḥ hya va da t
te ṣāṃ ca yo ni ro dha
e vaṃ vā dī ma hā śra ma ṇaḥ

Ye dharmā hetu prabhāvā
hetuṃ teṣāṃ tathāgataḥ hy avadat
teṣāṃ ca yo nirodha
evaṃ vādī mahāśramaṇaḥ

Translation

Of those things that arise from a cause,
The Tathāgata has told the cause,
And also what their cessation is:
This is the doctrine of the Great Recluse

or alternatively

Of those experiences that arise from a cause
The Tathāgata has said, "this is their cause,
And this is their cessation":
Thus the Great Śramaṇa teaches.

Tibetan Uchen

༄༅། ཡེ་དྷ་རྨཱ་ཧེ་ཏུ་པྲ་བྷ་ཝཱ།
ཧེ་ཏུཾ་ཏེ་ཥཱཾ་ཏ་ཐཱ་ག་ཏཿ་ཧྱ་ཝ་དཏ།
ཏེ་ཥཱཾ་ཙ་ཡོ་ནི་རོ་དྷ།
ཨེ་ཝཾ་ཝཱདཱི་མ་ཧཱ་ཤྲ་མ་ཎཿ།།

This is the Sanskrit text transliterated using the Tibetan Uchen script – it is not a Tibetan translation.

Devanāgarī

ये धर्मा हेतुप्रभवा
हेतुं तेषां तथागतः ह्यवदत् ।
तेषां च यो निरोध
एवं वादी महाश्रमणः॥

Pali

Devanāgari

ये धम्मा हेतुप्पभवा
तेसं हेतुं तथागतो आह।
तेसञ्च यो निरोधो
एवं वादी महासमणो॥

Sinhala

යේ ධම්මා හේතුප්පභවා
තේසං හේතුං තථාගතෝ ආහ|
තේසඤ්ච යෝ නිරෝධෝ
ඒවං වාදී මහාසමණෝ||

Aśokan Brāhmī script

𑀬𑁂 𑀥𑀫𑁆𑀫𑀸 𑀳𑁂𑀢𑀼𑀧𑁆𑀧𑀪𑀯𑀸
𑀢𑁂𑀲𑀁 𑀳𑁂𑀢𑀼𑀁 𑀢𑀣𑀸𑀕𑀢𑁄 𑀆𑀳
𑀢𑁂𑀲𑀜𑁆𑀘 𑀬𑁄 𑀦𑀺𑀭𑁄𑀥𑁄
𑀏𑀯𑀁 𑀯𑀸𑀤𑀻 𑀫𑀳𑀸𑀲𑀫𑀡𑁄

Transliteration

Ye dhammā hetuppabhavā
tesaṃ hetuṃ tathāgato āha,
tesañca yo nirodho
evaṃ vādī mahāsamaṇo

Comments

This verse has been referred to a kind of Buddhist *credo* (Latin: *I believe*). It is very commonly seen inscribed on statues of the Buddha, or on the backs of paintings (see above). That "things" arise in dependence on causes, and cease when the causes are no longer present is taken not as a statement of faith by Buddhists, but as a statement of empirical truth; a fact which may be confirmed through observation. Buddhists do not follow the Christian idea: *credo quia absurdum est* – "I believe it because it is unreasonable". Belief, if it is to be at all relevant, must be reasonable.

The "things" refered to are in fact *dharmas* (Pāli *dhamma*) which are mental phenomena - the experience of a thing through the senses and the mind, rather than actual objects themselves. The phrase is: "of those dharmas which arise from causes..." All knowledge of any "objective" reality is mediated through the senses and the mind, and therefore all knowledge is subjective. This does not deny the possibility of an objective reality, only that it can be known directly. In contemporary terms then, it is experience (the knowledge of dharmas) which arises from a cause, and ceases when the cause is no longer present. By claiming to know the origins of experience, the Buddha is not claiming omniscience, or indeed any knowledge of objective reality. His gnosis is related to the nature of experience, why experience is ultimately disappointing, and what to do about it.

May all beings be happy!

THIS PHRASE in Pāli has taken on the status of a mantra - it is chanted repeatedly in Pāli by Buddhists. Siddhaṃ can be used to write any Indic language including Pāli, although it is unlikely, historically speaking, that it was.

Transliteration

Siddhaṃ

सब्बे सत्ता सुखि होन्तु

Devanāgarī

සබ්බෙ සත්තා සුඛි හෝන්තු

Sinhala

sa bbe sa ttā su khi ho ntu

sabbe sattā sukhi hontu

Translation

May all beings be happy!

Notes

The Wildmind online meditation site has more info on this phrase as a mantra as well as some sound files for how it sounds chanted.[240]

[240] http://www.wildmind.org/mantras/figures/sabbesatta/

Truths of the Noble Ones

The Four Noble Truths[241] is one of the best known and succinct summaries of the Buddha's teaching. Briefly the truths are: that all experiences are ultimately disappointing (duḥkha), that this disappointment has a cause (samudaya), the disappointment can cease (nirodha) and there is a way (marga) to make it cease.

Transliteration

ā rya sa tyā
duḥ kha
sa mu da ya
ni ro dha
mā rga

ārya satyā: duḥkha samudaya nirodha mārga

आर्य सत्या दुःख समुदय निरोध मार्ग

Devanāgarī

Translation

Noble truths: suffering, cause, cessation, path.

[241] *Āryasatyā* is typically translated as 'Noble Truths'. However philologist Professor K.R. Norman has recently drawn attention to a problem with this translation. Norman's conclusion is that while Noble Truths is a possible translation, "truth of the Noble Ones" is the more likely I have explored this on my blog: 'The Four Noble Truths' http://jayarava.blogspot.com/2007/07/four-noble-truths.html

This being, that becomes...

THIS VERSE IS ONE OF THE MOST FAMOUS explanantions of the central insight of the Buddha. It describes the workings of dependent arising, in Pāli is *paṭicca-samuppāda*, and in Sanskrit *pratītya-samutpāda*. The basic idea is that phenomena arise in dependence on other phenomena. This formula is found in many places in the Pāli canon, for instance *Assutava Sutta*, SN 12.61, the *Cūḷasakuludāyi Sutta*, MN 79 (PTS M ii.32) etc.

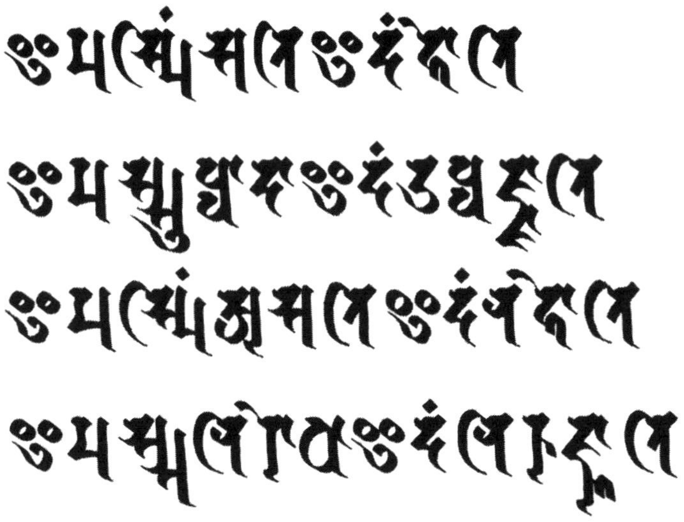

Siddhaṃ

ඉමස්මිං සති ඉදං හෝති

ඉමස්සුප්පාදා ඉදං උප්පජ්ජති

ඉමස්මිං අසති ඉදං න හෝති

ඉමස්ස නිරෝධා ඉදං නිරුජ්ඣති

Sinhala

इमस्मिं सति इदं होति
इमस्सुप्पादा इदं उप्पज्जति
इमस्मिं असति इदं न होति
इमस्स निरोधा इदं निरुज्झति

Devanāgarī

Transliteration

i ma smiṃ sa ti i daṃ ho ti
i ma ss'u ppā dā i daṃ u ppa jja ti
i ma smiṃ a sa ti i daṃ na ho ti
i ma ssa ni ro dhā i daṃ ni ru jjha ti

imasmiṃ sati idaṃ hoti
imass' uppādā idaṃ uppajjati
imasmiṃ asati idaṃ na hoti
imassa nirodhā idaṃ nirujjhati

Translation

This being, that becomes;
On the arising of this, that arises.
This not being, that does not become;
On the cessation of this, that ceases.

Notes

Of course Pāli was never written in the Siddhaṃ script - the Pāli tradition headed south a long time before Siddhaṃ emerged as a distinct script. Pāli was first written in the Sinhala script. However there is no reason not to write Pāli in Siddhaṃ or Devanāgarī.

The Three Refuges

CHANTING THE THREE REFUGES, in Pāli or Sanskrit or some other language, is a universal practice in Buddhism. Going for refuge to the Three Refuges or Jewels (S. *triratna* P. *tiratana*) is what makes one a Buddhist, and it is the unifying factor of all the wildly varying forms of Buddhism.

The Three Refuges in Sanskrit

Siddhaṃ

बुद्धं शरणं गच्छामि
धर्मं शरणं गच्छामि
संघं शरणं गच्छामि

Devanāgarī

བུདྡྷཾ་ཤ་ར་ཎཾ་ག་ཙྪཱ་མི།
དྷརྨཾ་ཤ་ར་ཎཾ་ག་ཙྪཱ་མི།
སཾ་གྷཾ་ཤ་ར་ཎཾ་ག་ཙྪཱ་མི།

Tibetan

Lantsa

Sanskrit Transliteration

Bu ddhaṃ śa ra ṇaṃ ga cchā mi
Dha rmaṃ śa ra ṇaṃ ga cchā mi
Saṃ ghaṃ śa ra ṇaṃ ga cchā mi

Buddhaṃ śaraṇaṃ gacchāmi
Dharmaṃ śaraṇaṃ gacchāmi
Saṃghaṃ śaraṇaṃ gacchāmi

The Three Refuges in Pāli

बुद्धं सरणं गच्छामि
धम्मं सरणं गच्छामि
संघं सरणं गच्छामि

Devanāgarī

බුද්ධං සරණං ගච්ඡාමි
ධම්මං සරණං ගච්ඡාමි
සංඝං සරණං ගච්ඡාමි

Sinhala

Pāli Transliteration

Bu ddhaṃ sa ra ṇaṃ ga cchā mi
Dha rmaṃ sa ra ṇaṃ ga cchā mi
Saṃ ghaṃ sa ra ṇaṃ ga cchā mi

Buddhaṃ saraṇaṃ gacchāmi
Dharmaṃ saraṇaṃ gacchāmi
Saṃghaṃ saraṇaṃ gacchāmi

Translation

To the Buddha for refuge I go
To the Dharma for refuge I go
To the Sangha for refuge I go

Notes on the Three Refuges

Sometimes you will see the phrases translated as "I take refuge.." but the verb in this sentence is *gacchāmi* which is the first person singlular of the verb √*gam* 'to go'. So it is very definitely 'I go' rather than 'I take'. Verbs of motion use the accusative case for the destination in this case the Buddha (with the *-ṃ* ending). Another, perhaps more grammatical correct, way of reading this would be 'I go to the Buddha refuge'. More correct because if it was 'for refuge' we would expect the dative case (which indicates the indirect object or the purpose of the action, and is usually to be translated 'to' or 'for') – compare the salutation *namo buddhaya,* where 'Buddha' is in the dative case, translated "homage to the Buddha".

Note the minor difference between Pāli and Sanskrit in this case. Where Sanskrit has *śaraṇaṃ* the Pāli has *saraṇaṃ* - Both *śa* and *ṣa* become *sa* in Pāli. Sanskrit *dharma* becomes Pāli *dhamma*.

Glossary

(in English alphabetical order, ignoring diacritics)
q.v. in the glossary means the term is defined elsewhere in the glossary
see references to other parts of the book.

ādibuddha

Ādi means 'primordial, beginning, commencement'. The *ādibuddha* is similar to the *dharmakāya* Buddha, and similar in concept to the Vedic idea of *brahman* in that he predates the universe and everything in it springs from him. An idea from late Mahāyāna Buddhism, possibly originating in Tibet. In the Nyingma he is identified as Samantabhadra, in Kagyu lineages Vajradhara.

anunāsika

Nasal sound, like the *anusvāra* (q.v.), but indicated in Indic scripts with a *candra-bindu* (q.v.) or half-moon and dot.

anusvāra

'Aftersound'. The diacritical mark that nasalises a vowel – in Indic scripts a dot or small circle above the letter; sometimes also a *candra-bindu* (qv). Romanised as *ṃ* or *ṁ*. See also p. 31.

avagraha

A mark which functions like an apostrophe for letters omitted due to *sandhi* (q.v.) changes, e.g. *–ātmaḥ ahaṃ* > *–ātmo 'haṃ*. Devanāgarī ऽ, Tibetan ྅, Romanised as an apostrophe.

bīja

A single Sanskrit syllable. See also p. 179.

bodhicitta

'The mind (*citta*) of awakening (*bodhi*)'. It usually refers to the decisive break-through in Buddhist practice from which there is no falling back – rather like 'stream entry' (*sotapana*) in Pāli. Bodhicitta is later said to have two aspects: that which individuals experience or relative bodhicitta; and something more akin to the *Dharmakāya* which is called 'absolute'.

candra-bindu

A more elaborate form of *anusvāra* (q.v.) sometimes also called *anunāsika*. Literally "moon and dot" from the way it is written as an upturned half-circle and dot. There is no Roman equivalent. Not much used in Sanskrit except or seed-syllables; whereas used routinely in Hindi for *anusvāra*. See also p. 31.

cintāmani

Translated as 'wishfulfilling jewel'. Literally thought (*cintā*) jewel (*mani*).

conjunct consonants

A 'conjunct' is any two different consonants without an intervening vowel. These are a feature of Sanskrit in particular, e.g. *jñ*, *sth*, *skr*, etc. The earlier Indic scripts stacked such consonants vertically e.g.*ṣ* + *ṭa* = *ṣṭa* ष् + ट = ष्ट, but later scripts used modified forms horizontally e.g. *s* + *ta* = *sta* स् + त = स्त. Devanāgarī combines both forms of conjunct. Computer fonts tend to favour horizontal forms, which have less effect on line height. Two similar consonants together e.g. *mma* are referred to as 'double' or 'geminate' consonants.

daṇḍa

punctuation mark used in Indic writing. In verse a single *daṇḍa* | is used to mark the end of a *pada* or line, while a double *daṇḍa* || is used to mark the end of a *gāthā* or stanza. The *daṇḍa* is also used, without much consistency, in place of the comma, semicolon and fullstop in prose.

ḍākiṇī

A tantric adept or *yoginī* (qv) who may originally have been a tribal shaman. The meaning 'sky dancer' comes from Tibetan translation *khandroma* (*mkha' 'gro ma*). S. may derive via Prakrit from √*śak* 'able, powerful' (with ś > ḍ). According to Śubhakarasiṃha (637-735 CE) they were originally demons who ate human flesh, hence Monier-Williams' definition "flesh-eating imp". Mahāvairocana subdued the ḍākiṇī in the guise of Mahākāla (a form of Śiva) and they now eat the defilements of the "hearts of men".[242] Ḍākiṇī's are depicted in the earliest Buddhist *maṇḍalas* as attending on Mahākāla.

dharma-kāya

'The body of the Dharma'. In terms of mantra it refers to the cosmic order is one sense of the word *dharma*. Equivalent, or at least encompassing, *śūnyatā* (qv) and *pratītyasamutpāda*. Personified in various Buddhas: Vajrasattva in many Tibetan traditions (and the Triratna Order), Mahāvairocana in Shingon. See also *trikāya.*

diacritic

Diacritic means 'distinguishing from' and refers to the various dots, dashes and squiggles added to Roman letters to accomadate the phonetics of languages other than English. For Sanskrit we add the *under-dot* (ṭ), *over-dot* (ṅ), the *tilde* (ñ), the *macron* (ā), and the *acute* (ś). Diacritics in Pinyin Chinese transliterations indicate *tone*. Tibetan uses the *umlaut* (ö).

dialect

The language spoken by people of a particular region, community or group. A variety of a language. The defition of a dialect as distinct from a language is often simply conventional, rather than scientific.

kana

Japanese syllabic scripts as opposed to *kanji* (qv), the logographic scripts based on Chinese. Hiragana[243] is mainly used to write Japanese, while Katakana is used to write loan words, onomatopoeia and for transcribing the sounds of *kanji*. The *kana* scripts are said to have been influenced by the syllabic *Siddhaṃ* script used to write Sanskrit in China and Japan.

kanji (漢字)

Chinese characters (漢字; hànzì) used in writing Japanese. Each character represents a word or concept – hence they are called 'logographs' or 'ideographs'. See also *kana*.

mantra

sound symbols; individual sounds or series of phonemes chanted in Buddhist rituals (may include actual words). see *What is a Mantra*? (p.50)

mudrā

Literally 'a seal' (i.e. stamp or certification). Symbolic positions of the hands during *sādhana* (q.v.). *Bīja's* are also known as doctrine-knowledge seals (*dharmajñāna-mudrā*).

mūla-yoga

"foundation practices". A set of preliminary practices, or yoga (q.v.), often with an emphasis on purification, which are carried out prior to Tantric initiation (see *abhiṣeka*). A common set consists of 100,000 repetitions of four practices: visualising a refuge tree and prostrating to it; visualising Vajrasattva and chanting the 100 syllable Vajrasattva mantra; offering a maṇḍala; and visualising one's guru.

nāga

"water god or spirt; serpent; elephant". Early *nāga* and *yakṣa* were simply chthonic nature spirits, often both associated with trees and the distinctions developed over time. The *nāga* became particularly associated with serpents and water. With respect to elephants often applied to especially magnificent animals. Also an early epithet for the Buddha. In later mythology the *nāga* were the source of the *Prajñāpāramitā* scriptures. Possibly related to the IE root *√*sneg* 'to crawl, snake' whence E. *snake*, *snail*; or *√*nag*^{w}*o* 'tree'.

nirmāṇa-kāya

Nirmāṇa means 'to measure' or 'to form, make, create'. It refers to the physical manifestation of the historical Buddha. See also *trikāya.*

phoneme

The smallest unit of spoken sound. Phonemes are written between slashes: /a/ /b/ /c/. The letters of the English alphabet are phonemes, but a complete set English phonemes includes conjuncts

[242] cited in Snodgrass, p.485.
[243] The /k/ sound changes to /g/ in this case.

like /bl/ and /br/. Also the English letter *c* may represent the phonemes /k/ or /s/; *j* is always /j/ (though /y/ in Spanish words); while *g* can sound like either /g/ or /j/.

Proto-Indo-European
: The common features of ancient North Indian (especially Sanskrit) and Iranian languages (especially Avestan) have lead to the postulation of a more ancient common language which is known and Indo-Iranian. Similarly the commonality between Indo-Iranian languages and ancient European languages (Latin, Greek, Anatolian, Armenia, Slavonic) suggests that they are all descended from a common language (of which we have no direct evidence) that they have dubbed: Proto-Indo-European.

Roman
: This is the generic name for the alphabet used to write English and other European languages. Modified by diacritics (q.v.), it can be used to write Indic, Tibetan and Chinese – such writing being referred to as a transliteration in the Roman script, or simply a Romanisation.

sādhana
: Literally 'leading or accomplishing'. Generally any spiritual practice, but specifically meditations characteristic of Tantric Buddhism involving *mudrā*, *mantra*, and *maṇḍala*. See also *yoga*.

sādhaka
: one who performs a sādhana (q.v.). A *yogin* (q.v.)

saṃbhoga-kāya
: *Saṃbhogakāya* is variously translated as 'body of mutual enjoyment', etc. but the Sanskrit word *saṃbhoga* literally mean 'union' or 'embrace'. See also *trikāya*

sandhi
: *Sandhi* literally means 'juncture'. In Sanskrit grammar *sandhi* refers to the rules which affect the spelling when two words come together. In English for example we say 'a bear' but 'an apple' (a > an before a vowel sound); note also the creations of plurals with -s compare the final sound and spelling in the words: weeks, bears, fishes. In Sanskrit these changes affect both vowels and consonants and the rules are complex. In writing Sanskrit all of these changes are notated.

Shingon
: A school of Tantric Buddhism in Japan founded in the 9th century by Kūkai (see p. 168).

śūnyatā
: 'Emptiness' but only and always in the sense that both the subject and object of cognition (*dharma*) lack *svabhāva* (literally own-being) or independent existence. That is both consciousness and the objects of consciousness arise in dependence on conditions.

tantra
: A general movement in Indian religion dating from about the 6th Century CE which synthesised elements from a number of different traditions including Buddhist, Vedic, and Śaiva.

trikāya
: A theory developed in the Yogacāra school in which the Buddha exists in three different forms or *kāya* (body, assemblage, principal, substance) at different levels: an historical physical form (*nirmāṇa-kāya*, created body); and archetypal form which may be experienced in yoga, i.e. meditation (*saṃbhoga-kāya* union body); and a cosmic form which is entirely abstract but represents the principle of the Dharma (*dharma-kāya* reality body). See also individual terms.

Vajra
: Diamond or thunderbolt, but typically depicted as a stylized lightening bolt. Symbol originally of the Vedic god Indra, but adopted by Vajrapāṇi and other Vajrayāna Buddhist deities.

Veda
: Literally 'knowledge'. The Vedas are the core texts of the Brahmanical religion. The main texts are the Ṛgveda, Samaveda, Yajurveda and Atharvaveda. They consist of several sections: the *saṃhita* portion contain the hymns to various gods and are usually what is referred to as 'The Vedas'. The other sections – brāhmaṇas, aranyakas, and upaniṣads – are technically included, but also form their own corpus.

Vedic
: Can refer to a time period or a culture of that time period. The early Vedic period from before 1500 BCE to about 1000 BCE saw the composition of the Vedas (q.v.) and relates to a culture

centred around worship of the gods found in especially the Ṛgveda through fire rituals. The Middle Vedic period ca 1000-500 BCE saw the composition of the commetarial texts (Brāhmanas and Aranyakas) and the Upaniṣads; and is associated with the Vendanta style of Indian religion. The late Vedic Period begins around 500 BCE and begins to end, but overlaps with the foundation of the great Indian Empires beginning ca mind 200's BCE; and is associated with the rise of *śramaṇa* movements including Buddhism and Jainism. Hinduism post-dates the Vedic period.

Virāma

The virāma is a diactric (q.v.) used in Indic scripts to indicate that the syllable has no vowel. This is required because unmarked syllables are assumed to a consonant followed by the short a vowel. In modern scripts this is usually a dash below the letter: e.g. ka क, k (with virāma) क्

visarga

Unvoiced aspiration of a vowel. Can be articulated as a soft 'h' or an echo of the vowel sound. Indicated by two vertical dots (or small circles) in Indic and Tibetan scripts, and by *ḥ* in Roman script. See also p. 32.

wishfulfilling jewel

See *cintāmaṇi*.

yimgo (yig gmo)

Sign for marking the beginning of texts and mantras, see p.25.

yoga

literally 'union' (cognate with English *yoke*). Can refer to any spiritual practice, but in Vajrayāna practice specifically one merges with and becomes the Buddha. See also *sādhana*.

yogin

One who does yoga (q.v.).

Names

Sanskrit	Tibetan			Japanese	
	Anglicised	**dbu can**	**Wylie**	**Romanji**	**Kanji**
Acala-vidyārāja	Miyowa	མི་གཡོ་བ་	mi gyo ba	fudō myōō	不動明
Ākāśadhātvīśvarī	Chukma	དབྱིངས་ཕྱུག་མ་	dbyings phyug ma		
Ākāśagarbha	Namkhé Nyingpo	ནམ་མཁའི་སྙིང་པོ་	nam mkha'i snying po	Kokūzō	虚空蔵
Akṣobhya	Mikyöpa	མི་བསྐྱོད་པ་	mi bskyod pa	Ashuku	阿閦
Amitābha	Öpamé	འོད་དཔག་མེད་	'od dpag med	Amida	阿弥陀
Amitāyus	Tsepakmé	ཚེ་དཔག་མེད་	tshe dpag med	Amida	阿弥陀
Amoghasiddhi	Dönyö Drubpa	དོན་ཡོད་གྲུབ་པ་	don yod grub pa	Fukūjōju	不空成就
Avalokiteśvara	Chenrezik	སྤྱན་རས་གཟིགས་	spyan ras gzigs	Kannon	観音
Bhaiṣajyaguru	Sangyé Menla	སངས་རྒྱས་སྨན་བླ་	sangs rgyas sman bla	Yakushi	薬師
Caturmahārāja	Gyelchen Dezhi	རྒྱལ་ཆེན་སྡེ་བཞི་	rgyal chen sde bzhi	Shitennō	四天王
Dhṛtarāṣṭra	Yulkhor Sun	ཡུལ་འཁོར་བསྲུང་	yul 'kor bsrung	Jikoku-ten	持国天
Virūdhaka	Pak Kyepo	འཕགས་སྐྱེས་པོ་	'phags skyes po	Zōjō-ten	増長天
Virūpakṣa	Chen Mi Zang	སྤྱན་མི་བཟང་	spyan mi bzang	Kōmoku-ten	広目天
Vaiśravaṇa	Namtösé	རྣམ་ཐོས་སྲས	rnam thos sras	Bishamon-ten	毘沙門天
Kṣitigarbha	Sa Yi Nyingpo	ས་ཡི་སྙིང་པོ་	sa yi snying po	Jizō	地蔵
Locanā	Sangyé Chenma	སངས་རྒྱས་སྤྱན་མ་	sangs rgyas spyan ma		
Mahāsthāmaprapta	Thuchentop	མཐུ་ཆེན་ཐོབ་	mshu tsen thob	Seishi	勢至
Maitreya	Jampa	བྱམས་པ་	byams pa	Miroku	弥勒
Māmakī	Mamaki	མ་མ་ཀི་	ma ma ki	Mōmōkei	
Mañjuśrī	Jampal	འཇམས་དཔལ་	'jams dpal		
Mañjughoṣa	Jamyang	འཇམས་དབྱངས་	'jams dbyangs	Monju	文殊;
Milarepa	Milarepa	མི་ལ་རས་པ་	mi la ras pa		
Padmasambhava	Guru Pema Jungné	པད་མ་འབྱུང་གནས་	pad ma 'byung gnas		
Paṇḍāravāsinī	Gökarmo	གོས་དཀར་མོ་	gos dkar mo	Byakusho	
Prajñāpāramitā	sherchin	ཤེར་ཕྱིན་	sher phyin	hannya-haramitta	般若波羅蜜多
Ratnasambhava	Rinchen Jungné	རིན་ཆེན་འབྱུང་གནས་	rin chen 'byung gnas	Hōshō	宝生
Śākyamuni	Sangyé Shakya Tuppa	སངས་རྒྱས་ཤཱ་ཀྱ་ཐུབ་པ་	sangs rgyas shā kya thub pa	Shaka	釈迦
Samantabhadra	Kuntuzangpo	ཀུན་ཏུ་བཟང་པོ་	kun tu bzang po	Fugen	普賢
Sarasvatī	Yangchenma	དབྱངས་ཅན་མ་	dbyangs can ma		
Tārā	Drolma	སྒྲོལ་མ་	sgrol ma	Tarani	多羅
Green Tārā	Drol Jang	སྒྲོལ་ལྗང་	sgrol ljang		
Sita Tārā	Drolkar	སྒྲོལ་དཀར	sgrol dkar		
Vairocana	Nampar Nangdzé	རྣམ་པར་སྣང་མཛད་	rnam par snang mdzad	Dainich	大日
Vajrapaṇi	Chakna Dorje	ཕྱག་ན་རྡོ་རྗེ	phyag na rdo rje	Kongōshu	金剛手
Vajrasattva	Dorje Sempa	རྡོ་རྗེ་སེམས་དཔའ་	rdo rje sems dpa'	Kongōsatta	金剛薩埵
Vajrayoginī	Dorje naljorma	རྡོ་རྗེ་རྣལ་འབྱོར་མ་	rdo rje rnal 'byor ma		

The Japanese routinely add *Tathāgata* (J. *nyorai* 如来) to the names of Buddhas. Especially Śakyamuṇi, Bhaiṣajyaguru, and the Buddhas of the Five Buddha Maṇḍala. They also add *bodhisattva* (J. *bosatsu* 菩薩) to bodhisattva names. I've left it off here to fit the name on a page. Most of the Tibetan names and transliterations come from the *Rigpa Shedra Wiki,*[244]but have been checked in the THL Tibetan Dictionary.[245] I was not able to identify all of the Japanese equivalents – not all of the figures are popular in both countries.

[244] http://www.rigpawiki.org.
[245] http://www.thlib.org/reference/dictionaries/tibetan-dictionary/index.php

Bibliography

Canonical Sources in Primary Languages

大正新脩大藏經第八冊 No. 223. 摩訶般若波羅蜜經. [= 'Mahāprajñāpāramitā Sūtra'. *Taisho Tripitaka*, New Revised [Ed], Volume VIII, no.223.] (Translated by Kumārajīva). CBETA. Online: http://www.cbeta.org/result/normal/T08/0223_005.htm

大正新脩大藏經第七冊 No. 220. 大般若波羅蜜多經 [= 'Mahāprajñāpāramitā Sūtra'. *Taisho Tripitaka*, New Revised [Ed.], Volume VII, no.220.] (Translated by Xuánzàng). CBETA. Online: http://www.cbeta.org/result/T07/T07n0220.htm

Chandra, Lokesh and Snellgrove, David L. (1981) *Sarvatathāgatatattva Saṅgraha*, New Delhi: Sharada Rani.

Cone, Margaret. (1989) *Patna Dharmapada* [transcription]. Pali Text Society. Reproduced online with Pāli Parallels, Metrical Commentary, Notes, and Indexes compiled by Ānandajoti Bhikkhu (2007). Online: http://www.ancient-buddhist-texts.net/Buddhist-Texts/C5-Patna/Patna.pdf

'De-bshin-gśegs-pa thams-cad-kyi de-kho-na-ñid bsdusp-pa shes-bya-ba theg-pa chen-poḥi mdo (Sarvatathāgata-tattvasaṃgraha-nāma-mahāyāna Sūtra).' *Derge: The Sde-dge Mtshal-par Bka'-'gyur: A Facsimile Edition of the 18th Century Redaction of Si-tu Chos-kyi-'byuṅ-gnas* Prepared under the Direction of H.H the 16th Rgyal-dbaṅ Karma-pa. Delhi: Delhi Karmapae Chodhey Gyalwae Sungrab Partun Khang, 1976-1979.

Dutt, N. (1934) *Pañcaviṃśatisāhasrikā Prajñāpāramitā Sūtra: edited with critical notes and introduction*. London, Luzac & Co.

Pāli Tipiṭaka.

Chaṭṭha Saṅgāyana Tipitaka Version 4.0. Dhamma Giri: Vipassana Research Institute. http://www.tipitaka.org/romn/

Buddha Jayanti ed. Via the *Pali Canon Online Database*. http://www.bodhgayanews.net/pali.htm

Pali Text Society ed. various volumes and editors.

Kimura, Takayasu. (1986-2009) *Pañcaviṃśatisāhasrikā Prajñāpāramitā*. Tokyo: Sankibo Busshorin. Vols. I-VIII. Online: http://www.sub.uni-goettingen.de/ebene_1/fiindolo/gret_utf.htm#PvsPrp

Vaidya, P.L. (1960) 'Saddharmapuṇḍarīkasūtram' in *Buddhist Sanskrit Texts, No. 6.* Online: www.sub.uni-goettingen.de.

Vaidya, P.L. (1961) *Mahāyāna-sūtra-saṁgrahaḥ (part 1). Buddhist Sanskrit Texts No. 17.* Darbhanga: The Mithila Institute http://dsbc.uwest.edu/

Sources in English and Translations

Abe, Ryuchi. (1999) *The Weaving of Mantra*. New York: Columbia University Press.

Allen, Charles. (2002) *The Buddha and the Sahibs: The Men Who Discovered India's Lost Religion*. London: John Murray.

Anandajyoti. (1994) 'Manjusri: origins, role and significance (Part 3).' *Western Buddhist Review*. No. 1, Dec.

Anandajyoti. (1997) 'Manjusri: origins, role and significance (Parts 1 & 2).' *Western Buddhist Review*. No. 2, Aug.

Attwood, Jayarava Michael. (2008) 'Did King Ajātasattu Confess to the Buddha, and did the Buddha Forgive Him?', *Journal of Buddhist Ethics*, vol. 15.

Bharati, A. (1965) *The Tantric Tradition*. London: Rider, 1992.

Basham, A.L. (1967) *The Wonder that was India*. 3rd rev. ed. New Delhi: Rupa and Co, 2001.

Bays, G. [trans.] 1983. *The Lalitavistara Sūtra. 2 vol. The Voice of the Buddha: the beauty of compassion*. Berkeley: Dharma Publishing.

Beyer, Stephan. (1973) *Magic and Ritual in Tibet: the Cult of Tara*. Delhi: Motilal Banarsidass, 1996.

Bhattasali, Nalinikanta. (1924). Some Image Inscriptions from East Bengal. *Epigraphia Indica*, 17, p.349-362.

Boucher, Daniel. (1998) 'Gāndhārī and the early Chinese Buddhist translations reconsidered: the case of the Saddharmapuṇḍarīkasūtra.' *Journal of the American Oriental Society* 118 (4), p.471-506.

Brough, John. (1977) 'The arapacana syllabary in the old Lalitavistara.' *Bulletin of the School of Oriental and African Studies*. 40 (1), p.85-95.

Bühler, Georg. (1904) *Indian Paleography*. Oriental Books Reprint Corporation, 1980.

Bunnō, K. et al. (1986) *The Threefold Lotus Sutra: Innumerable Meanings; The lotus flower of the Wonderful Law; Meditation on the Bodhisattva Universal Virtue*. Tokyo: Kosei Publishing.

Chandra, Lokesh. (1979) 'Origin of the Avalokitesvara of Potala.' *Kailash: A Journal of Himalayan Studies*, 7 (1).

Chandra, Lokesh. (1982). *Indian scripts in Tibet.* New Delhi: Sharada Rani.

Chandra, Lokesh. (1988) *Thousand-Armed Avalokitesvara*. New Delhi : Indira Gandhi National Centre for the Arts : Abhinav Publications.

Chandra, Lokesh. (1999-2004) *Dictionary of Buddhist iconography* [15 vols.] New Delhi: International Academy of Indian Culture and Aditya Prakashan.

Cleary, Thomas. [trans.] (1989). *Entry into the realm of reality: the text: a translation of the Gandavyuha, the final book of the Avatamsaka Sutra*. Boston: Shambhala.

Conze, Edward. (1967) *Materials for a Dictionary of the Prajñāpāramitā Literature.* Tokyo: Suzuki Research Foundaion.

Conze, Edward. (1973) *Perfect Wisdom : The Short Prajñāpāramitā Texts*. Buddhist Publishing Group

Conze, Edward. (1975a) *Buddhist Wisdom Books: Containing the Diamond Sutra and the Heart Sutra*. London: George Allen & Unwin. (first published 1958)

Conze, Edward. (1975b) *The large sutra on perfect wisdom ; with the divisions of the Abhisamayālaṅkāra.* (Delhi, Motilal Banarsidass: 1990)

Conze, Edward. (1978) *The prajñāpāramita literature*. (2nd rev. ed.) Tokyo: The Reiyukai.

Conze, Edward. (1983) *Perfection of Wisdom in Eight Thousand Lines and its Verse Summary.* San Francisco, Four Seasons Foundation.

Cunningham, Alexander. (1854) *The Bhilsa topes, or, Buddhist monuments of central India : comprising a brief historical sketch of the rise, progress, and decline of Buddhism; with an account of the opening and examination of the various groups of topes around Bhilsa.* London : Smith, Elder.

Davidson, R. M. (1995) 'The Litany of names of Mañjuśrī' in Lopez, Donald S. [ed.] *Religions of India in Practice*. University of Princeton Press.

Deussen, Paul. (1906) *The philosophy of the Upanishads*. (trans. by Geden, A. S.) New York, Dover Publications, 1966.

Edgerton, Franklin. (1953) *Buddhist Hybrid Sanskrit Grammar and Dictionary.* New Delhi: Munshiram Monoharlal, 2004.

Eidson, Eijun. [ed.] (1997) *Shingon Esoteric Buddhism: A Handbook for Followers*. Kōyasan Shingon Buddhism.

English, Elizabeth (2002). *Vajrayogini: Her Visualizations, Rituals, & Forms*. Boston: Wisdom Publications.

Everson, Michael. (2009) *Preliminary proposal for encoding the Rañjana script in the SMP of the UCS*. http://std.dkuug.dk/jtc1/sc2/wg2/docs/n3649.pdf

Farrow, G.W. and Menon, I. (1992) *The concealed Essence of the Hevajra Tantra: with the commentary Yogaratnamālā.* Delhi: Motilal Banarsidass, 2001 printing.

Fishman, Alex. (2006) *Silver coinage of the Kunindas* (ca.2nd-1st century BC). Website: http://www.ancientcoins.ca/kuninda/kuninda.htm

Foucault, Michel. (1966) *The Order of Things: an Archaeology of the Human Sciences*. London: Tavistock (translated 1970).

FWBO Puja Book, 5th ed. (1990) Windhorse Publications; also 7th ed. retitled: *Puja: The FWBO Book of Buddhist Devotional Texts,* 2008.

Gair, J.W. and Karunatillake, W.S. (1998) *A New Course in Reading Pāli*. Motilal Banarsidass.

Gethin, Rupert. (1992) 'The mātikās: memorizations, mindfulness, and the list' in *In the mirror of memory: reflections on mindfulness and remembrance in Indian and Tibetan Buddhism*. State University of New York Press, p.149-172.

Glucklich, Ariel. (1997) *The end of magic*. New York: Oxford University Press.

Gombrich, R. (2009) *What the Buddha Thought*. London: Equinox.

Gonda, J. (1963) 'The Indian Mantra,' *Oriens*. Vo.16, Jan. 244-297.

Govinda [Lama Anagarika]. (1959) *Foundations of Tibetan Mysticism*. London: Rider.

Gulik, R. H. van (1956) *Siddham: An Essay on the History of Sanskrit Studies in China and Japan*, Nagpur: International Academy of Indian Culture. (Also available as a reprint from Aditya Prakashan, Delhi).

Gyatso, Janet. (1992) 'Letter magic: a Peircean perspective on the semiotics of Rdo Grub-chen's dharani memory' in *In the mirror of memory: reflections on mindfulness and remembrance in Indian and Tibetan Buddhism*. State University of New York Press, 1992, p.173-213

Hakeda, Y.S. (1972) *Kūkai: major works: translated and with an account of his life and a study of his thought*. New York: Columbia University Press.

Hodge, Stephen. (2003) *The Mahāvairocana Abhisaṃbodhi Tantra: with Buddhaguhya's commentary*. London, Routledge Curzon.

Hopkins, J. [trans. and ed.] (1977) *Tantra in Tibet: the Great Exposition of Secret Mantra, by Tsong-ka-pa*. London: Allen and Unwin.

Jayarava. (2006) *The last words of the Buddha*. Unpublished essay. http://www.jayarava.org/buddhas-last-words.html

Jayarava. (2006a) 'Buddhism as a path of Gracefulness' in *Jayarava's Raves* [18-7-2006]. http://jayarava.blogspot.com/2006/07/buddhism-as-path-of-gracefulness.html

Jayarava. (2007) 'The Four Noble Truths.' *Jayarava's Raves* [6-7-2007]. http://jayarava.blogspot.com/2007/07/four-noble-truths.html

Jayarava. (2008) 'Persian Influences on Indian Buddhism.' *Jayarava's Raves* [20-06-2008] http://jayarava.blogspot.com/2008/06/persian-influences-on-indian-buddhism.html

Jayarava. (2009a) 'Words in Mantras that end in –e' in *Jayarava's Raves* [6-3-2009]. http://jayarava.blogspot.com/2009/03/words-in-mantras-that-end-in-e.html

Jayarava. (2009b) 'Dharma: Early History' in *Jayarava's Raves* [9-10-2009]. http://jayarava.blogspot.com/2009/10/dharma-early-history.html,

Jayarava. (2009c) 'Dharma: Buddhist Terminology' in *Jayarava's Raves* [19-6-2009]. http://jayarava.blogspot.com/2009/09/dharma-buddhist-terminology.html

Jayarava. (2009d) 'Dharma as Mental Event' in *Jayarava's Raves* [23-10-2009]. http://jayarava.blogspot.com/2009/10/dharma-as-mental-event.html

Jayarava. (2010) 'The Hundred Syllable Vajrasattva Mantra.' *Western Buddhist Review*. 5. Online: http://www.westernbuddhistreview.com/vol5/vajrasattva-mantra.pdf

Jayarava. (2010) 'How the Karaṇīya Mettā Sutta Came About.' *Jayarava's Raves*. http://jayarava.blogspot.com/2010/06/how-karaniya-metta-sutta-came-about.html

Lakoff, G. and Johnson, M. (1981) *Metaphors we live*. Chicago University Press.

Lamotte, Étienne. (1958) *History of Indian Buddhism: from origins to the Śaka era.* [trans. 1988 Sara Webb-Boin] Louvain-la-neuve: Université Catholique de Louvain.

Linrothe, Rob. (1999) *Ruthless Compassion: Wrathful Deities in Early Indo-Tibetan Esoteric Buddhist Art*. London: Serindia.

Lopez, Donald S. (1998) *Prisoners of Shangri-La : Tibetan Buddhism and the West*. University of Chicago Press.

Kak, Subhash. (2000) *The Astronomical Code of the Ṛgveda.* Munshiram Manoharlal.

Kern, H. (1884) *The saddharma-pundarīka or the lotus of the true law*. Delhi: Motilal Banarsidass, 1980. [1st pub. 1884. Sacred books of the East Vol.21.]

Kodama Yoshitaka. (1991) *Bonji Hikkei: Shosha to kaidoku [= Siddhaṃ Manual: writing and deciphering*]. Tōkyō: Toki Shobo. [児玉 義隆. (1991) 梵字必携: 書写と解読. 朱鷺書房].

Macdonell, Arthur A. A (1926) *Sanskrit Grammar for Students*. (3rd ed.) New Delhi D.K Printworld, 2008.

MacQueen, G. (1988) *A Study of the Śrāmaṇyaphala-sūtra*, Wiesbaden: Otto Harrassowitz.

Magnus, Margaret. *The Magic Letter Page.* http://www.trismegistos.com/MagicalLetterPage/

McRae, John R. (1988) 'Ch'an Commentaries on the Heart Sūtra: Preliminary Inferences on the Permutation of Chinese Buddhism.' *Journal of the International Association of Buddhist Studies* 11.2: 87-115.

Monier-Williams, M. (1899) *A Sanskrit-English Dictionary*. [New Edition greatly Enlarged and improved by Leumann, E. and Cappeller, C.] Reprinted by Delhi: Asian Educational Services, 2008.

Mukherjee, B. N. (1999) 'Arapacana: a mystic Buddhist script' in Bhattacharya, N. N. (ed) *Tantric Buddhism*. New Delhi: Manohar Publishers & Distributors, p.303-317.

Mullin, Glenn H. (1997) *Meditations on the Lower Tantras: from the Collected Works of the Previous Dalai Lamas*. New Delhi: Library of Tibetan Works & Archives, 2004.

Ñānamoli. [trans.] (1964) *The Path of Purification*. (= Visuddhimagga by Buddhaghosa). Colombo: Semage. (reprinted by Singapore Buddhist Meditation Centre, 1997)

Nattier, Jan. (2005) *A few good men: the Bodhisattva Path According to the Inquiry of Ugra (Ugraparipṛcchā)*. University of Hawaii Press.

Nattier, Jan. (1992) 'The Heart Sūtra: a Chinese apocryphal text?' *Journal of the International Association of Buddhist Studies*, 15 (2), p.153-223.

Nyanatiloka and Bodhi (1999). Numerical Discourses of the Buddha: an Anthology of Sutta from the Aṅguttara Nikāya, Walnut Creek, Maryland: Altamira Press.

Padoux, André. (1990) *Vāc: the concept of the word in selected Hindu Tantras*. [Trans. 1992 by Jacques Gontier] Delhi: Sri Satguru Publications.

Ramachandran, V.S. (2003). Purple numbers and sharp cheese. *BBC Reith Lectures 2003*. http://www.bbc.co.uk/radio4/reith2003/lecture4.shtml

Rigpa Shedra Wiki: An Online Encyclopedia of Tibetan Buddhism. http://www.rigpawiki.org/

Roth, Gustav. (1986) 'Mangala-Symbols in Buddhist Sanskrit Manuscripts and Inscriptions' in Bhattacharya, G. (ed.) *Deyadharma: Studies in memory of Dr D. C. Sirdar*. Sri Satguru Publications. Delhi.

Salomon, Richard. (1990) 'New Evidence for a Gāndhārī Origin of the Arapacana Syllabary.' *Journal of the American Oriental Society*, 110 (2), Apr–Jun, p. 255-273.

Salomon, Richard. (1993) 'An additional note on arapacana.' *Journal of the American Oriental Society*, 113 (2), p.275-6.

Salomon, Richard. (1995) 'On the origins of the Early Indian Scripts.' *Journal of the American Oriental Society*, 115 (2), p.271-279. Online: http://indology.info/papers/salomon/

Salomon, Richard. (1998) *Indian Epigraphy: A Guide to the Study of Inscriptions in Sanskrit, Prakrit, and the other Indo-Aryan Languages*. New York: Oxford University Press.

Salomon, Richard. (1999) *Ancient Buddhist scrolls from Gandhāra: the British Library Kharoṣṭhī Fragments*. London: The British Library.

Salomon, Richard. (2006) 'Kharoṣṭhī syllables used as location markers in Gandhāran stūpa architecture.' in Pierfrancesco Callieri, ed., *Architetti, Capomastri, Artigiani: L'organizzazione dei cantieri e della produzione artistica nell'asia ellenistica*. Studi offerti a Domenico Faccenna nel suo ottantesimo compleanno. (Serie Orientale Rome 100; Rome: Istituto Italiano per l'Africa e l'Oriente, 2006), p. 181-224.

Sander, Lore. (1986) 'Oṃ or Siddhaṃ: Remarks on Openings of Buddhist Manuscripts and Inscriptions from Gilgit and Central Asia.' in Bhattacharya, G. (ed.) *Deyadharma: Studies in memory of Dr D. C. Sirdar*. Delhi: Sri Satguru Publications.

Sangharakshita. *Vajrasattva Mantra*. Unpublished seminar. *Free Buddhist Audio*. http://www.freebuddhistaudio.com/texts/seminartexts/SEM152_Vajrasattva_Mantra.pdf

Sangharakshita (1968) 'The Meditation and Mantra Recitation of Vajrasattva: purification', in *The Four Foundation Yogas of the Tibetan Buddhist Tantra* [track 7]. Online: http://www.freebuddhistaudio.com/talks/details?num=60

Sangharakshita (1981) *Concluding Remarks. Preordination Course 1981* [Tuscany 29.11.81]. Online: http://www.freebuddhistaudio.com/texts/seminartexts/SEM092P1_Mitrata_Omnibus_-_Pre_-_ordination_Course_Tuscany_1981_and_1982_-_Part_1.pdf

Sangharakshita (1993) *Wisdom Beyond words: Sense and Non-sense in the Buddhist Prajnaparamita Tradition*. Birmingham: Windhorse Publications.

Sangharakshita (1994) *Was the Buddha a Bhikkhu? A Rejoinder to a Reply to Forty-Three Years Ago.* Glasgow: Windhorse Publications.

Sangharakshita. (1995) *Transforming Self and World: Themes from the Sūtra of Golden Light.* Birmingham: Windhorse.

Scharfe, Harmut. (2002) Kharoṣṭhī and Brahmī. *Journal of the American Oriental Society*, 122 (2), p.391-3.

Shinjo Hinonishi (2002) 'The Hōgō (treasure name) of Kōbō Daishi and the development of beliefs associated with it,' [Translated by William Londo] *Japanese religions*, 27 (1), p. 5-18.

Sircar, D. C. (1965) *Indian Epigraphy*. Dehli : Motilal Banarsidass, 1965.

Skilling, P. (1992) 'The Rakṣā Literature of the Śrāvakayāna.' *Journal of the Pali Text Society,* 16, p.109-82.

Skilling, Peter. (1996). 'An arapacana syllabary in the Bhadrakalpika-sūtra.' *Journal of the American Oriental Society*, 116 (3), p.522-3.

Snellgrove, David. (1987) *Indo-Tibetan Buddhism: Indian Buddhists and their Tibetan Successors*. Boston: Shambhala, 2002.

Snodgrass, Adrian. (1988) *The Matrix and Diamond World Mandalas in Shingon Buddhism*. [2 vols.] Delhi: Aditya Prakashan.

Staal, Frits. (2008) *Discovering the Vedas : Origins, Mantras, Rituals, Insights*. Penguin.

Sthiramati [aka Skilton, Andrew.] (1990) 'The Vajrasattva Mantra : notes on a corrected Sanskrit text'. [*Western Buddhist*] *Order Journal*, vol.3 Nov.

Stevens, John. (1995) *Sacred Calligraphy of the East*. Shambala.

Strauch, Ingo. (2007-8). *The Bajaur collection: A new collection of Kharoṣṭhī manuscripts. A preliminary catalogue and survey (in progress)*. Online: http://www.geschkult.fu-berlin.de/e/indologie/bajaur/publication/strauch_2007_1_0.pdf.

Studholme, Alexander. (2002) *The Origins of Oṃ Maṇipadme Hūṃ: a Study of the Kāraṇḍavyūha Sūtra*. New York: State University of New York Press.

Shuchiin Daigaku Mikkyô Gakkai. (1983) *Bonji Taikan* [梵字大鑑]. Tōkyō: Meicho Fukyūkai.

Sutherland, G. H. (1991) *The Disguises of the Demon: The Development of the Yakṣa in Hinduism and Buddhism*. Albany: State University of New York Press.

Van Dam, Eva. (1991) *The Magic Life of Milarepa*. Boston: Shambhala.

Van Gulik, R.H. (1956). *Siddham: An Essay on the History of Sanskrit Studies in China and Japan*. New Delhi, Jayyed Press, 2001.

Verhagen, P.C. (1990) 'The mantra oṃ maṇi-padme hūṃ in an early Tibetan Grammatical Treatise,' *Journal of the International Association of Buddhist Studies*, 13 (2), p.134-5

Vessantara. (1993) *Meeting the Buddhas: a Guide to Buddhas, Bodhisattvas, and Tantric Deities*. Glasgow: Windhorse, 1993. [subsequently published as three separate books]

Vessantara. (2003) *Female Deities in Buddhism.* Windhorse,

Vessantara. (2004). *The Five Female Buddhas: A Commentary on Their Sadhanas and Pujas*. Prinvately published. Online: http://vessantara.net/wp-content/uploads/five-female-buddhas.pdf

Vira, Raghu and Chandra, Lokesh. (1965) *Sanskrit bījas and mantras in Japan*. New Delhi: International Academy of Indian Culture.

Ward, Nigel. *Responsive systems project*. http://www.cs.utep.edu/nigel/responsive.html

Wayman, A. (1985) *Chanting the names of Mañjuśrī: the Mañjuśrī -nāma-saṃgīti: Sanskrit and Tibetan texts*. Delhi: Motilal Banarsidass, 1999.

Wayman, A. (1984) 'The Significance of Mantras from the Veda Down to Buddhist Tantric Practice,' in Wayman, A. *Buddhist Insight.* Delhi: Motilal Banarsidass.

West, Andrew. (2005) *Proposal to encode two archaic Tibetan punctuation marks*. http://std.dkuug.dk/jtc1/sc2/wg2/docs/n3033.pdf

West, Andrew. (2006a) *Proposal to encode three archaic Tibetan characters*. http://std.dkuug.dk/jtc1/sc2/wg2/docs/n3012.pdf

West Andrew (2006b) 'When is a Swastika not a Swastika?' *BabelStone*. [blog] http://babelstone.blogspot.com/2006/02/when-is-swastika-not-swastika.html

Whitney, William Dwight. (1885). *The Roots, Verb-forms and Primary Derivatives of the Sanskrit Language*. Delhi: Motilal Banarsidass, 2006.

Index

A

a 78, 94, **180**.

Acala Vidyārāja 120.

ādibuddha 77, 81, 150, 251.

āḥ 108, **184.**

Ākāśadhātvīśvarī 93, **110**-111.

Ākāśagarbha **123-5**, 197.

Akṣobhya 77, 81, **98-100**, 103, 112, 121, 160, 195.

alphabet

as mantra 208; calligraphy 23, 34, 170-1; Sanskrit 14.

aṃ 110, 150, 181.

Ambedkar, Dr. Bhimrao Ramji 166-7.

āṃḥ 94, 181.

Amitābha 50-1, **103-7**, 116, 126, 128, 137, 139, 152, 155, 169-70, 187, 195.

Amitāyus 106.

Amoghasiddhi 101, **108-9**, 152, 184, 195.

Ānanda 228.

anusvāra 31-2.

Arapacana 34-46, 49, 65, 74, 142, 143-4, 182.

Arapacana Alphabet, meditation 36.

Aśoka 19-20, 23.

Aṣṭasāhasrikā Prajñāpāramitā Sūtra 143, 147.

Āṭānāṭiya Sutta 133.

auṃ, see *oṃ*.

avagraha 106, 224, 251.

Avalokiteśvara 16, 50-2, 70, 107, **128-130**, 187, 219-221.

Avataṃsaka Sūtra 49, 69-70, 150, 190.

B

Bajaur 35.

beginning and end marks 25-30.

bhaḥ 80.

bhai 89

Bhaiṣajyaguru 89-92.

bīja 24, 32-33, **179-201**, 251.

bīja, complex 199-201.

bodhisattva, the word 119.

Bodhisattvas 119-164; see under individual names.

Bonji 20. See also Siddhaṃ.

Brāhmī 19-23, 26, 29,31, 180-2, 234, 242; examples 19, 242.

Buddha, last words. 235.

Buddhas 77-118.

C

Caturmahārāja (The Four Great Kings) 130-4.

chants & phrases 239-250.

Chinese Buddhism 16, 20, 23-24, 70, 76, 103, 126, 216, 219.

Chinese Calligraphy 170, 187, 189, 193.

Chinese Language and Writing 12-13, 16-7, 20, 24, 35, 42, 46, 109, 126, 170, 187-9, 193, 252.

Conze, Edward 35-6, 38-9, 42, 51, 73, 75-9, 148-9, 206, 212-3, 236.

D

ḍākiṇī, see Vajrayoginī.

daṇḍa 12, 27-8, 75-6, 251.

dhāraṇī 12, 35-7, 48-9, **65-7**, 72, 91-3, 193, 200-1, 206-7, 213, 216-21. see also: Karaṇḍamudrā Dhāraṇī, Nīlakaṇṭha Dhāraṇī.

dharmacakra 93, 110, 141.

dhīḥ 52, 143-4, 147-8, 179, **185-6**, 199-200, 211.

Dhṛtarāṣṭra 130.

diacritics 12, 14-15, **17**, 74, 169, 182, 209, 252-3.

doors to the deathless 237.

dorje, see *vajra*.

E

e ending in Sanskrit 72-75

end marks 27-30.

F

Four Great Kings, see Caturmahārāja.

Four Noble Truths, see Truths of the Noble Ones.

Fudō Myōō, see Acala.

G

Gandhāra 21, 35, 38, 182-3.

Gāndhārī 21, 35, 38-40, 49, 65, 73-4, 144, 182.

Govinda, Lama Anagarika 52, 85, 111, 187, 193.

Guānyīn: see Avalokiteśvara.

H

hāṃ 120.

Heart Sutra, Mantra 75-6, **211-3.**

hrīḥ 104-5, 137-8, **187-8.**

hūṃ (seed syllable) 69, 81, 88, 99, 128, 160, 179, **189-191**, 210, 214; hūṃ also occurs in many mantras.

J

jaḥ hūṃ vaṃ hoḥ 214-5.

Japan 23-4, 168, 198, 200, 253.

Japanese Language 12-13, 15, 17, 20, 23, 27, 31-2, 105-6, 124-5, 160, 168-9, 181, 185, 252.

Japanese Buddhism 11, 20, 23, 92, 96, 105, 124, 135, 139, 168, 185, 198, 200, 216, 253.

K

Karaṇḍamudrā Dhāraṇī 200, **216-7.**

Kāraṇḍavyūha Sūtra 50, 128.

Karaṇīya Mettā Sutta 230-234.

Kharoṣṭhī 21-3, 35, 38, 42, 182-3.

khaṭvāṅga 162, 175.

Kōbōdaishi, see Kūkai.

Kṣitigarbha 135-6.

Kūkai 23-4, 49-50, 69, 87, 105, 123, **168-172**, 181, 187, 190-1, 253.

Kūkai, calligraphy 170-1.

Kurukullā 137-8.

Kwanyin: see Avalokiteśvara.

L

Locanā 98, **112-4.**

Lotus Sutra, see *Saddharmapuṇḍarīka Sūtra.*

M

ma (maṃ, maiṃ, muḥ) 192.

Mahāparinibbāna Sutta 235.

Mahāsthāmaprāpta 139-40.

Mahāvairocana, see Vairocana.

Mahāvairocana Abhisaṃbodhi Tantra 38-40, 52, 74, 80, 93, 95, 106, 120-1, 142, 180, 183, 187, 193, 203, 208.

Mahāvairocana Sūtra, see *Mahāvairocana Abhisaṃbodhi Tantra.*

Maitreya 141-2.

Māmakī 101, **114-5.**

Mañjughoṣa 143-6; see also Mañjuśrī

Mañjuśrī 52, **143-6**, 150, 185-6, 192, 200-1, 211; see also Mañjughoṣa.

mantra 11-13, 16-17, 19-24, 25-28, 32, 34, 36, 48-59. See also dhāraṇī.

mantra, etymology 54-58.

mantra, magic, and interconnectedness 70-71.

mantra, non-lexical utterances, stobhas 68-69.

Mantra of Light 96-7.

Mantrayāna 23.

mantric words 202-6.

mantras, miscellaneous 207-226.

May all beings be happy! 243.

Medicine Buddha 89-92.

Meditation 36-41, 48-49, 51, 57, 65, 70, 74, 87, 103, 106, 152, 173, 180, 187, 190, 213, 243, 253.

Mediation Posture 152, 155.

Milarepa 173-4.

mudrā 50, 53, 97, 214, 216-7, 252-3; *abhaya* (fearlessness) 108, 195; *añjali* (salutation) 116, 139, *bhumisparśa* (earth touching) 98, 112; *bodyagrī* (fist of wisdom) 93; *cakravartin* (wheel turning) 93, 112, 141; *dana* (generosity) 101; *dhyāna* (meditation) 93, 103, 112, 147; *Maitreya* 141; varada (giving) 89, 114, 123, 150, 195; warding off evil 177.

N

namas, namaḥ, namo 203-4.

names 255.

Nembutsu 105-6.

Nīlakaṇṭha Dhāraṇī 119-121.

O

oṃ 15, 20, 25, 48, 52, 69, 85, 134, **193-4**.

oṃ āḥ hūṃ 176, 210.

P

Padmasambhava **175-8**, 210.

Padmasambhava, seven line invocation 177-8.

Padmasattva mantra 88.

Pañcaviṃśatisāhasrikā Prajñāpāramitā Sūtra 35-6, 39, 42, 65-6, 73, 144.

Pāṇḍaravāsinī 103, **116-8**.

Perfection of Wisdom Sūtras
see: Aṣṭasāhasrika, Pañcaviṃśatisāhasrikā, Ratnaguṇasaṁcayagāthā, Vajracchedikā.

phaṭ 52, 88, **205.**

phonosemantics 59-63.

Prajñāpāramitā, Bodhisattva 147-9.

pronunciation **14-18**, 26.

punctuation 25-30.

R

Ratnaguṇasaṁcayagāthā 236-7.

Ratnasambhava **101-2**, 108, 114, 195, 197.

Ṛgveda 48, 68, 185, 254.

Rites 93, 98, 101, 103, 108, 137, 238.

S

Sabbe satta sukhi hontu 243.

Saddharmapuṇḍarīka Sūtra 66, 72-3, 206.

Śākyamuni 49, 77, **78-80**, 93, 141, 150.

Samantabhadra 150-1.

Sangharakshita 51, 86-7, 116, 156, **158-9**.

Śānti Mantra 222.

Sarvatathāgata-tattvasaṃgraha 44, 77, 84, 101, 108, 119, 160, 183, 214; see also Vajraśekhara Sūtra.

scripts 19-33.

Seed Syllables see *bīja*.

Shingon 11, 20, 23-4, 32, 40, 80-1, 93, 95-7, 105, 120, 124, 136, 139, 141-2, 150, 168-9, 176, 180-1, 211, 252-3.

Siddhaṃ 11-12, 16-19, 20-21, **23-24**, 25-7, 31-2, 105, 168-9, 172, 180, 182, 189, 194, 216, 234, 243, 246, 252.

Śiva 126, 145, 160, 193, 219, 252.

Skull Garland Mantra, see Thöthrengtsal Mantra.

sotaba 198.

sound symbolism, see phonosemantics.

Sukhāvatīvyūha Sūtra 73, 103, 128.

śūnyatā 31, 37, 50, 65, 88, 145, 162, 168, 181, 207, 223, 225, 252-3.

Śūnyatā Mantra 223-5.

sūtras 227-238.

svāhā 17, 52, 92, 113, 115, 134, **206**.

svastika 25-6, 29.

T

tadyathā 75-6.

tāṃ 152-6, 195-6.

tantric rites see rites.

Tārā, Green 108, **152-4.**

Tārā, Red, see Kurukullā.

Tārā, White 155-9, 195-6.

This being, that becomes... 245-6.

Thöthrengtsal Mantra 176-7.

Three Refuges 247-9.

Thus have I heard 228-9.

trāḥ 123, 197.

traṃ 101, 197.

Truths of the Noble Ones 244.

V

vāc 145-6, 198.

Vāgīśvara 143-6. See also Mañjuśrī.

Vairocana 77, 81, **93-7**, 110, 120, 160, 180-1, 190, 195, 198, 252.

Vaiśravaṇa 132-3.

vajra 12, 28, 52, 81, 85-87, 104, 160, 162, 174-5, 195, 223-4.

vajra bell (*vajraghaṇṭā*) 110, 112, 114, 116

Vajra Family 81, 98-99, 160.

Vajracchedika Sūtra 73.

Vajraguru, see Padmasambhava.

Vajrapāṇi 85, 119, 133, **160-1**, 219, 253.

Vajrasattva 49, 77, **81-88**, 99, 160, 205, 252.

Vajraśekhara Sūtra 94, 198; see also Sarvatathāgata-tattvasaṃgraha.

Vajrayāna 40, 81, 96, 133, 160, 168, 190, 253-4.

Vajrayoginī Ḍākiṇī 162-4.

vaṃ 94, 198.

vāṃḥ 94, 184, 198.

virāma 167, 205, 254.

Virūḍhaka 131.

Virūpākṣa 131-2.

visarga **32-3**, 80, 108, 179, 181, 184-5, 187, 200, 209, 254.

W

White Lotus Sutra, see *Saddharmapuṇḍarīka Sūtra*.

Wildmind 243.

Wisdom Alphabet: see Arapacana.

Y

yakṣa (P. *yakkha*) 119, 131-3, 160, 252.

ye dharmā hetuprabhava 240-2.

yimgo (*yig gmo*) 25-28, 254.

The Author

The name Jayarava is Sanskrit and means 'cry of victory'. It refers, according to Nāgabodhi who gave it to me, both to personal victories (*jaya* 'victory') along the way (of which this book is one); and to the victory to come, the *jayamaṅgalaṃ*, the Buddha's victory; and also to my desire to communicate (*rava* meaning 'song, cry, shout!').

I was born and bought up in a small town in New Zealand, but later moved to Auckland and then studied chemistry at Waikato University. After a stint as a unprofessional musician I worked as a librarian for 15 years, including a year out at Victoria University, Wellington for a post-graduate diploma in Librarianship. I moved to the UK in 2002 to pursue a deeper involvement in the Triratna Buddhist Community, and have lived in Cambridge since then. I was ordained into the Triratna Buddhist Order in 2005.

As a child I was always singing and I'm grateful to my mother for sending me to singing lessons. I still sing and play music. The first mantra I chanted was *oṃ namaḥ śivaya* with a Sahaja Yoga group in New Zealand. On becoming Buddhist in 1994 I was immediately attracted to communual mantra chanting, and fascinated by the exotic sounds of Pāli and Sanskrit. I taught myself calligraphy, initially from John Steven's book *Sared Calligraphy of the East*, and then later through various more obscure books and websites. I don't recommend being one's own teacher, as one usually develops bad habits that are difficult to correct later, but sometimes one has no choice.

I have been writing about Buddhism for several years, with articles published in the *Western Buddhst Review* and in the *Journal of Buddhist Ethics*, as well as writing a weekly blog which often dwells on aspects of linguistics. In 2011 I published a guide to the Sanskrit and Pāli names used by members of the Triratna Buddhist Order.

My websites:
visiblemantra.org
jayarava.blogspot.com